Trade Unions, Immigration, and Immigrants in Europe, 1960–1993

International Studies in Social History
General Editor: Marcel van der Linden,
International Institute of Social History, Amsterdam

Volume 1
Trade Unions, Immigration, and Immigrants in Europe, 1960–1993
Edited by Rinus Penninx and Judith Roosblad

Forthcoming Volumes:
Class and Other Identities
Edited by Lex Heerma van Voss and Marcel van der Linden

TRADE UNIONS, IMMIGRATION, AND IMMIGRANTS IN EUROPE, 1960–1993

A Comparative Study of the Attitudes and Actions of Trade Unions in Seven West European Countries

EDITED BY RINUS PENNINX AND JUDITH ROOSBLAD

Berghahn Books
New York • Oxford

First published in 2000 by

Berghahn Books

This study was commissioned by the International Institute of Social History, Amsterdam.

The study was prepared and coordinated by the Institute for Migration and Ethnic Studies of the University of Amsterdam.

Library of Congress Cataloging-in-Publication Data

Library of Congress Cataloging-in-Publication Data

Trade unions, immigration, and immigrants in Europe, 1960-1993 : a comparative study of the attitudes and actions of the trade unions in seven West European countries / edited by Rinus Penninx and Judith Roosblad.
p. cm. -- (International studies in social history ; v. 1)
"The study was prepared and coordinated by the Institute for Migration and Ethnic Studies of the University of Amsterdam"--Coyr. p.
Includes bibliographical references and index.
ISBN 1-57181-764-6 (alk. paper)
1. Labor unions--Europe, Western--Case studies. 2. Alien labor--Europe, Western--Case studies. 3. Emigration and immigration--Government policy--Europe, Western--Case studies. I. Penninx, Rinus. II. Roosblad, Judith. III. Universiteit van Amsterdam. Instituut voor Migratie- en Etnische Studies. IV. Series.

HD6657 .T69 2000
331.88'094--dc21

99-045029

British Library Cataloguing in Publication Data
A catalogue record for this book is available from the British Library.

Printed in the United States on acid-free paper.

ISBN 1-57181-764-6

Contents

List of Tables

Foreword

Jan Lucassen

For more than a decade, the Research Department of the International Institute of Social History (IISH) in Amsterdam has been concerned with approaching labour history by way of international comparisons, in regard to the 'basics' of labour circumstances and labour relations, and to labour organisations. In the first of those fields, volumes have been published on global issues such as free and unfree labour, labour migrations, and racism in the labour market,[1] and in the second field on topics such as the history of mutual benefit societies, internationalism in the labour movement, and the national sections of the Second International and of the Comintern.[2]

At the same time, the interest of the Institute has been moving eastward towards the Middle East and South and Southeast Asia. In this regard, Professor Erik Zürcher has built up impressive research collections on the social and labour history of the Ottoman Empire, Turkey, and Turkish 'guest workers' abroad.[3] He has also initiated a series of comparative studies in this field.[4]

These three developments have led to Erik Zürcher's initiative to launch this project on trade unions and immigrants in postwar Europe. It emerged from previous studies that mechanisms of exclusion of 'the other' operated rather as a rule than as an exception in labour history – contrary to what the socialist ideal of internationalism might lead us to believe. The 'organisational studies' referred to earlier provided us with considerations for and against the ideologically desirable inclusion of 'the other', including the foreign worker. The studies of Turkish labour history have emphasised the long-standing tradition of Turkish labour organisation in political parties and trade unions, on which emigrants could build once they were abroad.

The historical case of the relations between trade unions and 'guest worker' immigration in Western Europe seemed to be well suited to linking the three research themes of the Institute within one new project. Because of the recent character of this history, Erik Zürcher decided to commission the Institute for Migration and Ethnic Studies of the University of Amsterdam (IMES) to carry out this research project, including this final publication. Its Director, the anthropologist Rinus Penninx, combines a thorough and intimate knowledge of Turkish migration – reaching back more than twenty-five years – with expertise on migration and settlement studies in Western Europe in general. Some members of the IMES staff also work on the relations between trade unions and immigrants.

At the close of this project, I would first like to thank Erik Zürcher for taking the opportunity to link the different themes of IISH research in such an inventive and fruitful way. Secondly, thanks are due to IMES, and especially to Rinus Penninx and Judith Roosblad, for the preparation and coordination of the project. Finally we are grateful to Michael Wintle for his translation and correction of the English, and to Aad Blok, Ineke Kellij and Bart de Cort (IISH) for their role in the publication of this volume.

NOTES

1 T. Brass and M. van der Linden (eds), *Free and Unfree Labour: The Debate Continues*, Bern, 1997; M. van der Linden and J. Lucassen (eds), *Racism and the Labour Market: Historical Studies*, Bern, 1995; J. Lucassen and L. Lucassen (eds), *Migration, Migration History, History: Old Paradigms and New Perspectives*, Bern, 1997; see also the Supplements to the *International Review of Social History*, issued since 1993.

2 F. van Holthoon and M. van der Linden (eds), *Internationalism in the Labour Movement 1830–1940*, 2 vols, Leiden, 1988; M. van der Linden (ed.), *Social Security Mutualism: The Comparative History of Mutual Benefit* Societies, Bern, 1996; M. Linden and J. Rojahn (eds), *The Formation of Labour Movements: A Comparative Approach*, 2 vols, Leiden, 1990; J. Rojahn (ed.), *The Communist International and its National Sections, 1919–1943*, Bern, fortcoming; see also the reference to the *IRSH* in note 1.

3 E. Schwidder (ed.), *Guide to the Asia collections at the International Institute of Social History*, Amsterdam, 1996.

4 D. Quataert and E.J. Zürcher (eds), *Workers and the Working Class in the Ottoman Empire and the Turkish Republic 1839–1950*, London and New York, 1995; M. Tunçay and E.J. Zürcher (eds), *Socialism and Nationalism in the Ottoman Empire 1876–1923*, London and New York, 1994.

CHAPTER 1

INTRODUCTION

Rinus Penninx and Judith Roosblad

In the period after the Second World War, the economies of the West European countries involved in that war began a period of reconstruction. In a dominantly national context, some of the old forms of cooperation between employers, organised workers and state authorities were reinforced, and in part new forms were created to regain economic viability.[1] The political climate in which this took place was that of the emerging Cold War. This on the one hand led to the exclusion of those potential partners among trade unions that were suspected of overly internationalist or Communist sympathies. On the other hand the aims of reconstruction – building a new viable and stable economy, and creating employment – were primarily nationally defined goals (the fruits of which were designed for national citizens). These goals strengthened the national character of these reconstruction projects.

After a decade or so such reconstruction projects proved so successful that labour markets in some of these West European economies were confronted with labour shortages. Depending on factors such as the speed of economic reconstruction, the demographic situation, and the labour market participation (e.g., of women), these shortages were manifested sooner or later in all countries. By the mid-1950s most West European countries had become importers of labour. Systems for the recruitment and employment of these imported workers were developed. Recruitment areas differed from country to country: the historical ties (colonial or otherwise) of immigration countries with emigration countries or regions played a significant role in the first recruitment phase, while more diversification took place in all countries later on, not least because the migration movement, once well under way, gained its own momentum and sought new destinations.

The opportunities for migrants to find a place in that labour market, and the characteristics and qualities of that place, depend on a great number of factors relating to the number and type of the job opportunities themselves, and also on the way established participants in that labour market structure look at migrants and how they behave towards these newcomers: this includes not only potential employers in the first place, but also a number of other influential groups such as indigenous workers and their organisations in general, and public authorities, to name the most important ones. These established groups within the labour market have existing rules and regulations and have created special institutions to regulate the labour market. The functioning of such regulations and specific institutions may – independently of the structure of job opportunities – have a great influence on opportunities for newcomers, positively or negatively. In this study we will focus on organised workers and their unions.

Although the organisation of workers, particularly at the direct level of production units and at the local level of cities or small regions, is well established, the trade union movement (as we know it today) is relatively recent.[2] The launch of this modern trade union movement is related to the transition from the preindustrial to the industrialisation period, but the nature of that relationship is certainly not a direct and unique one. Lis and others have shown that the modern organised union movement did not start with industrialisation itself, but with the gradual growth of the nation state in the nineteenth century. The importance of this third party, the state, representing the common interests of all citizens within a clearly defined territory, fundamentally changed the dual relationship between employers and workers. Within the triangle – employers, workers, state – that gradually evolved, the three separate relationships had sometimes common and sometimes divergent interests. Changing coalitions within the triangle and the exertion of a mediation function by the authorities, legitimised by the wider tasks of state authorities for the benefit of the nation as a whole, were the practices that steered the development of industrial relations.

For the purpose of our study it is relevant to draw attention to some important implications of this development. The growth in importance of the nation state as a third party in the triangle meant the introduction of new elements that had previously been alien to both organised employers and workers. In the first place there is the concept itself of nation states: at the end of the nineteenth century an imagined community within a national territory became the dominant framework for the organisation of workers and employers alike; and indirectly citizenship – being a legitimate member of the national community – was introduced as an important distinction against aliens.[3] Not only did the presence of aliens within the borders of the nation state become an anomaly, but to a certain extent the immigrant alien worker also became by implication an anomaly in the organisation of labour, the more so in cases when such immigrants were regarded both as alien and temporary. The reverse was also true: the very definition of such workers as alien and temporary by both state authorities and unions, and the stubbornness with which they clung to that definition when it had become empirically untenable, seem a consequence of such thinking in terms of national communities and territories.

A second important implication for this study pertains to the special relationship between state and trade unions within the triangle. In the course of the last century in Western Europe, the trade union movement as an emancipatory force has contributed significantly to the development of nation states towards democratic welfare states. Looking at the developments during the last century, it is fair to state that the coalition between state authorities and trade unions has been the primary motor for the institutionalisation of the political, industrial, and social citizenship of all members of the nation state.[4]

Since European trade unions had become one of the potentially influential and powerful institutions within Western economies, in many cases cooperating with the government and employers' associations in the socio-economic decision-making process, they had to take their stand with regard to newcomers to these nation states. Not only employers and governments but also trade unions, as important intermediaries, had to formulate their policies relating to immigration and the migrant workers, who were actually arriving and becoming part of the workforce the unions were intended to represent. This made trade unions very important organisations for the socio-economic position of foreign workers in the host countries. Through membership of a trade union, foreign workers in theory gained indirect political influence. This could help to improve their socio-economic and political position in society. The main goal of trade unions was to protect the individual and collective interests of workers against the employers and other authorities who could affect the socio-economic position of the workers. It was in the interest of trade unions to represent as many workers as possible. Therefore, trade unions seemed to be the obvious organisations to protect the interests of foreign workers. However, for various reasons this was not always the case. And even if they tried to stand up for immigrants, this often appeared not to be an easy task.

Stating the Problem: Three Dilemmas of Trade Unions

It is within this roughly sketched historical context that we posit the question: how have trade unions[5] in West European countries reacted to immigration in general in the postwar period? How did they treat the immigrants who might potentially swell their rank and file? And what arguments did they use to legitimise their positions and actions (or nonactivity)? In order to answer these questions in a comparative research project, we have formulated three basic dilemmas with which trade unions are confronted regarding immigration and immigrant workers.[6] The first relates to immigration itself: should trade unions cooperate with employers and authorities in the employment of foreign workers or should they resist? The second dilemma emerges as soon as foreign workers appear: should trade unions include them fully in their ranks or exclude them as a special category? If trade unions in principle follow a line of inclusion, they are confronted with a third dilemma: should they advocate and implement special measures for these immigrants or should they insist on general, equal treatment for all workers? We will contextualize and specify these three dilemmas briefly below.

Immigration: Resistance or Co-operation?

A first dilemma, that was often not an easy one for trade unions, was: should they resist the claims of employers for the employment and recruitment of workers from abroad to fill vacancies, or should they cooperate, and if so, what terms should they try to lay down in the employment of foreigners?

Trade unions on the one hand feared that labour migration would be to the disadvantage of indigenous workers, since wages could be kept low and obsolete industrial sectors could be maintained because of the influx of foreign labour. They also had fears of a labour surplus and the opportunity for employers to turn to an alternative source of labour in industrial disputes. On the other hand they realised that in particular sectors of industry, migrant labour was indispensable, at least in times of economic expansion. Moreover, trade unions had always shown a tradition of international solidarity (at least verbally). Too open a resistance against immigrant workers (if that were the policy) would therefore not be in keeping with this ideology.[7]

Whatever the position held by trade unions in different countries and however variable their actual influence on the size and terms of foreign employment (which will be analysed in detail subsequently) the outcome has been that in the period between approximately 1960 and 1973 a specific labour migration system came into existence that connected most of the northwest European countries with a number of countries bordering the Mediterranean Sea as suppliers.[8]

One of the dominant specificities of that labour migration system was that the work of foreigners was defined as temporary employment.[9] The immediate argument was that capital investments should not lie idle because of a shortage of mainly unskilled and semi-skilled workers. The longer-term argument was initially that such employment would function as a buffer against conjunctural downturns, so avoiding unemployment in such circumstances by exporting it back to the country of origin. Later, new arguments were added: the necessary transition from increasingly obsolete labour-intensive production to a more modern, capital-intensive and automated production could be smoothed by the temporary employment of foreigners.

Temporary employment of foreign workers was also used as a buffer for industries that were on the verge of being exported abroad, for example the textile industry.

These arguments imply a strong element of protecting nationally defined goals, whether that refers to the entire economy, the labour market, or even the national community as a whole. The temporary nature was engrained in all the institutions and regulations that were brought about by the migration movement. And initially it was certainly also endorsed by the goals and motivations of the migrants involved. This definition made recruitment for trade unions more acceptable or at least more difficult to refuse, because it seemed to neutralize one of the basic fears of unions: the undermining of their bargaining power.

The migration movement of workers to West European countries has known various phases and has taken different forms. In the initial phase just described it started as a migration movement of workers who initially went on their own initiative or were later recruited to work in Europe temporarily, to save money and ultimately to return home. In the first phase many of the migrants did indeed return. Initially the system also functioned as a buffer against cyclical economic downturn. This aspect was clearly illustrated during the short recession of 1966/67. Kayser calculated that more than 400,000 migrant workers returned home from Europe as a consequence of that recession.[10]

On the other hand, the majority of the so-called temporary workers stayed, even in recession periods: migrant workers had become a structural part of the West European labour markets. Labour migration proved to be not quite so temporary and only partially manageable. For this reason a better directability of labour migration, and the development of a range of policy instruments to control the process, were of central importance in the ensuing period. To illustrate this general European development with the Dutch case,[11] as early as 1968/69 a rule was introduced in the Netherlands requiring that a temporary residence permit should be applied for prior to arrival in the Netherlands. In other words, permission in advance became a condition.

In addition to such entry policies, regulations were developed in a later phase to control the employment of foreign labour: not only did migrants need a work permit, but employers needed an employment permit and their number could be made subject to limitations, for example in the Netherlands by specifying a maximum number of foreigners for each firm. In the light of the dilemma of trade unions in relation to immigration it seems logical that most of these instruments were developed by the authorities with the explicit or tacit consent of the trade unions; the former tried to protect the interests of national prosperity, but at the same time the position of trade unions seemed to be strengthened in relation to employers.

The development of such instruments and the discussion about the temporary nature of migration took place at the zenith of the recruitment boom for foreign labour between 1968 and 1973. It was only after the first oil crisis of 1973 that the instruments were actually applied. A recruitment ban, in the form of a decision not to issue any more temporary residence or work permits to labour migrants, marked the formal cessation of the labour migration system.

Migration after 1973 did not dry up, but its character did undergo a change. The immigrant populations from the countries north of the Mediterranean Sea reacted quite differently to the recruitment ban and the restrictive measures and return migration policies that followed it, in comparison with those from, for example, Turkey and North Africa.[12] In the second half of the 1970s, the Italians, Spaniards, Greeks and Yugoslavs, and to some extent the Portuguese located in Northern Europe returned home on a substantial scale, and so Northern Europe witnessed a reduction in the size of these immigrant groups.[13] In the case of the Turks and North Africans, on the other hand, only minor and dwindling percentages returned to the country of origin, while there was a powerful wave of family reunion in the second half of the 1970s and early 1980s.

This state of affairs radically changed the discussion on labour migration in the 1970s. A growing number of the migrant workers stayed longer and longer and many of them brought their families to Western Europe, if opportunities to do so presented themselves. In the twenty years since then, immigrant populations in all major West

European countries have grown, notwithstanding restrictive policies, mainly through family reunion.[14] This also changed the character of the immigrant population. Although labour migration had been mainly a migration of male workers, women had also been recruited prior to the restrictive policies. But it was after the restrictive measures that the West European countries saw a significant feminisation of the immigrant populations and also, where policies were favourable, a feminisation of the immigrant workforce.

These immigrant populations have established their own communities and built up their own social infrastructure: religious organisations such as mosques and Koran schools, but also leisure and sports clubs, political organisations and pressure groups. They have established their own meeting places and coffee houses, shops, travel agencies and social service bureaus, and in some cases even their own primary schools. The existence of these settled immigrant populations as such led to further migration, including bringing over marriage partners for legally resident migrants, an immigration which is not induced by labour market needs, but which forms the consequence of the growing rights of long-settled immigrants.[15]

Not only did the migration patterns of the former labour migrants change, but new immigration also took place in spite of restrictive admission policies. The most important of these changes has been the growth of refugees and asylum seekers in West European countries since the mid-1980s.[16]

As a consequence of these developments the involvement of trade unions in immigration and the nature of the dilemma changed after the mid-1970s. In the direct sense trade unions were relieved of their original dilemma in so far as most governments implemented very restrictive policies relating to immigration for reasons of employment, and trade unions had only to endorse such policies.[17] But the picture turned out to be more complicated for trade unions when legally resident alien workers asked for the right to bring in their family members, and when in a later phase their children wanted to bring in marriage partners. As far as trade unions had included migrant workers and were prepared to defend their rights, it seemed logical to back these workers in their demands and plead for lenient admission policies in such cases. On the other hand these lenient policies would swell the number of new immigrants, some of whom would immediately or eventually enter the labour market. The dilemma of co-operation or resistance thus took a new form, and was intertwined with the second dilemma of inclusion or exclusion of migrants in the trade unions; a dilemma to which we shall turn shortly.

A comparable problem for trade unions arose in the mid-1980s when asylum migration gained momentum. There were similarities with the question of family reunion and family formation of settled immigrants: here too, trade unions were at best only indirectly involved in decision making and the eventual effects of their admission for the labour market could be anticipated. But there were also differences: the possible admission of refugees and asylum seekers is based on humanitarian grounds and international obligations to people who did not have any direct previous relations with trade unions or rights derived from their long residence. The decision of trade unions to involve themselves actively in this question in favour of these potential immigrants was thus of a more voluntary nature. If they engaged actively they did so more as part of a social movement than as trade unions in the strict sense.

Finally there is the very specific version of the first dilemma related to 'illegal' or 'undocumented' labour migrants. This question gained momentum after 1974, when recruitment was banned and restrictive policies implemented. In other words, whereas until that time it was fairly easy for 'spontaneous' migrants (as they were previously called) to regularise their position after finding work, the new system of control after 1974 made and kept them 'illegal'. For those trade unions which had previously had a close direct involvement in decision-making on immigration policies, one may assume that they also endorsed the stricter measures controlling illegals. Presumably, trade unions that had not been involved in such policies have more choice in taking a position in this respect.

Trade Union Inclusion or Exclusion of Migrant Workers?

The fact that from the late 1950s and early 1960s onwards large numbers of foreign workers had actually become part of the labour force, whatever the definition of their status, confronted the trade unions with a second dilemma, one that needed to be solved internally within the unions: should foreign workers be regarded as an integral part of the rank and file of the trade union movement and therefore actively recruited as members, having the same rights as any worker, or should they, as foreigners and/or temporary employees, be excluded partly or completely from full union membership or at least from the privileges of protected worker status? That question had both an ideological and a strategic component.

On the one hand trade unions were well aware of the fact that it was of the utmost importance that migrant workers should join the trade unions. Exclusion of immigrants would lead to a rift in the labour movement which would result in a weaker position of the unions during negotiations. This argument gained momentum in the course of time, once it had become clear that a large number of immigrants intended to stay permanently and that immigrant workers themselves were attempting to improve their labour position by a number of means.

On the other hand the inclusion of migrant workers might be seen as a threat to nationally defined labour market or trade union interests: it might clash with the interests of indigenous members, or at any rate certain factions within the labour movement might come to hold this view.[18]

To complicate matters even more, the two options with regard to immigration on the one hand and inclusion or exclusion on the other were inextricably linked. Castles and Kosack have expressed this as follows:[19]

> It may seem logical to oppose immigration, but once there are immigrant workers in the country, it is essential to organize them – not only in their own interests, but also in the interests of the workers. If the unions oppose immigration initially and even continue to do so, they may find that the immigrants do not trust them and are unwilling to join. Where this happens, the unions have the worst of both worlds. Not strong enough to prevent immigration, their attempts to do so only serve to alienate the new workers from them. The result is a weakening of the unions and the deepening of the split in the working class.[20]

As noted earlier, this initial link between the two dilemmas took a specific turn from the mid-1970s onwards, when settled immigrant workers started to bring in their families, and later their children wanted to bring in their marriage partners.

This second dilemma had in fact existed since the earliest presence of labour migrants in Europe, but as time went on, and particularly from the mid-1970s onwards, it took on new dimensions. As communities of immigrants gradually emerged and an organisational infrastructure took form in these communities, at least some of these immigrant organisations developed activities in relation to the labour market and the position of immigrants in it. Although there have been no serious indications that immigrants have tried to establish their own trade unions (often not a feasible option in any case),[21] they still could mobilise organisational forces within their community, especially in cases of troublesome incidents. In such cases the dilemma of the trade union was once again: to cooperate with these immigrant organisations, or to define them as a threat to the 'unity of the labour movement', or more directly, as impinging on the monopoly position of the unions?

Another new dimension arose as a consequence of the actions of the third partner in the triangle, the state, in relation to immigrants and their position in society. The manifest transition from a temporary labour migration system to permanent immigration on the part of a large percentage of these immigrants made urgent the question of whether and how West European societies had to adapt their policies regarding these immigrant populations. The outcomes have varied greatly in different countries. Some designed explicit integration policies relating to these immigrant groups as early as the late 1970s (Sweden) and early 1980s (the Netherlands); others have followed the path of ambivalent ad hoc policies, vacillating between insisting on return migration and partial integration policies; some stuck to the old definition of temporary migration and therefore saw measures that would facilitate integration as counterproductive.[22]

The way these developments in government policies have affected trade unions and the extent to which they have been involved varies greatly, as we shall see later. As a consequence of the stances that trade unions had developed in relation to the first and second dilemma, they also took a stance, explicitly or tacitly, in relation to those government policies: an active integration policy on the part of the government, one could assume, would be called for and welcomed by those unions that had opted for inclusive policies for immigrants within their own ranks. By the same token those unions that tried to resist immigration, and had insisted on the temporary nature of the employment of foreigners, would not be expected to support integration policies.

The Equal-versus-Special-Treatment Dilemma

If trade unions solve the second dilemma in favour of including migrant workers, based on the view that indigenous and migrant workers belong to the same class, and fundamentally share the same rights, they are still confronted on a daily basis with actual or alleged differences between the two categories.[23] These differences may be due to a range of factors: there is the specific position as a migrant; there may also be specific problems which relate to the cultural, ethnic or racial characteristics of the immigrant groups and the significance attached to such characteristics by society and trade unions and their members on the one hand, and by the immigrants themselves on the other; and there may be specific problems which immigrants experience as newcomers and/or ethnic minorities in participating and functioning within existing trade union structures which had formed long before their arrival. Although one can distinguish the source of these differences analytically, in practice they are often seen as intertwined.

Whatever the sources of such differences and specificities, they lead, in the case of policies which are in principle inclusionist, to a third dilemma: should trade unions be concerned only with the common interests of indigenous and migrant workers, and practise general policies for all workers, or should they also stand up for the specific interests and needs of their migrant members, and devise specific policies in order to attain material equality? In the former case the trade union will run the risk of acting unjustly when it does not make a distinction in its treatment of cases which are not equal. Migrant workers may be in a disadvantageous starting position, and if given the same treatment as indigenous workers this disadvantage will remain. However, if a trade union pays special attention to its migrant members, there is a chance that indigenous workers will feel slighted and might even resist the special treatment of migrant workers. The trade unions are faced with a choice between two alternatives which each show negative consequences. This has been termed the 'equal-versus-special-treatment dilemma' by De Jongh *et al.*[24]

In general terms, the decisive criterion is the extent to which trade unions give special attention to and create special policies for immigrants, minorities, or migrant workers. In practice, however, special policies may be of quite a different kind, having different implications. The most obvious practical specific measures pertain to communication (translated documents, bulletins, special counsellors, etc.), which are intended to remove barriers and make participation possible in the initial phases shortly after migration. More far-reaching are those special policies that take into account the position of a migrant, for example by stipulating in agreements that employers must take care of housing, or in special regulations that make possible a longer summer vacation in the country of origin. One step further again is to negotiate cultural or religious facilities such as the right to take time off for non-Christian religious holidays, or the provision of a place for worship and Hallal food for Muslim workers.

Special policies may also pertain to the integration of immigrant and minority workers into the organisational structure of the union itself. If unions recognise the specific needs of immigrants or minority workers, the question arises of how to organise them. At one extreme there is the minimal variant that creates facilities for immigrant workers to organise themselves as special groups within the union, but outside the existing core organisation, for example as subsidiary, often advisory bodies. At the other end of the scale are unions that have become conscious of the culturally and ethnically bound nature of their organisation and the barriers that immigrants have to surmount to participate fully and equally. They may implement more drastic specific measures to adapt that organisation to the new composition of its membership and try to guarantee the influence of the new membership in decision-making. Such unions may launch active anti-discrimination policies within their own ranks (as opposed to the 'colour-blind' approach), implement positive action in training and employing immigrants or minority members within their own ranks, and in getting them more strongly represented in the higher decision-making ranks of the unions. It may be assumed that such policies will meet with much more resistance.

The Study: Aims, Sources and Procedures

In the original proposal for this study we formulated the aim of the project as follows:

> … to make an international comparative study of the policies of trade unions, the arguments trade unions put forward to justify these policies, and their actual behaviour with regard to a) the immigration of workers and b) the presence of immigrant workers. This study will not be restricted just to labour migration and labour immigrants, but will also pay attention to the other categories of migrants such as ethnic minorities, refugees, asylum seekers and 'illegal' or 'undocumented' migrants. … The study should describe and analyse the development of trade union policies, actual behaviour, and legitimations in the course of the post-war period, with the emphasis on the period 1960–1993. Through comparison of such developments in West European countries and analysis of the contexts in which they have taken place, the study tentatively aims at an accounting for differences of policies, actual behaviour, and legitimations of trade unions in various countries and periods.

The basic strategy was to mobilise and bring together existing expertise by recruiting experts who had conducted research (preferably empirical) in northwest European, labour importing countries. These experts would be invited to contribute to the project, each providing relevant information about trade unions in the country they had studied. An ex-post analysis or comparative analysis based on existing research would be the result.

To guarantee comparability of the country accounts, an analytical framework was prepared. In general terms, that framework corresponds with the dilemmas outlined above. It also contains a number of reflections on factors that might explain the evolution within countries over time and differences and the variations between these countries. In the interests of comparability we have listed a number of questions and items, derived from the general framework, to which we have asked the specialists to pay attention in their country reports. The initiators and the invited specialists discussed the general framework and agreed upon the topic list in a workshop, held in Amsterdam in November 1993. First drafts of each chapter were discussed in a second workshop, held in Amsterdam in February 1995.

The resulting country reports fall somewhere between the categories of description and thoroughgoing comparison. On the one hand rigid comparison, in the sense that for all cases the same information would be made available and compared, turned out to be impossible, since the authors had to rely on the data and research available in the country concerned. But neither was it desirable: applying too rigid a comparative framework would have led to the neglect of the special characteristics and contexts relevant in the different cases. It could even possibly have led to a misunderstanding of important characteristics or developments in certain countries. That is why the authors have demanded and have been given the freedom to report in such a way that, using the analytical framework and the topic list as much as possible, they could also do justice to particularities and the internal logic (or 'socio-logic') of their cases. This also implies that the terminology used varies in the different contributions.

Specific terminology is an integral part of the dominant discourses in the various countries and thus a relevant subject of analysis. Pressing for uniform terminology cross-nationally would yield greater losses in information and analytical insight than gains. In the course of the exercise a firm agreement grew among all participants that historical and national contextual factors are of overriding importance in understanding the attitudes and behaviour of trade unions, and thus in explaining differences between countries. The terminology used is both a part and a reflection of these historical and national contexts.

Central Questions and Organisation of the Material

In the first section of this introduction we have positioned the problem to be studied with the help of a systematic instrument for description in which three basic dilemmas take a central place. The fundamental question demands a descriptive answer: how have trade unions faced these three dilemmas over the postwar period up to 1993? What variance can we register in the reactions of trade unions?

A much more complicated second question that we have mentioned in passing concerns the next step, that of systematic comparison: which factors account for the different stances of trade unions in different countries and periods? In the original proposal for the project an inventory was made of the existing literature. That literature proved to be poor on this specific question. But still we formulated four possible explanatory factors or sets of factors, summarised below.

The first concerns the power position of the trade unions in a society[25] and the structure of the national trade union movement. It was assumed that the more powerful a trade union is, the more effectively it will be able to use its influence to steer government policy relating to immigration in a direction favourable to the union. This power position, however, is evidently related to the position occupied in the national socio-economic decision-making process. That in turn presupposes a strong centralisation of the trade unions themselves and at the same time a substantial membership. Apart from these factors the structural relationship between trade unions and strong ruling political parties may be of crucial importance. This enables trade unions to get special attention on the political agenda for their demands.

Finally it was assumed that the internal structure of unions could be an important explanatory factor: some trade unions can have strongly centralised organisation, which makes substantial influence on the national level more likely, but at the same time can be weak on the shop-floor level, which can negatively affect their ability to protect the interests of immigrants within the immediate working environment.[26] Trade unions with a more decentralised organisation, on the other hand, will not have the same influence on a national level, but they can be rather more powerful at the local level.[27]

Secondly it was supposed that the policy of trade unions would be strongly linked with the condition of the economy and the labour market in that society. Obviously in times of ample national labour supply, trade unions will tend to oppose further immigration of labour, often in coalition with the authorities which protect the national welfare state. In the reverse case, pressure will be exerted on the unions to stop resisting immigration and to cooperate. Hence economic and labour market factors may be seen as important conditions for the scope within which trade unions, government and employers may operate.

These same economic and labour market conditions may also influence the stance of trade unions relating to the second and third dilemma: in times of widespread unemployment the competition (whether actual or supposed) between indigenous and migrant workers could increase, making a trade union policy of inclusion much more problematic. In the same vein one may suppose that there is much more room for special measures for the improvement of the socio-economic position of immigrants, such as positive action, language courses, management training, and suchlike, in times of economic affluence.

A third complex of factors explaining the differences is connected with society as a whole. Trade unions are inextricably linked with the society of which they are a part. Several students of the labour unions have stressed that it is the national arena in which trade unions have taken their form and in which they have to exert their influence.[28] They are not only influenced by national histories, but are indeed the product of those histories. National identity and ideology, public discourse, institutional arrangements, legislation, political structure and orientations: all these may influence the policy of trade unions towards immigration and immigrants. The way other important institutional actors, such as national authorities, churches, or political parties and movements, react to immigration and immigrants are important factors for trade unions to take into account. In stressing such national historical factors it is not suggested, however, that trade unions are always and unilaterally influenced by such developments in society at large. On the contrary, they may explicitly offer resistance and try to change the balance.

Fourthly and finally, factors connected with the characteristics and perceptions of immigrants may help to explain differences of attitude between trade unions in the various countries. The extent to which immigration is accepted by unions may be different for the various categories of immigrants. Acceptance may be determined by a special historical tie and the legal status that goes with it, as when there is competition between ex-colonial migrants and other immigrants.

Trade unions may be more sympathetic towards immigrants from those countries where unions are organised according to the same ideologies. Presumably this category of immigrants will be more easily accepted by the unions than immigrants coming from countries where there is no such trade union tradition.[29] Moreover, trade union tolerance may depend on the extent to which a particular immigrant culture or religion is considered different. Trade unions will be more sympathetic towards immigrants who are considered less ‘different’.

Furthermore, immigrants themselves may display characteristics which will determine the extent to which they can or want to be organised within trade unions (or possibly be organised outside the existing unions). One might think of their experience in an industrial working environment, or their perception of such work. Migrants who consider both their employment and their stay in the host country to be temporary, and who want to earn as much money as possible and return to their country of origin as soon as possible, are less likely to join a trade union; at the same time they may be looked upon as less promising members by the unions. In the course of their stay abroad this perception may change, however. Finally the legal status of migrant workers may be an important factor from the point of view of migrants themselves: the stronger the legal status of migrant workers, the less they have to fear when they participate in industrial action (e.g., fear of losing their work permit, or of deportation).

The factors mentioned in this last section apply to the individual level. However, characteristics of migrants could also be considered at the group or organisational level. Immigrant and minority organisations can affect the policies of trade unions by pressing unions to pay attention to the interests of their members. The more powerful minority organisations are, the more pressure they can put on trade unions to take their demands into consideration, and the better they are able to get their interests onto the agendas of trade unions.

In drawing up the descriptive instrument for the country accounts we have incorporated these possible explanatory factors alongside the descriptive device of the three dilemmas. It means that we have asked contributors to provide information on these points to facilitate the comparative analysis.

This ultimate analysis then results in the crucial question that we have referred to earlier: has there been, apart from the obvious externally caused parallel developments in the various countries, a convergence in the attitudes and actions of trade unions over the period since the Second World War?

In Chapters 2–8, country reports on seven West European countries will be presented: Switzerland, the Federal Republic of Germany, Austria, the Netherlands, France, the United Kingdom and Sweden.[30] In Chapter 9 the comparative analysis is presented, in the first instance by recording the variance of attitude and action on the part of trade unions in relation to the three dilemmas. Thereafter an attempt is made to account for the differences established. Finally, in the conclusion, we shall address the question of parallelism and convergence. In a brief look to the future, we draw some conclusions on the prospects of trade unions within the developing context of the European Union, and on the lessons to be learned from the present analysis.

NOTES

1. The general picture outlined here applies particularly to four of the seven countries we have studied: the Federal Republic of Germany, Austria, the United Kingdom and the Netherlands. The economic infrastructure of other countries like France (and Belgium) were hit much less severely by the Second World War. Sweden and Switzerland did not experience any direct consequences in that sense. The latter two countries in particular, and Belgium too, profited from that favourable start after the war and were also the first countries to employ and recruit foreign workers, in all three cases continuing prewar patterns. Switzerland and Belgium turned once more to Italy as the prime supplier of workers, while Sweden initially attracted workers mainly from Finland (which formed part of the Common Nordic Market already established in 1954).
2. C. Lis, J. Lucassen and H. Soly, 'Introduction', in C. Lis, J. Lucassen and H. Soly, 'Before the Unions: Wage Earners and collective Action in Europe, 1300–1850'. Supplement 2 of the *International Review of Social History* (1994): 1–11.
3. This is not to say that before the introduction of these new elements of distinction immigrants and immigrant workers were not discriminated against or excluded; discrimination on the basis of political, cultural, religious and ethnic

prejudices also occurred in earlier periods (see for example, J. Lucassen and R. Penninx, *Nieuwkomers, Nakomelingen, Nederlanders: Immigranten in Nederland 1550–1993*, Amsterdam, 1994, but such distinctions and actions were not legitimised by a strong alien-versus-indigenous or citizen ideology, nor reinforced by national institutions and policies (like migration and admission policies) that in principle include citizens and exclude aliens and in this way make migration and immigrants an anomaly within nation states. (A.R. Zolberg, A. Suhrke and S. Agayo, *Escape from Violence: Conflict and the Refugee Crisis in the Developing World*. New York/Oxford, 1989.)

4. Such observations seem to be valid at least for the period up to the 1970s. Recently a shift in coalitions has taken place, at least in some West European countries. The high burdens of the welfare state, partly as a consequence of the new division of labour in the world economy leading to structural unemployment particularly of low-skilled workers in West European countries, and the necessity of reform in the system and of austerity measures for national expenditure, have severed relations between state authorities and trade unions. In addition, political changes in some countries to more *laissez-faire* regimes have led to a fundamental shift on the part of authorities from coalitions with trade unions to closer cooperation with capital and employers. See Chapter 7 for examples, and also: J. Visser, 'Tussen nationale ontwikkeling en Europese uitdaging', in J. Visser (ed.), *De vakbeweging op de eeuwgrens: Vijf sociologische studies over de vakbeweging*. Amsterdam, 1996, 7–19; J. Visser and B. Ebbinghaus, 'Een halve eeuw verandering: Verklaringen voor convergentie en diversiteit van werknemersorganisatie in West-Europa', in Jelle Visser (ed.), *De vakbeweging op de eeuwgrens: Vijf sociologische studies over de vakbeweging*, Amsterdam, 1996, 20–53.
5. In this study we will focus on the major trade union confederations of the West European countries involved.
6. The descriptive and analytical instrument for the study was developed on the basis of existing literature before the project started. Important sources included: R. Bauböck and H. Wimmer, 'Social partnership and "foreigners policy": On special features of Austria's guest-worker system', *European Journal of Political Research* 16, no. 6 (1988): 659–81; S. Castles and G. Kosack, *Immigrant Workers and Class Structure in Western Europe*, London, 1973; S. Castles and G. Kosack, 'How the Trade Unions Try to Control and Integrate Immigrant Workers in the German Federal Republic', *Race* 15, no. 4 (1974): 497–514; S. Castles and M.J. Miller, *The Age of Migration: International Population Movements in the Modern World*, Basingstoke/London, 1993; D. Edye, *Immigrant Labour and Government Policy*, (Hants, 1987); G.P. Freeman, *Immigrant Labor and Racial Conflict in Industrial Societies: The French and British experience 1945–1975*, New Jersey, 1979; G.P. Freeman, 'The Consequences of Immigration Policies for Immigrant Status: A British and French Comparison', in A.M. Messina et al. (eds), *Ethnic and Racial Minorities in Advanced Industrial Democracies*, New York, 1992, 17–32; L. Gani, *Syndicats et travailleurs immigrés*, Paris, 1972; T. Hammar, (ed.), *European Immigration Policy: A Comparative Study*, Cambridge, 1985; R. de Jongh, M. van der Laan and J. Rath, *FNV'ers aan het woord over buitenlandse werknemers*, Uitgave 16, Leiden, 1984; M.J. Miller, *Foreign Workers in Western-Europe: An Emerging Political Force*, New York, 1981; J. Vranken, 'Industrial Rights', in Zig Layton-Henry (ed.), *The Political Rights of Migrant Workers in Western Europe*. Sage Modern Politics Series 9, vol. 25, London, 1990, 47–73; J. Wrench 'Unequal comrades: Trade unions, equal opportunity and racism', in R. Jenkins and J. Solomos (eds), *Racism and Equal Opportunity Policies in the 1980's*, Cambridge, 1987, 160–86; J. Wrench, 'Ethnic Minorities and Workplace Organisation in Britain: Trade Unions, Participation and Racism',

paper at the conference 'Ethnic Minorities and Their Chances of Participation: A Comparison between France, Great Britain, the Netherlands and the Federal Republic of Germany', Bonn, December 1992. It was discussed in a workshop with all contributors before starting the project.

7. Castles and Kosack, *Immigrant Workers and Class Structure in Western Europe*; Edye, *Immigrant Labour and Government Policy*; de Jongh et al., *FNV'ers aan het woord over buitenlandse werknemers.*
8. This applies to a lesser extent to Sweden and the United Kingdom. Although both countries recruited some workers from Mediterranean countries, Sweden attracted immigrants primarily from Finland and the United Kingdom experienced predominantly colonial and ex-colonial immigration.
9. This does not apply (or applies less) to colonial immigration.
10. B. Kayser, *Cyclically Determined Homewards flows of Migrant Workers*, Paris, 1972.
11. H. van Amersfoort and R. Penninx, 'Regulating Migration in Europe: The Dutch Experience, 1960–92', in: M.J. Miller, *Strategies for Immigration Control: An International Comparison*, Annals AAPPS, no. 534 (July) 1994, 133–46.
12. R. Penninx, *Immigrant Populations and Demographic Development in the Member States of the Council of Europe.* Part I (Analysis of general Trends and Possible Future Developments), Part II (Country reports), Part III (Statistical Annexes, Population Studies Series no. 12 and 13, Strasbourg, 1984); R. Penninx, 'International migration in Western Europe since 1973: Developments, Mechanisms and Controls', *International Migration Review* 20, no. 76 (1986): 951–72.
13. Political changes in the countries of origin may well have contributed to the return of migrants in the mid-1970s: the death of Franco in Spain, the retreat of the military regime in Greece, and the Revolution in Portugal.
14. In some cases the immigrant community also grew by the arrival of people requesting asylum. After the 1981 military coup in Turkey, for example, a considerable number of Turks asked for asylum in European countries. The escalation of the Kurdish problem in Turkey later also contributed to new inflows into Europe, based on asylum admission.
15. See for example, U-B. Engelbrektsson, *The force of tradition: Turkish Migrants at Home and Abroad*, Gothenburg, 1978, for Sweden; A. Gitmez and C. Wilpert, 'A Micro-Society or an Ethnic Community?: Social Organisation and Ethnicity among Turkish Migrants in Berlin', in J. Rex, D. Joly and C. Wilpert (eds), *Immigrant associations in Europe*, Aldershot, 1987, for Turks in the Federal Republic of Germany; and R. Penninx, 'Immigration, Minorities Policy and Multiculturalism in Dutch Society since 1960', in R. Bauböck, A. Heller and A.R. Zolberg (eds), *The Challenge of Diversity: Integration and Pluralism in Societies of Immigration*, Vienna/Aldershot, 1996, 187–206 for the Netherlands.
16. EUROSTAT *Demandeurs d'asile et réfugiées: Rapport statistique*, Vol. 1, 3D. Rapporteur R. van der Erf, Bruxelles/Luxembourg, 1994.
17. The restrictive policies and instruments with regard to labour migration have in fact implied that unskilled and low-skilled labour from non-European Union countries is heavily or totally restricted. Highly skilled workers, company-linked migration and other specific forms of labour migration, however, are not hampered in practice by such measures and have in fact also increased in recent decades. Labour migration within the European Economic Community, later the European Union, has gradually become free. The extent of exchange of labour between member states seems directly related to business cycles, although the general tendency is one of increase.
18. Castles and Kosack 'How the Trade Unions try to control and integrate immigrant Workers in the German Federal Republic', 497–514; Edye, *Immigrant Labour and Government Policy*; de Jongh et al., *FNV'ers aan het woord over*

buitenlandse werknemers; Vranken, 'Industrial rights', 47–73; H.J.J. Wubben, *Chineezen en ander Aziatisch ongedierte: Lotgevallen van Chinese immigranten in Nederland, 1911–1940*, Zutphen, 1986.
19. Castles et al., *Immigrant Workers and Class Structure in Western Europe.*
20. See R. Miles, and V. Satzewitch, 'Migration, Racism and "Postmodern" Capitalism', *Economy and Society* 19, no. 3 (1990): 334–58 for a critique on Castles and Kosack.
21. In several countries there are organisations of migrant workers, for example the Indian Workers' Association (IWA) in the United Kingdom and the Organisation for Moroccan Workers (Kommitee Marokkaanse Arbeiders Nederland – KMAN) in the Netherlands. Although these organisations protect migrant workers' interests and sometimes work together with trade unions, they are not meant as trade unions for immigrants or minorities and they do not consider themselves as such.
22. H. Vermeulen (ed.), *Immigrant Policy for a Multicultural Society: A Comparative Study of Integration, Language and Religion in five Western European Countries*, Brussels/Amsterdam, 1997.
23. de Jongh et al., *FNV'ers aan het woord over buitenlandse werknemers*,
24. de Jongh et al., *FNV'ers aan het woord over buitenlandse werknemers*, 219.
25. Cf. J. Vranken, 'Industrial rights', in Zig Layton-Henry (ed.), *The Political Rights of Migrant Workers in Western Europe.* Sage Modern Politics Series, London, 1990, vol. 25, 47–73.
26. H.P. Kriesi, *Political Mobilisation and Social Change: The Dutch Case in Comparative Perspective*, Aldershot, 1993.
27. B. Schmitter, 'Trade Unions and Immigration Politics in West Germany and Switzerland'. *Politics and Society*, 10, 3(1981): 323.
28. J. Visser, 'Tussen nationale ontwikkeling en Europese uitdaging', in J. Visser (ed.), *De vakbeweging op de eeuwgrens: Vijf sociologische studies over de vakbeweging*, Amsterdam, 1996, 7–19.
29. Cf. Wubben, *Chineezen en ander Aziatisch ongedierte.*
30. Originally Belgium was included as a relevant case. Unfortunately the Belgian contribution was not delivered. Consequently, in this book we will refer only incidentally to the Belgian case.

CHAPTER 2

TRAPPED IN THE CONSOCIATIONAL CAGE: TRADE UNIONS AND IMMIGRATION IN SWITZERLAND

Barbara Schmitter Heisler[1]

Introduction

The editorial of a recent issue of the quarterly journal of the Swiss Trade Union Confederation, SGB,[2] devoted to illuminating 'aspects of the foreigners policy', aptly sums up the main points made by the contributing articles: 'Much has changed, much has remained the same'.[3] As banal as this observation appears to be, it captures the developmental essence of Swiss 'foreigners policy' during the last fifteen years. The concept 'foreigners policy' clearly indicates what 'has remained the same': despite the fact that 18.1 per cent of the resident population and more than a quarter of the labour force were not Swiss citizens in 1993 (the largest percentage in Europe excluding Luxembourg and Liechtenstein), and the majority of the foreign population are in the possession of permanent residence permits, Switzerland does not have a policy on immigration, or migration, or minorities. The foreigners policy has been driven primarily by economic needs, or more specifically, labour market ones, and while it has undergone some changes (to be discussed below), its essential character as a foreigners policy oriented towards the labour market has not changed fundamentally, and is not likely to do so in the near future.[4]

In democratic societies, policy outcomes are shaped by complex political processes that typically involve a variety of interest groups. Immigration policy, or foreigners policy,[5] elicits the involvement of a wide range of interest groups and publics. Among them, employer organisations and trade unions play a central and frequently opposing role: seeking an abundance of preferably cheap labour, the former tend to favour the easy access of foreigners to national labour markets; fearing increased competition and downward pressures on wages and working conditions, the latter tend to favour restrictions. Once immigrants or foreign workers have legally entered a national labour market, their presence constitutes an additional challenge for trade unions. Writing in the 1970s, Castles and Kosack clearly identified the 'dilemma' faced by trade unions, as the 'potential contradiction between trade union policies towards immigration on the one hand and policies towards the immigrant workers once they are in the country, on the other'.[6]

In contrast to the government's foreigners policy, the position of Swiss trade unions has changed considerably, both in regard to immigration policy and in regard to their foreign colleagues. The majority of Swiss unions[7] have moved from an initial anti-immigration, restrictive position in the 1950s and 1960s to one favouring a liberalisation of policies; they have moved from modest support for defeating the 'over-foreignisation' campaigns of the 1960s and 1970s to campaigning for several initiatives aimed at improving the legal position of foreign workers in the 1980s and 1990s, and have supported a variety of measures to help integrate foreign residents into Swiss society. They have also moved from being guarded and typically uneager to organise their foreign colleagues in the 1960s, to actively welcoming them as members and seeking to organise them in their ranks.

Overall, Swiss trade unions have not been very effective in their attempts to shape the direction of Swiss foreigners policy. Although, as we shall see below, the unions' quest for policies restricting the number of foreigners permitted to work in Switzerland eventually met with some success, such success can be attributed to the oil crisis of the 1970s and the 'over-foreignisation' campaigns launched by conservative political elements. Despite the unions' long and vigorous lobbying efforts to abolish the lynchpin of Swiss labour market flexibility, the seasonal workers statute, it remains in place and is an integral part of the 1991 basis for the future of Swiss foreigners policy.[8] Their hope for change now rests with Switzerland's future integration into the European Union, a hope that has only recently been dashed by the Swiss electorate's refusal to join the European Economic Area.[9]

After years of ambivalence and a marked reluctance to organise foreign workers within their ranks, the unions slowly changed their attitudes and behaviour in the 1970s, and their attempts to recruit foreigners more actively have met with some success. For example, foreigners now represent 30 per cent of the membership in the Swiss Trade Union Confederation (SGB), which is the largest and most important trade union.[10] This percentage represents twice the figure of 15 per cent given for the late 1970s.[11] In short, in the eyes of many foreign workers, Swiss trade unions may no longer represent 'Swiss workers' guilds, which collaborate with the employers',[12] but organisations which represent the interests of their foreign and Swiss members.

To understand the trade unions' role in the making of Swiss foreigners policy and their changing relationship to immigrant workers, we need to understand the particular constraints and opportunities that have structured the Swiss trade unions' immigration dilemma. These are located in Swiss trade union structure and organisation (which is not independent of many other aspects of Swiss society and economy that cannot be discussed here) and the position of unions in the process of political decision-making.

Swiss Trade Unions: Political Position, Organisational Structures and Membership

As the primary organisations of the working class, trade unions are a mixture of bureaucratic organisation and social movement.[13] As such they function in two arenas, as representatives of members' interest at the workplace, bargaining for wages and working conditions, and as representatives of their members and the working class in the larger political process, in the process of policy and law making. As bureaucratic organisations, trade unions' effectiveness depends on their organisational structure (i.e., the degree of centralisation, the relative authority of peak associations, the degree of fragmentation), the relationship to other organisational structures (in particular employer organisations), and their integration into the system of political decision-making (i.e., the degree of corporatism). As a social movement, trade-union effectiveness and legitimacy is in large part derived from the membership (organisational density).

Political Position and Organisational Structure

Swiss politics is characterised by consensus building and power sharing.[14] Consultation and negotiations between government and interest groups play a crucial role in the political process. While the Swiss system of interest representation has many corporatist features, it also lacks some important elements of corporatism.[15] Comparing

Switzerland to Austria, Katzenstein refers to Swiss corporatism as 'liberal corporatism',[16] a corporatism characterised by a weak federal state, considerable entrepreneurial power, and weak trade unions.[17] However weak, the formal integration of unions into the process of consensus building and decision-making means that trade unions have some influence on the legislative and policy-making process.[18] Yet, as Kriesi has pointed out, such influence tends to be restricted to social issues, rather than economic ones.[19]

As representative interest groups, the unions' channel of influence is located in the pre-parliamentary decision-making process, where they formally participate in the *Vernehmlassung* (parliamentary hearing), and in various federal commissions set up to study legislative questions. Additional important channels of influence are provided by the mechanisms of direct democracy: the plebiscite (referendum) and the initiative. The plebiscite functions as an important veto instrument (only 50,000 signatures are needed by opponents of any act of parliament to call a referendum).[20] The threat of a referendum forces competing interests to find compromises and thus offers some influence for unions on commissions. The initiative, which requires 100,000 signatures, provides political groups with an avenue to change legislation. The SGB has made use of this provision nine times since 1940, all without success. In the area of foreigners policy, several initiatives supported by the SGB aimed at improving the position of the foreign population have also failed.

Swiss trade union structure is characterised by high levels of decentralisation and pluralism. The trade-union movement reflects Swiss federalism; most functions are delegated to individual unions which enjoy high levels of autonomy, while confederations have little power. In their extensive overview of Swiss unions and employee organisations, Fluder et al. distinguish between 'four sub-systems of associations'.[21] The interests of blue-collar workers are represented by a variety of unions organised into two major peak associations, the Swiss Trade-Union Confederation (SGB) and the Christian National Confederation (CNG).[22] White-collar workers in the private sector are represented by white-collar associations, organised into a peak association, the Organisation of Swiss White-Collar Employees (VSA).[23] Additional, separate associations are found in the public sector.

The organisations of blue-collar workers are fragmented along religious/ideological lines. The largest confederation, the SGB, is close to Social Democrat ideology, yet it has played a most accommodative role in the postwar period.[24] The CNG recruits from the same membership base, predominantly blue-collar workers in private industry. It has close ties to the Catholic workers' movement and the Christian People's Party,[25] and is more conservative politically than the SGB.[26] Several professional and occupational organisations not integrated in a confederation form an additional and separate structure.[27] The ideological, status, and religious divisions are among the sources of the relatively weak Swiss trade-union movement.[28] Yet while the differences between manual and white-collar workers and between the public and the private sectors are less easily bridged, the political-religious differences between the SGB and CNG have not prevented them from working together.

Membership

Many national labour movements have suffered loss of membership, power and legitimacy in the past twenty years. While the causes are multifarious – including structural changes in the economy, increased globalisation, more conservative political climates, and a trend toward deregulation and decentralisation – the increased diversity of the labour force (in terms of region, skill, gender, race, ethnicity, and nationality) has also had a negative effect on union membership. As pointed out above, immigration, a major source of labour force heterogeneity, represents a particular dilemma for trade unions. Once immigration has become a reality, trade unions should be interested in organising newcomers to maintain or increase their membership (and legitimacy). Yet in addition to introducing new dimensions for potential intra-organisational conflict based on ethnicity or ideology, the organisation of large percentages of immigrants, who are not citizens and who are not counted as full members of the political community, may spell a potential loss of power in collective bargaining and more importantly, in the larger policymaking process. As long as immigrants do not have the franchise, policymakers are less likely to pay much attention to organisations in which large percentages of the membership do not have full political rights.[29]

Currently, aggregate union density in Switzerland stands at 26 per cent.[30] While this figure is above those for France and Spain and approximately the same as for the Netherlands, it represents one of the lowest rates of unionisation in Europe. It also represents a decline from a postwar high of 32.9 per cent in 1975.[31]

Swiss Foreigners Policy

In his review of Swiss foreigners policy in 1989, the director of the Federal Office for Industry, Artisanship and Labour, BIGA,[32] noted that the change in terminology from *Fremdarbeiterpolitik* (foreign worker policy) to *Ausländerpolitik* (foreigners policy) signifies a recognition on the part of Swiss policy-makers that labour importation has turned into immigration. The essay begins with the following statement: 'As an important part of Swiss labour market policy, foreigners policy occupies a more important position in Switzerland than in other states.'[33] Indeed, while all the advanced industrial countries in Europe made use of foreign labour in the period following the Second World War, the conscious and deliberate use of foreign workers as instruments of labour market policy has deep roots in Swiss history, going back more than a hundred years.[34] Between 1888 and 1900 thousands of Italians worked in building the Gottardo and Simplon tunnels. In 1914, the percentage of foreigners in the population reached a first peak of 15.4 per cent. While the numbers of foreign residents dropped drastically in the following decades in the face of worldwide recession and two world wars, it seemed almost natural for Switzerland to reinitiate the recruitment of foreign workers when labour shortages first became apparent soon after the end of the Second World War. Following demands from employers and their organisations, the Swiss government concluded a recruitment agreement with Italy in 1948.[35]

The political history of postwar labour migration can be divided into three relatively distinct periods, with a fourth period emerging.[36] The first period, roughly from 1948 to 1963, was dominated by the rotation principle. The aim was to maximise the use of foreign labour according to labour market needs, and to minimise settlement and integration. The conditions imposed on migrant labour were stringent. Holders of annual permits (which had to be renewed each year) could not bring their families in for five years, and could not change occupation or employment during the first ten years. Despite such exacting conditions, the number of migrant workers increased rapidly in the 1950s, representing 16.8 per cent of the labour force in 1960 (10.8 per cent of the population). As the economic boom continued unabated and foreigners did not return home, more and more immigrants qualified for family migration, changing the demographic characteristics of the immigrant population to include more women and children.

The second period, roughly from 1964 to 1980, was characterised by the politicisation of the 'foreigners question'. The rapidly increasing number of foreign residents who qualified for family reunion was placing unanticipated pressure on the local infrastructure (especially housing and education) which was ill prepared. It was feared that the presence of so many foreigners, for the most part Catholic, and occupying low socio-economic positions, would upset the delicate balance of cross-cutting cleavages of language, religion and class, the hallmark of Switzerland's stable yet heterogeneous social and political system.[37]

The general unease concerning the presence of a large foreign population was further fuelled by the Italian government's demand for a new treaty governing Italian workers.[38] The new treaty, commonly known as the *Italienerabkommen* (the Italian agreement), was signed in 1964. It provided several legal and social improvements for annual permit holders and seasonal workers, and reduced to five the number of years of service required before receipt of a permanent permit. It became the catalyst for an extensive national political debate involving all imaginable social and political groups. Yet, despite new efforts to tighten the quotas placed on employers, and new controls on the admission of foreigners from non-adjacent countries (in particular Turkey), the foreign population continued to increase rapidly.

Although fear of 'over-foreignisation' was not a new theme in Swiss history,[39] the 'over-foreignisation' initiatives launched during this period were more than simple expressions of xenophobia: they reflected a concern among many Swiss citizens and interest groups that the government was not doing enough to control the numbers of foreign workers and their families.

The most famous initiative, the 1969 initiative launched by the National Action against the Over-foreignisation of People and Homeland,[40] was known as the Schwarzenbach Initiative after the leader of the campaign, Zürich deputy James Schwarzenbach, and demanded that the proportion of foreign workers be reduced to 10 per cent of the total population.[41] Its narrow defeat in 1970 (a 54 per cent 'no' vote) provided increased legitimation for even stricter government controls, and the government imposed national ceilings on the total numbers of new workers to be admitted each year (rather than on employers). While this measure failed to reduce the foreign population, it prompted four more initiatives. Although all were defeated, each with increasing margins, they gradually contributed to calming public opinion. It took the oil crisis of 1973 and the recession that followed finally to accomplish what the Swiss government had been unable to do: between 1975 and 1979, 181,000 foreigners left Switzerland. Although seasonal workers bore the brunt of the recession, the returnees included significant numbers of yearly and full-resident permit holders.

The third period, roughly from 1980 to 1989, was marked by a relative depoliticisation of the foreigners question, a pronounced trend towards increasing settlement on the part of the foreign population, and a general recognition that foreigners had become an integral part of the Swiss economy. In connection with the fourth and fifth over-foreignisation initiatives, the government made it clear that immigrants played an important economic role even in times of recession and restructuring, necessitating greater efforts to integrate the long-term foreign resident population.[42]

Following this recognition, the government set out to revise the aliens legislation, ANAG,[43] which dated from 1931. The ANAG is the legal source for the complex system of residence and work permits that has permitted the Swiss to exercise considerable flexibility with regard to their foreign populations. It distinguishes between five types of permits: permit A for permanent residents, permit B for one year, permit C for seasonal workers (limited to nine months), work permits for frontier workers, and short-term permits for special objectives.[44] The goal of the revision was to adjust the law to reflect the changed position of foreign residents and to liberalise the conditions attached to each permit in order to harmonise them with several international treaties concerning migrant workers (e.g., the ILO, European Social Charter, European Convention on Human Rights). The revised legislation, however, was defeated by a small margin in a referendum in 1982.

The emergent fourth period (from 1990 to the present) is marked by a new debate concerning Switzerland's position in the changing European political landscape. Although Swiss voters have rejected membership of the European Union, the government is concerned that Switzerland will suffer should it be left out in the future. In their report on Swiss foreigners policy in the 1990s, the Federal Office for Industry and Labour (BIGA) and the Federal Office for Foreigners Questions[45] outlined the three factors shaping current and future Swiss policy: the continued need for foreign labour; the need to restrict the number of foreigners in order to maintain 'national and cultural identity'; and the need to help long-term residents to find a new home in Switzerland.[46]

The so-called three-circles model developed by the BIGA reflects the need for a common European strategy to deal with common migration pressures, the need to adjust foreigners policy to the global economy, the need to continue to satisfy seasonal work requirements, and the need to improve the integration of long-stay foreigners. The three circles consist of (1) Europe (EU and former EFTA countries); (2) countries similar in culture (primarily Canada and the United States); and (3) the rest of the world. While members of the first circle should have relatively free access to the Swiss labour market, their numbers can be restricted. Members of the third circle, which lumps together citizens of the former Yugoslavia (which used to be a major source of seasonal labour) and its successor states with countries in Africa and Asia, are to gain access only under exceptional circumstances.

This brief summary of Swiss postwar foreigners policy clearly supports the statement quoted at the beginning of this article. What then has been the role of Swiss unions in formulating the foreigners policy, and how have they responded to the presence of immigrants over the past thirty years?

Immigration and Union Politics

Our discussion and analysis of Swiss trade-union positions and activities on the subject of immigration will focus on the blue-collar unions, the SGB and the CNG, and their most important member unions. The reasons are clear: first, SGB and CNG enjoy an exclusive right of political representation,[47] and the SGB occupies 60 per cent of employee seats allocated to worker representation on non-parliamentary commissions.[48] Secondly, since the vast majority of immigrant workers have been blue-collar, they have been most directly affected. Thirdly, the SGB and CNG are the largest and third largest federations respectively. They are also the most active politically.

While the SGB is by far the larger and more influential of the two confederations, representing about 50 per cent of all union members (compared to 12 per cent for the CNG), it does not have a monopoly of representation in most industries (exceptions include railways and watches), and its organising efforts take place in a competitive environment. The second-largest confederation, the VSA, has virtually no foreign members and rarely gets involved in the 'foreigners question'. While the status differences between white- and blue-collar unions is not easily bridged, the two major blue-collar confederations, the CNG and SGB, often work together.[49]

Both confederations are numerically dominated by two or three member unions. In the case of the SGB the two largest unions, the SMUV or Swiss Metal and Watch Workers Association[50] and the GBI or Building and Industry Union,[51] together make up more than half the membership of the sixteen SGB affiliated unions. Among the eleven member unions in the CNG, the CHB or Christian Wood and Construction Workers Association[52] alone represents almost half the membership.[53]

The SGB argues in its official policy statement in 1990 that its approach to the foreigners policy has embraced two aims: a quantitative limitation of the number of foreigners admitted, and a qualitative demand to promote the legal and social equality of foreigners. However, the first goal has clearly taken precedence, especially during the first twenty-five years after the war. Indeed, most unions were slow to welcome their foreign colleagues and to pursue the cause of greater legal and social equality.

The unions did not initially oppose the importation of foreign workers. Yet beginning in the mid-1950s they became increasingly concerned.[54] While they accepted the prevailing *Konjunkturpuffer* (cushion for the economy) perspective that labour migration was temporary, some unions, notably the SMUV, raised concerns about a potential threat to workplace security and depression of wages.[55]

Although the SGB began lobbying in 1957 for greater government control and restrictions, it was not until 1963 that the federal government imposed a first mandatory control on employers' unlimited access to foreign labour by placing numerical ceilings on the number of foreign workers employed in each company.

Protectionism was also the prime motive for the SGB's position that foreign workers should enjoy legal and social equality at the workplace.[56] Yet in the 1960s the unions' political argumentation for controls and limitations changed from protectionist to more nationalistic themes. Although the SGB and CNG and most of their member unions rejected the Schwarzenbach Initiative, the political debates surrounding it revealed the deep-seated ambivalence of Swiss unions toward immigration, an ambivalence that can be traced to ideological divisions within the union movement, and which ultimately served to deepen the divisions. For example, an SGB brochure opposing the Schwarzenbach Initiative, entitled *Are Foreigners Superfluous?*, was criticised by several member unions for being too pro-foreign.[57] A survey conducted at the Institute for Sociology at the University of Zürich found that 54 per cent of SGB members and 45 per cent of CNG members actually favoured the initiative.[58]

In view of all this it is not surprising that Swiss unions were confronted with some difficulties in recruiting and integrating foreign workers, and that foreign membership was low in both confederations.[59] Yet, within the SGB, and to a lesser extent within the CNG, there are some important differences in attitudes and actions between the federation member unions. Such differences are evident when examining the two largest unions within the SGB: the GBH/GBI and the SMUV.[60] The former was first to recognise foreigners as potential members rather than wage depressors, while the latter came to this position only in the 1980s.

The pro-foreign worker position of the GBH/GBI is not surprising, considering that the construction industry has long relied heavily on foreign workers, and especially on seasonal ones. In the late 1950s, foreigners already made up half of the labour force in the construction industry, making the organisation of foreigners a question of union survival. In an industry characterised by seasonal work, the union moved from supporting the seasonal rotation of foreign workers in the 1950s and early 1960s to supporting their long-term settlement, and the abolition of the seasonal workers statute. It has also aggressively recruited seasonal foreign workers, who are notoriously difficult to organise, and pursues their equal treatment concerning wages and working conditions as well as housing and occupational training. To recruit foreign workers, the union employed foreign agents, and in 1969 changed the rules which had restricted membership of the central board to Swiss citizens.[61] The union sees the integration of foreigners into Swiss society primarily in terms of their integration into the union structure and hierarchy. Currently the majority of GBH/GBI membership (70–75 per cent) are foreigners.[62] Finally, on the larger political stage, the GBH/GBI was among the strongest supporters of the Mitenand Initiative, a pro-immigrant initiative which was soundly defeated in 1981.[63]

The machine sector (which includes watches and metals) has been among Switzerland's most important industries. Neither the SMUV nor its CNG competitor, the CMV, the Christian Metal Workers Association,[64] were favourably disposed towards foreign workers.[65] Unlike the construction industry, where foreign employment has a long history, it was a relatively new phenomenon in the metal and watch industry. The historically male and highly skilled workforce saw its power being eroded by structural changes in the industry and increased competition from less skilled workers, including women and foreigners. Accordingly, the SMUV expressed concerns that the increasing number of foreigners in the industry would threaten 'Swiss quality' and the 'principle of partnership'.[66] From the mid-1960s on, the union made some efforts to recruit foreigners by creating special sections, and in collaboration with the Centro Italo-Svizzero Addestramento Professionale (CISAP, founded in 1966 by unionised foreign workers) it offered vocational training.[67] Although the SMUV employed a foreign official as early as 1957 and expanded its Italian language newspaper in 1962, the union's leadership refused the request for an Italian-speaking central secretary (in 1960 foreign membership of the SMUV amounted to 12 per cent). Prevailing anti-foreign attitudes were also expressed in membership support for the Schwarzenbach Initiative.

Nevertheless, in the mid-1980s foreign membership in the union had increased to 30 per cent of the total. Unlike in the GBH/GBI, the increase must be attributed primarily to changes in the legal position of foreigners (the majority being in possession of permanent residence permits) rather than an aggressive recruitment campaign.

The changes in the position of Swiss unions (both the confederations and their member unions) regarding immigration and the presence of foreigners in the mid-1970s can be attributed to the fact that some union demands, especially the limits placed on the number of foreigners permitted to work in Switzerland, became federal policy. These limitations were not so much a direct result of union political pressure; rather it was the case that union demands increasingly happened to coincide with the interests of many other groups in Swiss society. In addition, in the eyes of many, the various over-foreignisation campaigns had posed a threat to Swiss political stability and consensus building. Under these circumstances, the limitations allowed the unions to save face, to recognize that immigration was a fait accompli, and to devote more attention to their second goal, the integration of the foreign population.

Today, the majority of foreigners in Switzerland enjoy considerable legal stability. In December 1993, the permanently resident foreign population (excluding seasonal workers, short-term permit holders and cross-border commuters) stood at 1,260,283. Of these, 928,555 (74 per cent) were in the possession of permit C (permanent resident permit). The remainder in this category are permit B holders (annual permit).[68]

The economic downturn of the early 1990s is a good indicator of the changed conditions. While Switzerland had exported unemployment during the 1973 recession,[69] the fivefold unemployment increase in the early 1990s (an increase from 0.7 to 5.7 per cent between June 1990 and October 1992) was not accompanied by returns.[70] Indeed, the same period registered an increase in immigration of 5.7 per cent. While foreigners are still disproportionately affected by unemployment (their unemployment rate being twice that of indigenous workers in 1993), the days when they were easy 'cushions for the economy' are clearly over.[71]

However, the unions have not been successful in their quest to abolish the most controversial aspect of Swiss foreigners policy, the seasonal workers' statute. In addition to frontier workers, the employment of seasonal workers remains the centrepiece of Swiss labour market flexibility.[72] In August 1993, there were 71,829 seasonal workers among the 950,434 foreigners employed (7.6 per cent of total foreign employment). According to the *Bundesamt für Ausländerfragen* the figure represents an absolute and relative decline in the use of seasonal labour.[73] The current aim is gradually to restrict the use of seasonal workers to certain industries, for the most part in agriculture and tourism in the mountain cantons. To that end, the unions favour further reductions in the annual contingents and a liberalisation of the rules for changing seasonal permits to yearly permits. The latter process (*Umwandlungen* – literally, transformations) requires seasonal workers to have worked in Switzerland for four consecutive seasons of nine months each.

And what of measures to improve the rights of the resident foreign population? Although the SGB and CNG called for improvements concerning family migration policy, changes in the restrictive legislation were only made when pressure mounted from outside Switzerland, and when employers feared that they could no longer compete with other labour-importing countries (in particular Germany).[74] While opposition to the various over-foreignisation initiatives was not overwhelming or unanimous, some unions actively supported the pro-immigrant Mitenand Initiative, foremost among them the CNG confederation, and within the SGB, the GBH/GBI.[75]

Since then, they have also supported other pro-foreigner initiatives, all defeated at the polls. The most recent (June 1994) concerned the easing of legal procedures for the naturalisation of second-generation foreigners. Swiss naturalisation procedures are the most complex (and expensive) in Europe, and naturalisation rates have been extremely low in Switzerland. As in Germany, Swiss law requires persons who want to become citizens to renounce their previous citizenship. The SGB favours dual citizenship as a means towards better integration.[76] At its congress in November 1986, the SGB passed a resolution supporting the 'active participation of foreigners'. More specifically, the confederation calls for representative foreigner organisations, and political rights at the level of commune and canton.[77]

These positions clearly represent a significant change from the early 1960s, when the SGB took a rather ambiguous position and many of its member unions were vehemently opposed to immigration. These changes are reflected in foreign membership of unions, which increased steadily. Thus, Fluder et al. place foreign membership in the SGB at 31 per cent and at 21 per cent in the CNG in the late 1980s.[78] Reflecting in part the sectoral distribution of foreign labour, the percentages of foreign members vary considerably between member unions. For example, in the GBI foreigners make up 70 per cent of total membership, while they represent 30 per cent in the SMUV.

Given its membership composition, and as indicated above, the GBH/GBI has pursued a strong pro-foreigner agenda. The union's position concerning seasonal workers is clearly stated in a document responding to a study on the human and social problems of foreign seasonal workers by the Swiss Consultative Commission on Foreigners Questions, EKA.[79] In this document, the union reproaches the EKA for wanting to solve these problems within existing legislation and demands the abolition of the statute, which it considers to be an insult to the countries of origin and a violation of human rights.[80]

It is particularly important that the right to transform seasonal permits into annual ones is safeguarded. The union notes that employers and officials have tried to undermine that right and that the latter have used different criteria in different cantons. In some cases, being two days short of the thirty-six months required for the *Umwandlung* (conversion) to a yearly permit results in a refusal to grant it. The margin of tolerance had already been reduced to seven days (from fourteen) in 1982.[81] The union demands a reinstatement of the old fourteen-day margin and legal safeguards against the rotation of seasonal workers used to prevent them from meeting the thirty-six month continuous employment requirement.[82]

As is the case elsewhere in Europe, the new asylum issue has introduced new challenges for foreigners policy. Until the early 1980s, refugee and asylum policy, which is separate from (but parallel to) foreigners policy, did not present problems. In the mid-1980s, more and more people sought asylum in Switzerland. While many asylum seekers came from countries (especially the former Yugoslavia and Turkey) most affected by the more stringent restrictions, and especially by the reduction in the number of seasonal worker contingents, the numbers of asylum seekers from non-European countries also increased rapidly.[83]

NOTES

1. The author wishes to extend her gratitude to Dr Robert Fluder, Soziologisches Institut der Universität Zürich, for sharing some of his time and knowledge on Swiss trade unions, and to Gettysburg College for travel assistance.
2. Schweizerischer Gewerkschaftsbund.
3. E. Ackermann, 'Editorial', *Gewerkschaftliche Rundschau*, 86, 2 (1994): 3.
4. It is no secret that current Swiss migration policy is the most restrictive, most controlled and labour market-oriented policy in Europe. Although it is currently opposed by many segments of Swiss society (including the majority of trade unions), in favour of greater liberalisation, Swiss voters rejected joining the European Union in December 1992, a move that would have forced a liberalisation of Swiss policy and that was strongly supported by the trade unions.
5. In this chapter I will use the terms 'foreigners policy' and 'immigration policy' interchangeably, keeping in mind that the official Swiss use of 'foreigners policy' reflects the reality of Swiss policy.
6. S. Castles and G. Kosack, *Immigrant Workers and Class Structure in Western Europe*, London, 1973, 128.
7. The Swiss union movement is characterised by a high level of fragmentation along professional and religious/ideological lines, which will be discussed later in this chapter.
8. Bundesamt für Industrie, Gewerbe und Arbeit and Bundesamt für Ausländerfragen (BIGA) *Bericht über Konzeption und Prioritäten der Schweizerischen Ausländerpolitik der Neunziger Jahre*, Bern, 1991.
9. Although membership was supported by most political parties and economic organisations, the Swiss people narrowly (50.3 per cent of the votes) turned down membership of the European Union in December 1992.
10. In the CNG (Christlichnationaler Gewerkschaftsbund-Christian National Confederation) it is 20 per cent. R. Fluder, H. Ruf, W. Schöni and M. Wicki, *Gewerkschaften und Angestelltenverbände in der schweizerischen Privatwirtschaft*, Zürich, 1991.
11. B. Schmitter, *Immigration and Citizenship in West Germany and Switzerland.* Unpublished dissertation, 1979.
12. P. Gessler, as quoted in Castles and Kosack, *Immigrant Workers and Class Structure in Western Europe.*

13. W. Streeck, *Gewerkschaftliche Organisationsprobleme in der sozialstaatlichen Demokratie*, Königstein/Ts., 1981.
14. B. Hotz-Hart, 'Switzerland: Still as Smooth as Clockwork?', in A. Ferner and R. Hyman (eds), *Industrial Relations in the New Europe,* Oxford, 1992; P. Katzenstein, 'Capitalism in One Country?: Switzerland in the International Economy', *International Organisation*, 34 (1980): 507–40; P. Katzenstein, *Corporatism and Change: Austria, Switzerland and the Politics of Industry*, Ithaca, NY, 1984; P. Katzenstein, 'Small Nations in an Open International Economy: The Converging Balance of State and Society in Switzerland and Austria', in P. Evans, D. Rueschemeyer and T. Skocpol (eds), *Bringing the State Back In*, Cambridge, 1985; H. Kriesi, *Entscheidungsstrukturen und Entscheidungsprozesse in der Schweizer Politik*, Frankfurt a.M./New York, 1980; W. Linder, *Swiss Democracy: Possible Solutions to Conflict in Multicultural Societies*, New York, 1994.
15. Katzenstein, *Corporatism and Change;* Kriesi, *Entscheidungsstrukturen und Entscheidungsprozesse in der Schweizer Politik.*
16. Katzenstein, *Corporatism and Change.*
17. In Austria corporatism is characterised by a central state, strong unions, and weak entrepreneurs.
18. The participation of interest groups is anchored in the constitution of 1947. Yet union influence has tended to be relegated to social policy and unions have not fared well in the field of economic policy. H. Kriesi, *Entscheidungsstrukturen und Entscheidungsprozesse in der Schweizer Politik.*
19. Ibid.
20. In a comparative analysis of union participation in economic policymaking in Austria, Switzerland, the Netherlands, Belgium and Ireland, Compston argues that the 'high level of union participation appears to be determined almost entirely by the existence of the referendum option, which can be used by unions (among others) to threaten legislation'. H. Compston, 'Union Participation in Economic Policy-Making in Austria, Switzerland, the Netherlands, Belgium and Ireland, 1970–1992'. *West European Politics*, 17 no. 1 (1994): 140.
21. Fluder et al., *Gewerkschaften und Angestelltenverbände in der schweizerischen Privatwirtschaft*; see also R. Fluder, *Stability Under Pluralist Conditions: Trade Unions and Collective Bargaining in Switzerland.* Paper presented at the 12th World Congress of Sociology, Madrid, 1990.
22. Christlichnationaler Gewerkschaftsbund.
23. The VSA (Vereinigung Schweizerischer Angestelltenverbände) is the second largest peak association.
24. The *Arbeitsfrieden* (literally, work peace, but better translated as 'social peace agreement'), which was concluded in 1937, represents a unique feature of Swiss labour relations. It is a kind of continuous contract between employers and unions, regulating wages, hours of work, holidays, child allowances, etc. The agreement needs to be renewed every five years and virtually precludes strike as a means for making demands. Although some union representatives have begun to question the attractiveness of the peace agreement, and although the 'general positive position' towards the agreement has declined somewhat since 1987, three quarters of workers recently surveyed favoured the agreement. Support was particularly strong among union members (*Neue Zürcher Zeitung*, 8 May 1993).
25. CVP, Christliche Volkspartei.
26. A Protestant workers' association, the SVEA (Swiss Association of Protestant Workers, Schweizer Verband Evangelischer Arbeiter) was founded in 1920, and merged with the CNG in 1982.
27. The largest of these, Zentralverband des Staats- und Gemeindepersonals (ZV), is an association of civil servants.

28. Other reasons for the weakness are the decentralised nature of Swiss industry, and the relatively small size of factories.
29. As will be discussed below, this is particularly important in the Swiss system of direct democracy.
30. This figure is not without its problems. It also includes some employee organisations that 'cannot be unproblematically classified as unions'. B. Hotz-Hart, 'Switzerland: Still as Smooth as Clockwork?', in A. Ferner and R. Hyman (eds), *Industrial Relations in the New Europe*, Oxford, 1992.
31. Europäisches Gewerkschaftsinstitut, *Gewerkschaften: Mitglieder in Europa*, Brussels, 1993.
32. Bundesamt für Industrie, Gewerbe und Arbeit.
33. K. Hug, 'Ausländerpolitik – eine mittel – und längerfristige Betrachtung', *Die Volkswirtschaft*, 5 (1989): 8–29.
34. H.-M. Hagmann, *Les travailleurs étrangers: Chance et tourment de la Suisse*, Lausanne, 1966; J. Niederberger, 'Die politisch-administrative Regelung von Einwanderung und Aufenthalt von Ausländern in der Schweiz: Strukturen, Prozesse, Wirkungen', in H.-J. Hoffmann-Nowotny and K.-O. Hondrich (eds), *Ausländer in der Bundesrepublik Deutschland und der Schweiz*, Frankfurt a.M., 1982.
35. A second labour agreement was concluded with Spain in 1961.
36. B.S. Heisler, 'From Conflict to Accommodation: The "Foreigners Question" in Switzerland', *European Journal of Political Research*, 16 (1988): 683–700.
37. K. Mayer, 'Migration, Cultural Tensions and Foreign Relations: Switserland', *The Journal of Conflict Resolution*, 11 (1967): 139–152.
38. The 'Italian agreement' of 1964 improved the position of Italian workers in Switzerland and these improvements were then extended to cover Spaniards as well. According to the agreement, family reunion could take place after eighteen months of residence, on the condition that 'proper housing was available'; changes of occupation and employment could be made after five years, and seasonal workers could apply for yearly permits after forty-five months (nine months a year for five years).
39. V. Willi, *Überfremdung: Schlagwort oder bittere Wahrheit*, Bern, 1970.
40. Nationale Aktion gegen die Überfremdung von Volk und Heimat.
41. A previous over-foreignisation initiative, submitted by the Democratic Party of the Kanton of Zürich in 1965, was withdrawn in 1968 when the government promised to increase its efforts to reduce the number of foreigners.
42. Recognising the need to take positive action, the government established the Eidgenossische Konsultativkommission für das Ausländerproblem-EKA (Consultative Commission for Foreigners Problems) in 1970. The task of the commission was to promote 'a conflict-free community between Swiss and foreigners'. As the name indicates, the commission's work is limited to studying problems and suggesting directions and proposals. The realisation of proposals is left to public and private organisations operating at the local level. In other words, the EKA has no policy-making power and did not include foreign members until 1980.
43. Bundesgesetz über Aufenthalt und Niederlassung für Ausländer (Federal Law Concerning the Stay and Residence of Foreigners).
44. It should be noted that neither frontier workers nor short-term permits for special objectives are subject to government control and limitations.
45. Bundesamt für Industrie, Gewerbe und Arbeit and the Bundesamt für Ausländerfragen.
46. Bundesamt für Industrie, Gewerbe und Arbeit & Bundesamt für Ausländerfragen (BIGA), *Bericht über Konzeption und Prioritäten der Schweizerischen Ausländerpolitik der Neunziger Jahre*, Bern, 1991.
47. L. Parri, 'Staat und Gewerkschaften in der Schweiz (1873–1981)', *Politische Vierteljahresschrift*, 28 (1987): 35–58.

48. H. Compston, 'Union Participation in Economic Policy-Making in Austria, Switzerland, the Netherlands, Belgium and Ireland, 1970–1992'. *West European Politics* 17, no. 1 (1994): 123–45; Fluder et al., *Gewerkschaften und Angestelltenverbände in der schweizerischen Privatwirtschaft.*
49. Early attempts of CNG unions to organise Italian workers in collaboration with the ACLI (Associazione Christiana Lavoratori Italiani) were the source of some hostility between the two confederations. B. Schmitter, 'Trade-unions and Immigration Politics in West Germany and Switzerland'. *Politics and Society* 10, no. 3 (1981): 317–34.
50. Schweizerischer Metall- und Uhrenarbeiterverband.
51. Gewerkschaft Bau und Industrie, formerly GBH, Gewerkschaft, Bau und Holz, Building and Wood Union.
52. Christlicher Holz- und Bauarbeiterverband.
53. While there have been some minor mergers in the past twenty years, the main lines of fragmentation remain in place. H. Anderegg, 'Stellenabbau wirkt sich auf Mitgliederzahl aus', *Dokumentation* no. 12, Bern, 1994.
54. F. Höpflinger, *Industriegewerkschaften in der Schweiz*, Zürich, 1976.
55. Schweizer Metall- und Uhrenarbeiterverband (SMUV) *Geschaftsbericht SMUV*, Bern, 1955.
56. F. Höpflinger, *Industriegewerkschaften in der Schweiz.*
57. R. Riedo, *Das Problem der ausländischen Arbeitskräfte in der schweizerischen Gewerkschaftspolitik von 1945–1970*, Bern, 1976.
58. For example, when the SMUV recommended that its members vote against the initiative, the number of resignations increased by 50 per cent compared to the previous year (Höpflinger, *Industriegewerkschaften in der Schweiz*; P. Heintz and H.J. Hoffmann- Nowotny, *Bericht über eine Survey Analyse des Fremdarbeiterproblems.* Part I: 1–120. Zürich, 1970.
59. According to estimates, 10 per cent of members in the SGB and 15 per cent of the CNG were foreigners in 1968 (Castles and Kosack, *Immigrant Workers and Class Structure in Western Europe*, London, 1973). The CNG was first to attempt to organise foreign workers (R. Riedo, *Das Problem der ausländischen Arbeitskräfte in der schweizerischen Gewerkschaftspolitik von 1945–1970*, Bern, 1976; J. Siegenthaler, *Die Politik der Gewerkschaften*, Bern, 1968). When the SGB unions started to pay more attention to their foreign colleagues, this produced some competition and divisions between the two federations.
60. The GBI represents the merger in 1992 of the GBH (Gewerkschaft Bau und Holz) and the GTCP (Gewerkschaft Textil, Chemie und Papier).
61. Foreigners have come to occupy important positions in the hierarchy, including the central secretary (Pacheco), and the commission that negotiates the union contracts.
62. The CHB (Christlicher Holz- und Bauarbeiterverband) is the CNG's rival. While the 1960s were marked by some competition, the current foreign CHB membership is only 30 per cent.
63. The Mitenand Initiative (literally, 'Together Initiative') was launched by the Catholic workers movement in 1977 and was supported by both the Catholic and Protestant churches, most immigrant organisations, and left-of-centre political parties and organisations (including the Social Democratic Party, but not the SGB). The initiative (which was soundly defeated) would have guaranteed human rights for all immigrants, choice of workplace and family migration, full social security coverage, the right to renew a permit, and the abolition of the seasonal workers statute.
64. Christlicher Metallarbeiterverein.
65. In the 1950s the SMUV and CMV favoured policies that would protect 'the indigenous workforce' from foreign competition. The CMV was first to recognise a need to organise foreigners.

66. One needs to keep in mind that the 1937 Peace Agreement began as an agreement between the SMUV and the employers' organisations; Riedo, *Das Problem der ausländischen Arbeitskräfte in der schweizerischen Gewerkschaftspolitik von 1945–1970*, 44.
67. Schweizer Metall- und Uhrenarbeiterverband (SMUV), *Unsere Zukunft hat Geschichte: Eine Festschrift zum hundertjährigen Bestehen des Schweizerischen Metall- und Uhrenarbeiter-verbandes*, Bern, 1988, 150.
68. These figures do not include international officials and their families, or asylum seekers (Bundesamt für Ausländerfragen, *Die Ausländer in der Schweiz: Bestandergebnisse Ende Dezember 1993*, Bern, 1993)
69. M. Schmidt, *Der Schweizerische Weg zur Vollbeschäftigung*, Frankfurt, 1985.
70. OECD/SOPEMI, *Trends in International Migration: Annual Report 1993*, Paris, 1994.
71. A. Frick, 'AusländerInnen sind nicht mehr Konjunkturpuffer', *Gewerkschaftliche Rundschau* 86, no. 2 (1994): 4–6.
72. They have succeeded in reducing the degree to which seasonal workers can be used as cushions for the economy, by fighting for restrictions on the numbers of seasonal workers (first introduced by the Federal Government in 1963).
73. Bundesamt für Ausländerfragen, *Die Ausländer in der Schweiz: Bestandergebnisse Ende Dezember 1993*, Bern, 1993.
74. These changes were made in the Italian Agreement. See note 38.
75. See note 38.
76. J.-F. Marquis and G. Grossi, *Einwanderer-Minderheit ohne politische Rechte*, Bern, 1990.
77. Ibid. It is important to note that the EKA does not support local voting rights for foreigners.
78. R. Fluder, H. Ruf, H. Schöni and M. Wicki, *Schweizerische Arbeitnehmerorganisationen im Vergleich: Binnenstruktur und Verbandspolitik*, Schlussbericht zum Forschungsprojekt Nr. 12–26587.89, Zürich, 1991.
79. Eidgenössische Konsultativkommission für das Ausländerproblem (EKA), 'Menschliche und Soziale Probleme der Ausländischen Saisonniers', *Information Nr. 17*, Bern, 1988.
80. Meanwhile the union demands that seasonal workers are legally protected. Seasonal workers (about 60,000 each year in construction) should have the right to a written contract specifying wages, working hours, and rent. Wages must be union wages.
81. Gewerkschaft Bau und Holz, *Saisonnierstatut im Wandel.* Schriftenreihe der Gewerkschaft Bau und Holz no. 5.1.1992.
82. The union draws attention to the increasing numbers of accidents that they attribute to the inexperience of seasonal workers, and notes that seasonal workers appear to be younger each year, replacing older workers.
83. In 1990, 36.1 per cent of the 35,425 asylum seekers were from Turkey and Yugoslavia, with 10 per cent coming from Africa and 13.3 per cent from Sri Lanka.

CHAPTER 3

THE FEDERAL REPUBLIC OF GERMANY: AMBIVALENT PROMOTION OF IMMIGRANTS' INTERESTS

Peter Kühne[1]

The German Trade Unions in the System of Labour Relations

When international comparisons are drawn, the trade unions in Germany, and particularly those organised in the German Trade Union Federation (DGB)[2] since 1949, are regarded as being relatively strong. The variant of a 'different' or 'Rhenish' capitalism, whose competence in economic efficiency and social balance is emphatically described by Michel Albert,[3] would not have been possible without strong trade unions which have been able to assert their weight in the tripartite structure of labour relations, comprising state, capital, and trade unions. But what is the reason for the relative strength of these trade unions?

As far as the degree of organisation or membership density is concerned, in a European comparison they are somewhere in mid-field at approximately 30 per cent. What is important is the principle applied in postwar Germany of a unified trade union: 'one company, one trade union'. This unified trade union regards itself as ideologically and politically neutral, as the common representative of all categories of employed persons (workers, salaried employees, civil servants), and as the integrating organisation of employees with different characteristics: young, old, men, women, Germans, immigrants, people of different ethnic origin.

Also of importance are the legal provisions governing labour relations which restrict the trade unions, but also strengthen them to a certain degree in times of economic crisis or loss of members. These legal provisions apply to all levels on which there are processes of dialogue between capital and labour: the macro-social level, with autonomy in collective bargaining as guaranteed by the Constitution; the level of large enterprises, in whose supervisory boards the trade unions have a seat and a voice; and the company level, with the system of dual representation of interests. 'Dual' means here that the works councils, as the legal representative bodies of the employees of a company, are not trade-union bodies: they are elected by the staff of the company. Nevertheless, the trade unions do decide on the composition and policies of most works councils, depending on trade union shop stewards in the companies.

As early as 1949 this system of legally regulated labour relations was identified by Theodor Geiger as a system of 'institutionalised class conflict', in which structurally produced class conflicts are transformed into limited and controllable conflicts of interest.[4] Walther Müller-Jentsch described the trade unions as 'intermediary organisations',[5] and thus accentuates a pragmatism characteristic of labour relations in Germany, and the orientation of the conflicting parties towards compatible interests, where consent and compromise are possible.

As legally recognised participants in the system of labour relations, trade unions have, according to Götz Briefs, the 'position of a quasi-public corporation'.[6] They have a place in all public and political institutions so that their voice at least is heard. They are represented, for example, in industrial jurisdiction, in social security institutions, in political advisory bodies ('concerted action'; round tables with the Federal Chancellor, etc.), in bodies that assist the Ministries, and in parliamentary hearings. They are also indirectly present in parliaments and governments through political parties and their representatives. Furthermore, trade unions may take part in public hearings in the Bundestag, as was the case in 1990 when the law on foreigners was amended.

As quasi-public bodies, the trade unions have also been involved in formulating government migration policy, even if, as is shown in more detail below, they have by no means been able to obtain all their demands. Through the board of administration of the Federal Institution for Labour,[7] a self-administering public institution with a tripartite structure (state, employers, trade unions), they were involved in the recruitment policy of the 1950s and 1960s, and in obtaining complete equality for immigrant workers in pay and in legislation on labour and welfare.

Another important interface between trade unions and the state is the 'coordinating group for foreign workers' at the Federal Ministry of Labour and Social Affairs. The members of this body represent trade unions and employers, the churches, welfare groups, the Federal Institution for Labour, the labour departments of two selected *Länder*, the parliamentary groups of the Bundestag, and other Federal Ministries.

At company level the Employees' Representation Act[8] stipulates that both the works council and the employer must ensure that no person is discriminated against for reasons of race, religion, nationality or origin (§ 75). The works council also has the task of 'integrating foreign workers at their place of work and promoting understanding between them and the German workers' (§ 80). This refers to all areas of cooperation and co-determination of the works council in social and staff matters. But it also refers to the election procedure for the works council and consideration of the proportion of non-German candidates, as well as the distribution of tasks and the release of employees from normal duties in order to sit on works councils.

The Federal Republic of Germany: An Immigration Country

Germany is not a classic country of immigration.[9] In fact, historically it was a country of considerable emigration; we only have to think of the five million Germans who settled in the USA in the nineteenth century. In the eighteenth and nineteenth centuries, millions of Germans also emigrated to Eastern and South-Eastern Europe. In the twentieth century there was a mass exodus because of the Nazi regime, emigrants and refugees, including a total number of approximately 300,000 German Jews.

In the first period of the German Reich (1871–1914) there was great demand for workers, and 1.2 million people from Poland and the Austro-Hungarian Empire were recruited, including some 350,000 so-called Ruhr Poles, who were employed in heavy industry (mainly coal and steel) on the Rhine and Ruhr. During the Second World War, eight million imported 'foreign workers', prisoners of war and concentration camp prisoners were used by the Nazis to maintain production. Then, after the Second World War, West Germany first took in refugees and expellees from the former German territories in the East, and then German settlers from non-German territories in Eastern and South-Eastern Europe. In addition, up to 1961 when the border was closed, a large number of refugees and immigrants came from the Soviet Occupation Zone or GDR. A total of 15 million people came to Germany by these means.

But the economic miracle meant that as early as 1955, the huge labour potential of all these people was insufficient. 'Guest workers' from Mediterranean countries were to be recruited for certain jobs, first in agriculture, then in industry. Recruitment agreements were signed for this purpose with Italy (1955), Greece and Spain (1960), Turkey (1961), and Morocco, Tunisia, and Portugal (1963–65).

In 1973 the recruitment and employment of these 'guest workers' was at its peak: 2,595,000 foreign workers, accounting for 11.6 per cent of the total number of employed persons. That same year turned out to be the year of the first serious economic and employment crisis in postwar Germany. In November 1973 the German government imposed a recruitment stop which has never since been lifted. Since then, immigration on a large scale has only been possible for family members who are joining their relatives in Germany, or for EU citizens as part of the growing free movement of labour within the European Union.

It was not until the end of the 1980s that a 'new immigration' was noticeable, for a variety of reasons:

- the collapse of the socialist systems in Eastern Europe and the opening of the borders, particularly the border with the GDR;
- outbreaks of fierce nationalism, ethnic cleansing, civil wars and pogroms in the same countries, and also in Turkey and other crisis areas;
- the possibility of return for hundreds of thousands of people from the East who regard themselves as Germans;
- abuse of human rights and political persecution in more than a hundred countries; and
- further recruitment of guest workers employed for a limited period, seasonal workers, and contract workers, particularly from Poland and Eastern Europe.

On 31 December 1993 a total of 6,878,117 non-Germans were living in the Federal Republic of Germany, including 1,918,395 from Turkey, 1,535,576 from other EU member states, 929,647 from the former Yugoslavia, and 260,514 from Poland. In June 1993 the number of foreign employees paying national insurance was 2,183,579. In addition there were 72,743 contract workers, who in 1993 were employed mainly in the building industry. The GDR also used to employ contract workers from various friendly states (e.g., Vietnam, Mozambique, Angola, Poland). Of the roughly 95,000 persons employed when the GDR and the Federal Republic were reunited, the majority were made redundant, received a very small amount of money, and were told to return to their home countries.

On 15 July 1993, 19,036 of those contract workers were still in the Federal Republic of Germany, including 16,635 Vietnamese. Unlike the foreign workers recruited to work in West Germany, they did not receive a residence permit. They were regarded as 'guest workers' in the strict sense of the term, obliging them to leave the country after being dismissed or after their contracts had expired. This discrimination at the level of foreign workers reflects the general East-West difference in the united Federal Republic. At the end of 1993 it was not yet clear whether the residence status of foreign workers in the East could be improved from a humanitarian point of view.

Migration: Support or Resistance by the German Trade Unions?

In 1955, the West German trade unions were first confronted with the issue of migrant workers, just six years after the re-establishment of their umbrella organisation the DGB. They found it difficult to give their approval: German nationals who had been expelled or had fled from the countries of Central and Eastern Europe were still arriving in West Germany. Among those coming from the GDR, many were highly qualified. At the same time, about a million West Germans were registered as unemployed. Would the majority of trade union members be prepared under these circumstances to agree to the recruitment of foreign labour, in the first instance from Italy? In the end the trade unions did agree. The initial reservation displayed by them towards the migrants clearly gave way later on to a readiness to become concerned with their interests. There was thus a definite change in trade-union migration policy. However, other considerations did not change, like those relating to the situation on the domestic labour market.

Trade-union migration policy was essentially reactive, and therefore turned on the state of government policy. Trade union migration policy either agreed or disagreed with it. Since 1955 there have been four distinct phases:

1. A phase of recruitment considered to be temporary. The trade unions tried to ensure equal rights for foreign workers at work and in social insurance (1955–73).
2. A phase of 'consolidation' of the employment of foreigners, which reached its zenith when the government ordered a recruitment stop and at the same time said it was prepared to integrate socially those migrants whose lives were firmly established in the Federal Republic (1973–82). This phase largely coincided with the SPD-

FDP coalition in West Germany, and met with the particular approval of the trade unions.

3. This no longer applied to a third phase which started with the Conservative-Liberal coalition, which wanted fewer migrant workers in Germany (1982–90). The government officially encouraged foreign workers to return home, and the trade unions reacted by demanding a secure right of residence and socio-political equality. For the trade unions the Federal Republic was now an 'immigration country'.
4. Since 1989 at the latest, the year when the East European political systems collapsed, the discussions and arguments about the status of the labour migrants have been overtaken by others concerning refugees and asylum seekers, who had been arriving in increasing numbers, especially from Eastern Europe. The trade unions wanted a humane approach to the issue, and article 16 of the German Constitution,[10] which anchored the right to asylum, to be maintained and observed. But for the first time they were also in favour of a regulatory mechanism which would on the one hand allow labour immigration and on the other consider the interests of the German labour market. They hoped that a regulatory mechanism of this sort would ease the debate in Germany on immigration, refugees and asylum.

Recruitment Phase

Although in 1955 about one million people were still registered as unemployed, it was already forecast that there would not be enough workers available for the labour market. The reasons for this included:

- the continuing postwar boom and the mobilisation of all domestic productivity potential;
- the unfavourable age structure of the population;
- social achievements, such as a reduction in working hours;
- more holiday time and a lower retirement age;
- longer compulsory education; and
- the development of the Bundeswehr (the German armed forces).

From 1960 the supply on the labour market was exhausted. For the first time in the postwar history of the Federal Republic, the number of vacancies registered with the labour office was higher than that of the unemployed. Full employment had been reached. When in 1961 the GDR built the Wall and so stopped the stream of qualified workers, the readiness to recruit foreign workers increased. It was seen as the cheapest and quickest way to solve the problems of shortages on the domestic labour market. At the same time the recruited workers functioned as an 'economic buffer'. Foreign workers should be easy to employ when the economy was doing well, but equally easy to dismiss and send back in a crisis. The 1965 Aliens Law and the 1969 Work Development Law formed the legal basis for this. In the first postwar recession of 1966–67 the number of employed foreigners fell from 1,314,031 (1966) to 1,014,774 (1968), or by over 300,000. They thus bore a disproportionate share of the labour market risk.

The DGB endeavoured from the very start to influence the opening of the labour market by making use of the Federal Institution for Labour,[11] and thus opened information and control possibilities for itself. It attained equal wages as well as labour and social security rights for the workers recruited from abroad, which was, of course, also in the interest of the majority of members who were German. In this way any doubts in the organisation about the employment of foreign workers were removed. As a result of the full employment, the growth in the economy and salaries, and a general improvement in the working conditions of German employees, the majority of them accepted the employment of foreign workers. However, everyone concerned, including the trade union leadership, considered the employment of foreigners to be temporary. For example, the DGB raised no objections to the Aliens Law of 1965, the objective of which was to control the presence of foreign workers in the Federal Republic, nor to the Work Development Law of 1969, section 19 of which states that Germans will be given priority in filling job vacancies.

The Phase of 'Consolidation'

The serious labour market crisis of 1973 led to many political discussions on how those workers who had been recruited could be sent back to their countries of origin. Labour market policy concerning foreigners thus became 'consolidation policy', which meant:

- the German labour market closed its doors to foreigners (recruitment stop in November 1973);
- labour migrants are encouraged to return home;
- social integration of some labour migrants whose work will probably always be in demand and who are also prepared to adapt to the situation in the Federal Republic;
- 'socially responsible control' of workers' families bringing in new members: restrictive regulations governing the opportunity for children of the first generation and spouses of the second and following generations to join their families or partners in Germany.

The employment crisis of 1973 also frustrated the further development of a trade union migration policy. The differing interests of the German majority and the foreign minority became very apparent. Opinion polls indicated a spectacular change in mood in working-class districts and in companies. The electoral successes of neo-fascist groups, particularly in working-class districts of big German industrial cities signalled the same message. The DGB's involvement in the official government programme of consolidating the employment of foreigners (i.e., integration of the foreigners living in Germany, but no new immigrants) was ambivalent: partly it endorsed it, partly the DGB simply tolerated it. Apart from closing the German market to foreign workers, there were further restrictive elements of trade union policy in this matter:

- emphasis on more priority for Germans in job vacancies;
- rules governing the interval that relatives joining their families in Germany had to wait before they could have access to the German labour market;
- a lowering of the maximum age of children joining their parents from eighteen (age of majority) to sixteen;
- receipt of social security remains grounds for deportation;
- foreigners are not allowed to participate in political elections.

On the other hand, those foreigners who by that time had genuinely made Germany their permanent home were not completely forgotten. It was, for example, due to the influence of the trade unions that the general rule on the implementation of the Aliens Law of 1 October 1978 was reworded. The new version made the so-called consolidation of the legal residence status of foreign workers easier: depending on the situation and the conditions they fulfil, they should generally receive, on application, an unlimited residence permit.

The Phase of Promoting the Return of Foreigners

The Conservative-Liberal coalition, which came to power in 1982, was not satisfied with the consolidation results achieved up to that point. They wanted to change the Aliens Law of 1965 in order to be able to send foreign workers home, and the CDU/CSU argued for a 50 per cent reduction in the number of foreigners in the Federal Republic by 1990. A commission with members from the national and some of the regional (*Länder*) governments prepared extensive amendments to the law, and presented them on 24 February 1983. The commission's report shows the restrictions considered by the different political groups. Among other things, there are two distinct categories of restrictive measures:

- an extension of the reasons and opportunities for deporting foreigners, for example, the receipt of unemployment benefit.[12]

What in the past had been a possible reason for deportation was rephrased and tightened to make it the rule.

- far-reaching restrictions on relatives who wished to join their families in Germany. The age of children of the first generation of foreign workers who were allowed to join their parents in Germany was to be reduced from sixteen to six. In order to be able to check the legality of the residence of children and adolescents in the Federal Republic, a residence permit was to become compulsory for them. The parents of any children who lived in the Federal Republic without a permit were to be forced by law to accompany the children back to the country of origin. And spouses of the second and following generations were hardly to be allowed to come to Germany at all.

Another law of the new Federal Government concerning labour migrants also aimed to send foreigners home: the Law to Support the Willingness of Foreign Workers to Return Home[13] of 29 November 1983. Section 1 of this law laid down that workers from Yugoslavia, Portugal, Spain, Turkey, Tunisia, Morocco, and Korea would receive 'return assistance' if, after 30 October 1983, they became unemployed because their company or large parts of their company closed down. The same would apply if they had been put on short time at least six months before applying for return assistance, and they had worked on average for at least 20 per cent lower wages. The grant they received to return home amounted to DM 10,500. It was based on an average unemployment period of seven months, and an average unemployment benefit for this period of DM 1,500. In addition to this sum, DM 1,500 would be paid for each returning child. The application for a grant to return home had to be made by the end of June 1984.

Departure was possible up to the end of 1984 without any reduction in the grant. Furthermore, under section 2 they could also apply for reimbursement of their contributions to the state pension scheme. Additional sums paid by some large companies, particularly in the coal and steel industry, led to a real re-emigration flow of foreign workers and their families. In 1984 a total of some 300,000 people returned to their countries of origin after claiming the government grants and assistance from their employers.

There were other items in the policy on foreigners promoted by the Conservative-Liberal government:

- The Federal Government rejected the right to freedom of residence for foreigners[14] as a preliminary stage or alternative to naturalisation.

- It rejected an option for foreigners from outside the EC to return to Germany after returning to their countries of origin for a trial period.
- A claim for social security remained grounds for deportation.
- Unemployed persons without a secure residence status should also expect to leave the country. Permanent residence permits were not issued to unemployed persons.
- The demand that it should be impossible to expel people after a certain period of residence was rejected. This also applied to foreigners who were born or grew up in the Federal Republic and who had no ties to any other country.

Such policy proposals, the very purpose of which was to make foreigners leave (which had already been manifested in the form of the Law to Support the Willingness of Foreign Workers to Return Home), led to sharp controversies between the DGB and the Conservative-Liberal Federal Government. In a decision of the national executive board of the DGB of 6 September 1983 on policy regarding foreigners, the DGB confirmed the positions it already held. Reference was made firstly to the options open to the authorities for expelling people: in view of the disproportionately high number of unemployed foreign workers and the above-average length of unemployment, the DGB stated that it no longer agreed to the expulsion of foreigners drawing social security. The Metal Workers' Union[15] even stated that under no circumstances should the drawing of social security[16] or unemployment benefit[17] lead to deportation.

The DGB also had new proposals regarding expulsion procedure: it demanded that the courts should decide what reasons justify an expulsion, so that the authorities would have to take legal action for an expulsion order. The DGB once again confirmed its demand made in 1973 that, after ten years' uninterrupted residence in the Federal Republic, expulsion should no longer be possible. The DGB furthermore rejected the so-called return assistance law. It sought a joint position with the churches on migration policy. At the same time, the distance from the employers' associations, who were the only other group also demanding a policy of repatriation of labour migrants, was growing. For the first time, the IG Metall demanded the right for all non-Germans to vote in local elections.

The new version of the Aliens Law[18] was passed by the Bundestag in 1990, despite the votes of all the opposition. The most important provisions of the new law were as follows. A foreigner was to receive a firm residence status only if he or she had regular, permanent employment. The special form of permanent residence permit granting the foreigner more security (*Aufenthaltsberechtigung*) required that the foreigner had sufficient living space, which could not be less than in socially subsidised housing. The law restricted the scope for family members to join their families in Germany by setting certain conditions which were very difficult to fulfil, for example proof of 'sufficient living space'. Juveniles might enter the country only if both parents were living in the Federal Republic. A visa or residence permit was compulsory for children and juveniles under the age of sixteen. The *Aufenthaltsberechtigung* would only be issued after the applicant had paid sixty monthly contributions to pension insurance, a condition which young people find extremely hard to fulfil. Members of the second or third generation who wanted their spouse to join them had to be over the age of eighteen, must have entered the country as a minor, needed to hold an unlimited residence permit, and must have been legally resident for at least eight years. The few progressive changes were implemented only half-heartedly and with many restrictive conditions; they included:

- that spouses and children of labour migrants have their own right of residence;
- juveniles and pensioners have the option to come and go at will;
- naturalisation became easier for juveniles.

Even if not all the intentions originally expressed by the CDU/CSU were implemented in this law, it was a definite rejection by the government of the trade unions' ideas on integration and equality. Non-Germans were still split up into a variety of different status groups. On the one hand there are the privileged groups with a firm residence status, and on the other there are those whose residence is limited to a certain term. In any conflict the interests of the Federal Republic of Germany rank above those of the foreigner.

In 1990 another fundamental decision was made – in this case by the High Court: the second senate of the Federal Constitutional Court declared void those laws of the *Länder* (states) of Schleswig-Holstein and Hamburg which would have given non-Germans the right to vote in local elections. At the time of the fourteenth Federal Congress of the DGB in May 1990, it was thus clear that all the initiatives with which the trade unions had prepared to give foreigners more equality had failed. The essentials stated in Application 258 of trade union policy could only be of a rhetorical nature – particularly the demand for a change in the Aliens Law which would acknowledge that immigration was a fact and would grant a right of residence to all those who have been living in the Federal Republic for eight years or who were born within the area where the Constitution was applicable. The demand that foreigners should be able to vote or to stand as candidates in local elections was similarly no more than an assertion: after the decision of the Federal Constitutional Court, the granting of voting rights to foreigners would require an amendment of the German Constitution, and the majority required for that is really nowhere in sight.

Another of the DGB's demands was the right of naturalisation and, at the same time, dual nationality, a demand which in view of some signs of agreement from members of the government coalition may have some chance of being met. An independent petition on dual nationality, supported by the DGB, was able to collect one million signatures in less than a year, and was then presented to the Bundestag.

Moreover, on the question of further immigration the DGB and IG Metall have shown a more open attitude, which goes far beyond the terms of the amended Aliens Law. While in the past the DGB supported the recruitment stop of 1973, and immigration was only possible within the framework of the freedom of movement in the European Union or family reunion, they now stress that this should not be misunderstood as a general ban on migration. Exceptions to the recruitment stop are possible, they maintain, as clearly defined exceptional rules which could come about with the participation of the self-governing bodies of the Federal Institution for Labour. It must be ensured, they say, that the social welfare and wage agreements of the Federal Republic are observed. The DGB also sees the possibility of legal labour immigration, even if subject to quotas and demands (the IG Metall took this position as early as 1991) and is calling for a national immigration law. Under no circumstances, they say, should there be any quotas on family reunion or on the number of politically persecuted persons accepted by the Federal Republic. It is also very important that the immigration policy of industrialised countries does not lead to a brain drain elsewhere, due to qualified persons leaving their countries, because this would lead to more impoverishment of those countries. As in the past the DGB is still opposed to all forms of limited employment (whether seasonal workers, guest workers, or contract workers),[19] which according to the new version of the Aliens Law are possible and are made use of by workers from Central and East European partner countries, particularly Poland. Bilateral agreements made between the Federal Government and the respective countries of origin plan an annual quota of a total of 100,000 employment contracts.

Refugees and Asylum in Trade Union Migration Policy

After the 1980s, when the annual number of refugees in the Federal Republic had already reached the 'magic number' of 100,000, the number of asylum seekers shot up even higher in the years 1989–93.

In 1992 no less than 438,191 non-Germans applied for asylum, and in 1993 a total of 322,842. Almost two thirds of these asylum seekers were refugees from countries in Eastern and South Eastern Europe. The majority were not labour migrants 'in disguise', but had genuine reasons for fleeing: the outbreak of dangerous nationalism in their countries of origin, war and civil war, discrimination, and even the pogrom-like persecution of ethnic minorities. The same applied to refugees from Turkish Kurdistan, from various African states, and from Afghanistan. The great majority of these people thought they would return if their countries managed to solve their political conflicts, and to achieve relative economic stability and social cohesion.

The Federal Government was clearly not prepared to recognise this, nor to implement it in new concepts of development cooperation or asylum policy. Neither was it prepared to act in a humanitarian, pragmatic manner on the basis of international agreements and existing laws. Instead the parties even made political use of the problems which some parts of the German population had in accepting these refugees, for example at various local and regional elections in 1991–93. This opened the gates for extreme right-wing parties, neo-Nazi groups, and spontaneous groupings of right-wing and violent young people to move into a political vacuum, and even to carry out acts of violence which are comparable with pogroms. In the year 1992 the Federal Office for the Protection of the Constitution registered a total of 2,285 acts of violence proven or suspected of being the acts of right-wing extremists, a 54 per cent increase over the previous year. Seventeen people were killed, including seven non-Germans. There were 598 cases of physical injury and 701 cases of arson and incendiary attacks. A further 77 cases of desecration of Jewish cemeteries, monuments and other buildings were registered.

The individual basic right to political asylum, derived from section 16 II 2 of the Constitution, collapsed. This was possible because the SPD leadership itself also signalled a change in its policy on asylum, with its 'Petersberg Immediate Programme'.[20] Earlier the SPD had been prepared to support changes in asylum proceedings with the coalition partners, namely a drastic acceleration of proceedings and a severe restriction of the guarantee of access to the courts. After the change in policy decided on in Petersberg in August 1992, the SPD leadership came to an agreement in December of that year with the coalition parties on an asylum compromise, and on a joint draft by the CDU/CSU, FDP, and SPD of a new asylum article 16a in the Constitution, and further bills for the accompanying laws. Although all this generated extensive internal problems for the SPD, and though only a very small majority of the SPD parliamentary group agreed to the draft, a majority which would allow an amendment to the Constitution was guaranteed.

In article 16a, passed with a two-thirds majority on 25 May 1993, paragraph 1 lays down the individual basic right to asylum only to restrict it seriously in paragraphs 2–4: it will be possible to turn away at the border any asylum seekers who come to Germany via third countries in which the application of the Geneva Convention on Refugees and the European Convention on Human Rights is ensured. The same applies to asylum seekers who come from countries which are believed to be safe countries. It is no longer possible to stop an expulsion order by appealing against a decision.

For the SPD it was, of course, important to see how its traditional partner, the DGB, would react to its new ideas. Would it act politically against the involvement of the SPD in the all-party compromise? Would it even put extra-parliamentary pressure on the party? Or would it also give in to the pressure of the SPD and the government parties and revise its own resolutions? In fact neither happened. Unlike the main religious organisations, the DGB and the trade unions maintained their resolutions without – apart from a few exceptions – seeking any conflict with the SPD. This was remarkable, since in previous years the trade unions had taken firm stands on the asylum issue.

For example, in 1990 at the fourteenth DGB Federal Congress, there was a total of nine motions on policy towards aliens, and four of them dealt in great detail with the issue of refugees. Motion 21 of the Berlin DGB group for a 'humane asylum policy' was fully adopted; it referred not only to those who may claim political asylum and how their basic right as determined in article 16 of the Constitution (as it was then) could be fully established again, but also to the so-called 'de facto refugees', and their situation. Their residence status had to be guaranteed, the congress asserted. They could not be deported 'as long as there is even any presumption of danger in their own country'. Motion 23 of the Federal Youth Committee clearly demanded that people who flee from war and civil war in their own countries should also be granted asylum, and it also stated: 'Torture is a reason for asylum in every case.' Motion 22 of the Bavarian DGB group referred specifically to reasons why women flee, and said that these reasons should be considered in asylum law and proceedings.

These resolutions show that at that time, the trade unions were actively discussing the situation of the refugees. This applies both to understanding who should be legitimately regarded as a refugee under current circumstances, and to resistance to procedural restrictions and harassing behaviour by state or local administrations. And above all it confirms the trade unions' wish to retain article 16 II 2 of the Constitution.

In the ensuing years, 1991 and 1992, this course was confirmed, through declarations of the DGB Federal Committee[21] of 7 November 1991 and 7 October 1992, and at trade union level through many motions at the seventeenth trade union conference of the IG Metall in October 1992, some of which were adopted. It was in particular the Foreign Workers' Department[22] and the politically responsible member of the national executive board of the DGB,[23] Jochen Richert, who reported on the positions prepared by the trade unions and the DGB on the asylum issue to the members and to the public. At the same time close co-operation developed with Pro Asyl (an organisation that helps refugees) and Amnesty International, which was also expressed in joint press statements. In association with Pro Asyl, a total of three discussion papers were developed. They were highly regarded and were published as pamphlets, but for reasons of cost only a relatively small number could appear, and so they probably did not reach companies or the grass roots of the trade unions. Interestingly enough, two of these discussion papers dealt with the basic right to asylum, and expressed – on behalf of the DGB – fierce criticism of the SPD in their change of opinion on asylum policy. But this remained the exception. The third paper dealt with the planned drastic reduction in social security benefits to refugees.

Generally speaking it can be said that the trade unions do not see themselves simply as the representatives of workers' interests, but feel they should take a stand on human rights particularly where the situation of asylum seekers and refugees is concerned. Their messages and declarations address not only their members, but also a wider public in the democracy. Furthermore, trade union members are reminded of the many opportunities they have to take action. For example staff committees and works councils are told that, together with employers, they should make any signs of racism in companies or public bodies the subject of company and staff meetings. Shop stewards and works councils can approach the small number of asylum seekers who can now take regular employment and make social-insurance payments. Any chances for Germans and foreigners to meet and get to know each other should be taken up, for example during breaks, or through taking part in in-company and trade union courses. In particular, trade-union representatives in companies have special responsibility here.

At a local level, DGB groups are urged to become involved with refugee councils and seek cooperation with foreigners' organisations and people or initiatives that work against racism. Special attention is to be paid to hostels or homes housing large numbers of foreigners. DGB groups, companies, and public sector administration are asked to 'adopt' such dwellings. And indeed many groups associated with the trade unions such as students, youth associations, and others have organised activities for the benefit of asylum seekers and refugees.

Overall it can be said that an inner-trade-union minority supported the refugees. Young trade unionists in particular have been very active. For example the DGB and trade unions have been involved in many demonstrations and informative or cultural events, and there have been appeals, sometimes together with employers and employers' associations, and sometimes together with human-rights organisations and church groups. On occasion, telephone chains have been set up to protect foreign colleagues and their families, for example by the DGB Hanover, or the works councils and IG Metall representatives of the Dortmund Krupp-Hoesch iron and steel works. Sometimes in big companies the chair of the works council has taken the initiative; in others they have been urged to speak openly about the racism found in certain companies, and in one case at least (IKEA) they have been asked to confront it through a petition.

But those who had expected great gestures, first towards asylum seekers, and then – after the arson attacks in Mölln and Solingen – towards Turkish immigrants and their demonstrating children and grandchildren, were to be disappointed. It was the Central Board of the Jews in Germany and its chairman, Ignatz Bubis, and Jewish intellectuals from Germany and abroad, who spoke out. It was left to Opel in Rüsselsheim and Ford in Cologne to donate money to the survivors and families of the murderous attacks in Mölln and Solingen.

Inclusion of Immigrants in Trade Union Work?

The existence of some 700,000 non-German trade union members, including tens of thousands of elected works officials, hundreds of works council chairs and deputies, and hundreds of trade-union delegates, manifests two things: in the first place a serious effort to activate foreign employees in the trade unions, and secondly a process of the opening of the trade unions and representation groups at work for their interests.

Trade-union rules and guidelines, as well as the industrial relations code, were altered in the course of time in order to open up the possibilities for democratic participation. There was thus no repetition of what had occurred in the past: the establishment of trade unions along ethnic lines. In 1902 the so-called Ruhr Poles, immigrant Polish miners in the Ruhr, founded the Polish Workers' Association, ZZP. They disassociated themselves from the politically adjacent Christian Trade Union, and also from the Social Democratic Old Association, whose German national loyalty was so marked that it was not capable of considering the interests of the Polish minority. The present involvement of migrants in trade-union structures can be measured by the following indicators:

1. The degree of organisation of immigrants;
2. the absolute and relative increase in the number of foreigners holding positions in worker representative bodies, like works councils and staff committees;
3. the involvement of foreign workers in wage disputes and strikes;
4. the increasing election of non-Germans to representative bodies of the trade unions, especially at local level;
5. the continuing increase in the interest of foreign workers in attending trade-union courses; and
6. the increase in the number of such immigrants who are employed by the trade unions and work as political secretaries.

We shall deal with these six indicators in more detail below.

Degree of Organisation

In 1973, of the approximately 2,500,000 foreign workers, some 500,000 were organised in trade unions affiliated to the DGB, and in 1985 of about 1,500,000 foreign workers, 600,000 were unionised. This represented an increase from 20 to 36 per cent in the membership density amongst foreign workers. By 1991 about 700,000 foreign workers were members of a DGB union, implying 33.9 per cent density. Thus foreign and German colleagues do not differ significantly in degree of organisation.

The degree of organisation among the main groups of immigrants from the former recruitment countries (Italy, Spain, Portugal, Yugoslavia, Greece and Turkey) is higher, at exactly the same levels as their German worker colleagues. In 1989, for example, in the DGB as a whole, 44.9 per cent of the workers from Turkey, 45 per cent of those from Greece, 41 per cent from Spain and 41.7 per cent from Italy were members of a trade union. In the IG Metall, which accounts for almost half of all foreign members of a trade union (325,859), these percentages are even a little higher. Remarkably, Turkish women have clearly surpassed their German colleagues in degree of organisation. For a long time, however, it has been noticeable and worrying that many young foreigners do not join trade unions. A breakthrough has not yet been achieved.

Trade-Union Representatives in Companies

In the elections for representatives at work as well, continuous progress has been made. In 1987 for the first time the number of foreign members of works councils was more than 7,000, and in 1990 a further increase to 8,381 was reached. Of these elected members of works councils, 558 became chair of the works council, including 45 women. In the 1991 IG Metall elections for members' representatives, 9,360 foreign workers were elected (out of a total of 80,949).

Together with the 3,000 foreign members of works councils and 390 representatives of young workers and apprentices, the IG Metall boasts 12,750 foreign workers' representatives, which is an increase of more than one thousand since 1987. But it must also be noted that the number of foreign members of works councils has stagnated since 1987, at 3,000.

Involvement in Industrial Disputes

It has become clear again and again that foreign colleagues are essential if the trade unions are to be successful in any company or wage dispute. This is also shown by the experience of warning strikes and other measures in the first half of the 1980s. The course of events in the major conflict on the 35–hour week in 1984 made this evident. The foreign members of the IG Metall conducted this strike as a struggle for jobs: more jobs would mean less racism in the workplace. They conducted this struggle differently, more emotionally, more vocally than their German colleagues. The intense involvement of the foreign workers aroused a very positive echo from the German trade union members, which also influenced the atmosphere in companies and the further development of trade-union policy on foreigners.

In this context, the support of the strikes by local and regional organisations of foreign workers and their joint activities with those of the workforce should be mentioned. Yilmaz Karahasan, Turkish secretary on the executive board of the IG Metall, reported that the reserved attitude of the trade unions towards these foreign workers' organisations had become noticeably more relaxed. He said that this was particularly true where good contacts between local strike leadership and the democratic worker associations had already existed before the conflict.

Foreign Delegates

Foreign workers are increasingly taking over delegate functions especially at a local level. The IG Metall produced details on foreigners for its federal conferences in 1989 and 1992. According to those data, 742 labour migrants in 1989, and 919 in 1992, were delegates in the local administration structures of their unions. That meant a share of, respectively, 4 and 5 per cent, with the proportion of members of local administrations at (respectively) 11.5 and 12 per cent.

The increases registered here are considerable, even if the IG Metall does not regard them yet as satisfactory.

Anyone familiar with trade-union structures, and who knows what preliminary agreements have to be made in these sorts of elections and that the candidates are finally elected by large majorities of the whole electorate, will come to the conclusion that things are on the move here. This is also shown by the fact that in 1992 at the seventeenth conference of the IG Metall in Hamburg, the delegates elected Yilmaz Karahasan, a Turk, to the executive body of their organisation for the first time.

Willingness to Attend Courses

The willingness of foreign workers to attend courses bears a close relationship to their increased willingness to take over functions at work and in the trade unions. Migrants make use of the regular courses offered by the trade unions, and there are also special courses, partly in foreign workers' languages. The foreign worker division of the DGB's national executive board[24] regularly organises seminars for foreign trade union officials. The purpose of the DGB seminars is to introduce foreign workers to the society, law, and trade unions of the Federal Republic of Germany, and to provide them with knowledge so that they may take over functions as workers' representatives and members of works and staff committees. These seminars usually last one week and are held at central course centres. They are also held with the assistance of the regional DGB groups on a regional level, as day or weekend courses. The IG Metall offers two-week 'basic' and 'function-holder' courses in the participants' mother tongues at both the central and regional level. Every year the IG Chemie-Papier-Keramik (the chemical, paper, and ceramic union) organises two 'one-week courses on foreigner issues' at central level. At these seminars special importance is attached to the dialogue and exchange of experience between Germans and immigrants. For this reason mixed target groups are invited, whose members are more or less half Germans and half foreigners.

Foreign Trade-Union Secretaries

It is still difficult for foreigners who hold voluntary offices to become employed by trade-union administrations as political secretaries. In the IG Metall, which employs by far the largest number, the board has sometimes helped. Foreign applicants have been engaged for a limited time as secretaries for special issues, and subsequently have been taken on permanently by the offices employing them. The total number of foreign political secretaries is now approximately 60. They mainly work at central administrations and DGB regional offices, and to a lesser degree at administrative and local DGB offices, and at their advisory centres.

Immigrants in Germany: Equal Treatment or Special Support from the German Trade Unions?

In the DGB and its member trade unions there were also plenty of people who preferred not to talk about the specific interests of foreign employees and to delay any discussion. At the company level there were repeatedly clear symptoms of a selective safeguarding of interests along ethnic lines. This affected the whole field of personnel planning and policy. At the national political level, the DGB (as described in the opening of section 1) was sometimes involved in selective government action directed against foreign employees and against further immigration. This applied in particular to the phase of the Social-Liberal coalition.

But there are also a number of signs pointing to a more open attitude of the trade unions regarding measures concerning equal treatment as well as those to do with special support of labour migrants. For example:

1. *The programmatic declaration of the equal status of trade union representation of interests for foreigners and Germans.* In this respect the paper dated 2 November 1971 from the DGB national executive board formed the first fundamental document on policy towards foreigners on the part of German postwar trade unions. It continued with the 1981 programme of the DGB, and many resolutions made at trade union conferences and DGB congresses on policy towards foreigners.
2. *Organisational measures, by means of which the trade unions opened their doors more widely to foreign members.* The signs were the establishment after 1973 of sections and departments for issues concerning foreign workers, at the central administrations of big trade unions, at the DGB national executive board, and at some DGB regional offices. Furthermore, special courses in the immigrants' mother tongues were organised. The distribution of printed media, also in the languages of the migrant workers, the setting up of trade-union advisory centres, and the extension of trade-union legal protection to cover the law on aliens too, form further indications of greater openness for the special interests of foreigners.
3. *Efforts to achieve adequate representation of foreign employees in bodies that represent interests at work.* The policy of works councils includes a commitment to equal treatment, and this should also be

reflected in the composition of works councils. According to the guidelines of the IG Metall and Chemie-Papier-Keramik, it is the task of the trade union representatives in companies to organise and decide on the nominations for works council elections. They do this under the supervision of the trade-union administration, which has the function of controlling and correcting power structures in firms. The composition of the labour force should be considered: apart from women and young workers, more foreign workers than in the past should be nominated as candidates.

The trade-union statistical services supply information on the increasing (but still disproportionately low) number of foreign chairs or deputy chairs of works councils. It is probably the foreign members of works councils in small and medium-size firms, with a high proportion of workers of one nationality, who have the chance to become chair of their works council. There are no statistics on how many foreign members of works councils have been released from their normal duties, or on what works council committees they are to be found. It is often heard that foreign members of works councils are urged to deal only with the problems of their compatriots, and to carry out the work of an interpreter. The German works council members would then feel relieved of the problems of foreign workers, and would deal with other tasks that they consider more important.

4. *Foreigner committees, which have been constituted since October 1984 in the IG Metall at the local, regional and national level.* Like other groups they have the right to hold their own conferences and the right to send motions to the trade-union decision making bodies. The aim of the committee work is, among other things, to motivate foreign colleagues to become involved in these bodies, to urge them to take on functions, and to strengthen the representation of foreign officials in the trade-union decision making bodies. By 1991 foreigner committees had been formed in 113 of the 192 administrative centres of the IG Metall. The self-presentation of the committees and their work reached a climax at the national foreigner conferences in 1986, 1988 and 1992. Here some 200 delegates clearly stated the needs and interests of their organised electorate. Critical questions and numerous proposals on how the situation could be improved were also directed to the trade-union organisation.

IG Chemie-Papier-Keramik, the second largest trade union, was not yet prepared for this sort of democratic approach. But it does also support working groups of foreign workers at the local and district level. At the national level it organised an advisory group of sixteen voluntary officials elected by the district boards of the organisation. This advisory group is called together as needed by the Foreign Workers' Department at the governing board. It is the responsibility of the central administration to set the agenda, so keeping the reins firmly in their hands.

5. *Demands for support of foreigners.* The national foreigner conferences of the IG Metall of 1989 and 1992 developed plans and proposals in a foreigner support programme to promote the representation of foreign members in all bodies and decision-making organs of the IG Metall. Accordingly motion 703 at the sixteenth trade-union conference of the IG Metall in 1989 was animatedly discussed. The motion asked,

   - that all bodies at all levels must nominate foreign candidates, and then place them in good positions for IG Metall elections;
   - that the representation of foreign members in all bodies and at all levels of the organisation must correspond to the proportion of foreign members;
   - that the full-time union officials have a special duty to work towards this goal and thus to prepare the ground for necessary changes;
   - that before and after the elections a report is to be made on the results achieved.

   After the intervention of the chairman Franz Steinkühler, however, the motion was only accepted as material for the board.

6. *Integration of foreigner-related work by the trade union.* A characteristic of trade-union work on issues of foreign workers is still its isolation. Foreign members have the opportunity to establish themselves as groups and to speak within the organisation, but what is lacking is the integration of their activities in the overall organisation. The responsibility for the foreign members is – to the satisfaction of many in the trade-union organisation – delegated to these particular bodies. This shortcoming is counteracted in some IG Metall administrations by making trade union organisation structures more flexible, and by responding to wishes for contacts from both immigrants and Germans. For example:

   - foreigner committees are complemented by German-foreign working groups;
   - regular discussions of the foreigner committees at all levels of the organisations with other groups and officials' committees, e.g., those of young people, women, and representatives;
   - joint seminars and conferences of foreign and German members and officials at all levels of the organisation, in which immigrants and Germans should appear together as speakers;

- organisation of local German-foreigner networks with non-trade union organisations, like human rights groups and youth associations that are able to provide legal advice and individual assistance, and to influence the authorities and local politics.

In view of pogrom-like violence against foreigners in general and refugees in particular, networks of this sort are increasingly important. It was thus a step in the right direction when in both 1991 and 1992 the DGB national committee urged its members to become involved in local or regional groups of this sort and urged them, as trade unionists, members of works councils, representative bodies, and so on to take the initiative themselves.

Final Observations

The effect of these appeals in companies, and at the local and regional level has now been documented.[25] Impressive as some of the examples are, both in quantity and quality they trail far behind the achievements of other social groups, like church and human rights organisations. Sometimes the efforts of individuals have met with internal resistance from certain organisations, such as the initiative of granting asylum symbolically to a group of gypsy refugees by the DGB regional group of Baden-Württemberg.[26] Although the trade unions have stuck to the decisions made by the DGB on foreigners and asylum, they only took part at certain points in the major socio-political debate in the early 1990s. With certain exceptions, there has been no debate with the SPD on their change of policy on asylum.[27]

The trade unions do not take part in the public discussions on the government practice of deporting particularly imperilled groups and individuals, such as Kurds from Turkey, Algerians, Sudanese, and others. They are not present in the debate on the future of former contract workers from Vietnam who were employed in the ex-GDR but who are now deprived of residence status because they have no work. Why are the trade unions so cautious? There are some well-founded reasons for the following assumptions:

- The German trade unions are politically on the defensive as never before. One and a half decades of political preference for market radicalism and subsequently a deregulation of labour relations and the massive cutbacks in the welfare state are not without their consequences. The concept of ‘Rhenish capitalism’, which held Germany up as a model for industry, is the subject of some doubt.
- The loss of trade unions’ ability to develop and achieve their aims has led to a legitimation crisis and heavy loss of members,

particularly in the new *Länder* in the East of Germany, where the old industries have largely collapsed. In the West of Germany the trade unions have not managed to achieve a breakthrough among young, qualified employees in technologically developed industries and in the private service sector. Thus from 1990 to 1993 the number of trade union members fell by about 1.5 million from 11,800,413 to 10,290,152. An enquiry on the developments in the *Länder* in the East showed for the period from the end of 1991 to mid-1994 that the number of members fell by 1,531,548, or 36.8 per cent.[28]

- A fall in the number of members also means a decline in financial resources. This has led to a fall in the number of staff and generally to a reduction in staff in the organisations, particularly at the level of the umbrella organisation DGB. Thus reforms which were necessary to change both concept and structure were sacrificed as savings measures.
- The reduction in the number of staff in the organisation means a restriction in the political mandate of the trade unions. In the future trade unions and the DGB want to restrict themselves to the so-called core tasks: assuring that certain industries and production centres remain in Germany; industrial, sectoral and structural policy; labour market and wage policy. In contrast, issues concerning human rights, ecology, gender equality, and ethnic minorities are rapidly becoming marginal matters.
- By definition, the core tasks do not include work with minority groups, including foreign workers, their committees or working groups and the board departments or divisions which deal with them. The 'foreign worker' department at the DGB board is under threat; in the IG Metall, similar far-reaching measures are being taken.

No precise answer can be given to the question of whether this downward spiral of trade-union activity, which is now affecting the German trade unions in a way similar to what has already taken place in the British, French, and Italian trade unions, can be arrested within the foreseeable future. But prospects are bleak.

NOTES

1. The Hans-Böckler-Stiftung financed the translation of the original German essay into English.
2. Deutscher Gewerkschaftsbund.
3. Michel Albert, *Kapitalismus contra Kapitalismus*, Frankfurt am M./New York, 1992.

4. Theodor Geiger, *Die Klassengesellschaft im Schmelztiegel*, Köln/Hagen, 1949.
5. Walther Müller-Jentsch, *Soziologie der industriellen Beziehungen*, Frankfurt am M./New York, 1986.
6. Götz Briefs, *Zwischen Kapitalismus und Sozialismus,* Bern, 1952, 88; see also Klaus Armingeon, *Die Entwicklung der westdeutschen Gewerkschaften 1950–1985*, Frankfurt am M./New York, 1986.
7. Bundesanstalt für Arbeitsvermittlung.
8. *Betriebsverfassungsgesetz.*
9. Klaus-J. Bade, et al. (eds), *Deutsche im Ausland, Fremde in Deutschland: Migration in Geschichte und Gegenwart*, München, 1992.
10. *Grundgesetz.*
11. Bundesanstalt für Arbeitsvermittlung.
12. *Arbeitslosenhilfe.*
13. *Gesetz zur Förderung der Rückkehrbereitschaft ausländischer Arbeitnehmer.*
14. *Niederlassungsrecht.*
15. IG Metall.
16. *Sozialhilfe.*
17. *Arbeitslosenhilfe.*
18. *Ausländergesetz.*
19. *Saisonarbeiter*, *Gastarbeiter*, *Werkvertragsarbeitnehmer.*
20. *Petersberger Sofortprogramm.*
21. DGB-Bundesausschuss.
22. Abteilung 'Ausländische Arbeitnehmer'.
23. DGB-Bundesvorstand.
24. Abteilung 'Ausländische Arbeitnehmer' beim DGB-Bundesvorstand.
25. DGB-Bundesvorstand, *'Es ist Zeit zu widerstehen…': Beispiele gewerrkschaftlicher Aktivitäten gegen Fremdenfeindlichkeit und Rassismus,* Düsseldorf, 1993.
26. Jürgen Klose, ' *"Die Zigeuner kommen!"*: Aufnahme von Roma-Familien durch den DGB-Landesbezirk Baden-Württemberg', in Peter Kühne et al., *Gewerkschaften und Einwanderung*, Köln, 1994, 62ff.
27. DGB-Bundesvorstand, *'Es ist Zeit zu widerstehen…'.*
28. Michael Kittner (ed.), *Gewerkschafter heute: Jahrbuch für Arbeitnehmerfragen*, Köln, 1995.

Chapter 4

Austria: Protecting Indigenous Workers from Immigrants

August Gächter

Introduction: Trade Unions in the Structure of Austrian Corporatism

Employers and workers in Austria are organised into tightly centralised bodies, known as chambers. Legislation provides for a chamber of agricultural employers, a chamber of non-agricultural employers, and a chamber of labour, in each of the nine provinces. Membership is compulsory. Each chamber has an assembly elected by the members every five years. At the provincial level the chambers are largely administrative bodies, while policy-making lies with their respective national federations. This structure was conceived immediately after the First World War. While the employers' chambers were a formalisation of earlier chambers of commerce, the chambers of labour had no precedent and were created, by a Social Democrat-led government, as an antidote to the power wielded by employers' associations.

The trade unions also have a highly centralised structure. The individual unions have neither their own legal entities nor their own money. They exist only through and by means of the Austrian Trade Union Federation, the ÖGB.[1] Collective agreements are made by the individual trade unions with relevant sections of the national Chamber of Employers, the BWK.[2] They are always made at the national level. The ÖGB controls the chambers of labour and treats them as wholly owned subsidiaries. This is more true of the national chamber and the seven provincial chambers with Social Democrat majorities than of the two provinces with Christian Democrat majorities. The high degree of centralisation and the formalised interaction with the equally centralised employers' organisation have led to a concentration on legislation and on influencing government policy rather than on shop-floor activity.[3]

In spite of the presence of corporatism, Austrian politics in the interwar period was marked by confrontation until it was superseded by Catholic dictatorship in early 1934. When the Republic was recreated in 1945, the old antagonism was buried and replaced by conscious cooperation between the representatives of labour and capital. This included the respective political parties, the Christian Democrats on the one hand and the Social Democrats on the other, neither of which, until 1966, was able to obtain an outright majority in parliament. The original cooperative framework was the Economic Commission, composed of labour and employers' officials in strict numerical parity and chaired by the Prime Minister. Between 1947 and 1953 it steered the economy and the state through the currency stabilisation. It was reconvened in 1956 in order to devise ways of combating inflationary pressures without pitting workers and employers against each other. At issue were prices and wages, and the mechanisms for setting them.

Under the moderating influence of a coalition government that could, for the sake of its own stability, ill afford economic or political instability, a halting process of compromises and trade-offs came into being within the Commission. This was institutionalised in 1961 under the name of the Parity Commission on Prices and Wages.[4] This body still exists today. At the same time, subcommittees were set up to monitor wages and prices. The Commission was given the power to intervene in price and wage fixing if it found rises to be unjustified. During the 1960s the government largely withdrew from the Commission. If anything this enhanced the Commission's importance for at the same time the government and parliament abdicated from economic or social policy-making without previous agreement within the Commission. Its members are now the presidents of the three national federations of chambers – labour, employers, and agriculture – and the president of the Trade Union Federation. In this way the trade unions' position in national policymaking became entrenched. Thirty-five years later, the trade unions still regard their elevation from influence at the level of the plant and the enterprise to the national level as their greatest success.

'An Orderly Labour Market': The Trade Unions' Stance on Immigration

In the mid-1950s labour shortages had begun to appear in the west of Austria and in Vienna. They were most obvious in certain industries, especially construction, but shortly also in textiles, and in low-grade service jobs. In the west this was partly due to workers being lost to much better paying industries just across the border in Switzerland and Liechtenstein. The western employers' reaction was to recruit people from less dynamic parts of the country, mainly in the south and south-east. In Vienna the government reacted by facilitating commuting.

In Germany, labour recruitment in Italy and other Mediterranean countries had started in the mid-1950s. Soon after, employers in Austria also began to call for immigration. Until 1960 the trade unions resisted. In 1961, under the influence of absolutely full employment, the Building and Timber Workers Union entered into a nationwide agreement with employers permitting the seasonal employment of up to 7,300 foreign workers in construction. The agreement was for specified periods of time during the peak season. Only about a quarter of the agreed quota did actually become employed.[5] The agreement could not have been struck without at least the approval of the Federation's presidency.[6] It was to turn into a pilot scheme for bigger things to come.

Accelerating inflation quickened the pace of negotiation between the government, trade unions and employers in the summer of 1961. In these negotiations, conducted by the trade unions as an attempt formally to become a partner in national policy-making, and by the employers as a bid to lay down once and for all the precedence of indirect policy measures over direct ones, the future volume and form of labour immigration was a central issue. At first the aim was to agree on a new labour immigration law. This proved to be impossible. Therefore a provisional solution for the 1962 calendar year had to be found. The agreement reached was to establish a procedure outside existing law which would grant businesses reasonably rapid access to a limited number of foreign workers. For 1962 a quota of 48,000 fast-track employment permits was agreed.

However, for the trade unions it was important that access to quota employment permits be tied to a number of conditions:

1. a health check paid for by employers was to be undergone before immigration;
2. an assurance had to be given by employers that repatriation after expiry of the contract would be guaranteed;
3. foreign workers had to be laid off before Austrian workers;

4. on demand, enterprises/firms had to make available all relevant information on their foreign employment practices to labour inspectors;
5. an employment permit could only be granted for employees whose proper housing was assured;
6. foreign workers were barred from employment in the jobs of striking Austrians but they could be transferred to departments or plants in the same company which were not on strike;
7. an application could only be granted if the company adhered *in general* to labour market and employment regulations. A grave violation could justify turning down the application. The normal non-quota application procedure would still be open to violators;
8. special conditions were agreed upon in various part-quotas. Most notably it was agreed that a maximum of half the jobs in a given construction company could be filled by foreigners.

From then on, every autumn trade-union executives and employers negotiated fifty separate industry and occupation quotas for each of the nine provinces, plus fifty 'federal reserve' quotas. In practice only about 340 of the provincial 450 were usually negotiated and agreed. Some of these were only nominal, and some of the part-quotas were available only during certain months of the year. This was true mostly of seasonal industries such as tourism and construction, which however are of great importance in the Austrian economy. They were then added up into a national quota. For the trade unions the size of each of the quotas was always a bargaining chip to be traded against concessions by employers in other regards.

Employment permits inside or outside the quota were issued to the employer, not the worker. They were always valid for a maximum of twelve months, but they were renewable. A permit issued through the quota procedure in one year could be renewed as part of next year's quota. The quota, consequently, was never about immigration or about labour market intake but about the stock of foreign nationals employed. A year-on-year reduction of the quota, as bargained for by the trade unions on various occasions,[7] signalled the intention to reduce not the intake but the number of those already employed and resident in the country. Whether this intention could be realised depended on an ability to preclude the compensatory issuing of employment permits through other procedures such as the 'quota overdraft' or the 'normal' (i.e., non-quota) procedure. In the event, employers discovered that the Labour Market Administration was hardly ever able to force them to consider seriously an Austrian national for the job when they applied for an employment permit, and was therefore seldom able to deny a permit outside the quota. As a result, from the mid-1970s, the 'normal procedure' became indeed normal, and the quota lost all meaning. This proved, in retrospect, that the quota had always been essentially meaningless, and the fight over its availability and size a proxy for the real issue: should there be any foreign employment and any immigration at all, and if so, who should control it and by what means?

The Trade Unions and the Regulation of Supply

The employers initially had a hard time recruiting in the Mediterranean countries. The Trade Union Federation had been expecting this. In its annual report for 1962, it noted that among European industrial countries only in Italy did employees earn less per hour than in Austria. There was therefore no reason to expect any enthusiasm for migrating to Austria.[8]

The decoupling of immigration from recruitment that occurred towards the end of the 1960s acquired the name in Austria of 'tourist employment'. People arrived as tourists, without a visa required for activity in the labour market, but found employment in Austria. The employers applied for a quota employment permit, which was granted, and subsequently the residence status was regularised. By 1969 the phenomenon had become so visible, especially in the west of the country, that the unions initiated a meeting with employers at the Ministry of Social Administration. It was agreed that employment permits for 'tourists' would in future only be granted if they were absolutely necessary. The employers were reminded of the measures available to the police for dealing with tourists looking for work, and the Ministry for Foreign Affairs was mobilised to alert embassies in the relevant countries to the problem.[9]

All this was of little use because employers had come to look upon tourist employment as the normal way of doing things. In this way sections of the labour market had ceased to be national. In 1972 the national Chamber of Employers explicitly defended the practice in public and in letters to various ministries.[10] In 1973 the public debate about immigration and the employment of immigrants became more heated. The Chamber of Employers argued that since Yugoslavia was trying to curb the outflow of skilled personnel, to hire them as tourists was the only way of getting them at all. The number of untrained and often effectively illiterate workers the Yugoslav government was willing to supply had dwindled.[11]

But in 1973 the trade unions became more insistent that the free flow of labour across the border ought to be curbed. Initially the aim was to stabilise the level of employment. The Building and Timber Workers Union, however, immediately formulated a reduction target.[12] As of 1 March 1974, the Minister of Social Administration decreed tighter regulations for employment permits. The aim was to restrict permits to cases in which the worker concerned held a valid visa marked as labour-related,[13] and to regions with lower than average shares of foreign employees.[14] Both conditions were further tightened in mid-April 1975, bringing to a halt not only tourist employment but official recruitment as well.[15] The percentage of foreign workers given documentation by the Labour Market Administration enabling them to obtain a re-entry visa (for the next season) became a much more important element of the annual negotiations between employers and unions than the mere quota. Clearly, in the recession the unions were finally getting their way in substance, and not just in verbiage.

Changing the Law

The legal basis for the employment of foreign workers until 1975 was the German *Decree on Foreign Workers*, dating from 17 January 1933. It became law in Austria on 1 April 1941. In 1945, unamended, it was taken over into post-Nazi Austrian law.[16] These regulations did not provide for the quota practice agreed upon in 1961–62, which remained provisional and existed solely on the basis of an annual agreement between trade unions and employers.

As early as 1960 a proposal for a new law existed, drawn up by the Ministry of Social Administration, dominated by Social Democrats and trade unions. The employers opposed it and at the end of 1961, when negotiations were resumed, proposed their own version of the law. They wanted a regulation whereby permits would automatically be granted, if unemployment over the previous twelve months had averaged less than 7.5 per cent, and they wanted the permits to be issued for substantially more than one year, ideally for an indefinite period. The trade unions defended the Ministry's proposal and insisted on permits being short-term and being accessible only as part of a quota. A commission was formed consisting of representatives of the government, of labour and of the employers, but no progress was made then or over the next decade.[17]

By 1975 the political tide had turned. There was a Social Democrat majority government up for re-election, and the trade unions had a vested interest in keeping it in power. The employers, in the crisis, had a much harder time demanding liberal labour immigration. Previously it had been the employers who were eager to have a new law, because it would have removed the provisional nature of foreign employment on which the trade unions kept insisting. Now it was the unions who wanted the law most eagerly. They wanted to have an instrument that would be sufficiently detailed and sufficiently restrictive to achieve a series of objectives: to make access to the labour market discretionary, to focus unemployment on immigrants, and to ensure trade-union leverage in the administrative process. When the Foreigners Employment Law (*Ausländerbeschäftigungsgesetz*) came into effect on 1 January 1976, it provided for a marked degree of continuity with the previous German decree (and to a degree with the 1925 Austrian Inland Workers Protection Law).[18] In the new law the quota system was legalised.[19] The gist was that foreign employment would not be provisional any more, but that each individual foreign employee's residence in the country would remain provisional.

When the government submitted the law to parliament, copious explanation of its *raison d'être* was provided. These explanations, as approved by the relevant parliamentary committee, tend to be more important than the law itself because they clarify the law makers' intent, and courts are likely to take this into account in interpreting the law. In this particular case the commentary was drafted by the Ministry of Social Administration's employment section, in close coordination with the trade unions' and the employers' negotiators in the drafting of the law itself.

However, given the Social Democrat majority in parliament, it reflected in the main the trade unions' position. According to the commentary the new law's primary concern was the protection of indigenous workers (against any possible ill-effects of immigration). A second concern was the protection of the foreign workers themselves (against employers). These protective aspects are clearly trade-union concerns. The employers' concern that the law should 'satisfy the justified [or justifiable] demand of the economy for labour' ranked only third.[20] The ranking was being justified in macro-economic terms. The advantages and disadvantages of employing foreigners had to be weighed against each other. Foreigners had made up 9.3 per cent of all employees in October 1973, and all experience in other countries had shown, the government told parliament, that the employment of foreigners became economically disadvantageous once it approached a share of 10 per cent. In addition, the population would start to take a more negative attitude towards the phenomenon. In particular, nationals had to be protected from being substituted in their jobs by foreigners.

However, the government continued, experience in other countries had shown that even where this danger did not exist, the short-term advantages of employing foreigners tended soon to be outweighed by disadvantages of an economic, demographic, and social kind. All these countries had therefore reversed their policies and become more restrictive: it had been shown that not only was the policy change more urgent the longer its implementation was postponed and the higher the share of foreigners had become, but also that the economic damage was the greater.[21] The economic burden was specified. It was argued at some length that continuous structural adjustment was hindered by the employment of foreigners. Consequently the growth of productivity, wages and labour force participation had suffered.[22] The employment of too large a share of foreigners also created externalities; in other words, there were costs to be borne by society if foreigners – 'possibly with family' – came to reside in greater numbers. There would be a demand shock on housing, schools and hospitals, aggravated by the fact that supply of these services was insufficient even for Austrian nationals.[23] This line of argument originated from a group of economists closely aligned with the trade unions and the institutions of corporatism,[24] and was also used in popular explanations of the law.[25]

From 1984 the new law was employed mainly to exclude resident foreign nationals from the labour market. Indications are that by 1989 between 45,000 and 50,000 persons willing to take up regular employment within the ambit of the law were either forced to do so outside the law or to forego employment and income. Due to high economic growth from 1988 to 1991, a number of measures were taken in 1990 which led to a reduction of this number to below 30,000. Since then, however, exclusion from the regular labour market has soared again to around 70,000 persons,[26] an estimate also arrived at by the Ministry of Labour and shared widely among organisations of labour and of employers.

Immigration Control in the 1990s: New Means, Old Goals, Same Effect

The trade unions' new prowess achieved its goals only in part. The employment of foreigners was reduced to about 170,000 in 1979 or just above two thirds of the 1973 level, and to below 140,000 in 1984 (about 5 per cent of total employment), but this proved to be the absolute floor. Overall unemployment rose from 2 per cent of the labour force in 1980 to 4 per cent in 1982 and 6 per cent in 1987, a level it reached again in 1991. While the intention had always been to reduce foreign employment in anticipation of domestic unemployment, and while the administrative discretion afforded by the 1975 Foreigners Employment Law was intended to support the link, it now proved impossible to maintain. This was especially obvious in

1990 and 1991, when real GDP growth exceeding 4 per cent coincided with a rapid rise in registered foreign employment and a renewed rise in unemployment. The trade unions also suspected substantial unregistered foreign employment.[27] Labour market economists, most of them firm Social Democrats, supported the notion that a supply shock of labour was being observed.[28] The trade unions were left with a sense of failure. The signal they sent to the Social Democrat Party and to the country's population was that immigration and the presence of immigrants was a cause of problems, and that the problems should be tackled. They eagerly connected the broken link between national unemployment and foreign employment with the gradual growth of anti-Social Democrat and right-wing populist sentiments from 1986 onwards.

The 1975 Foreigners Employment Law had been aimed primarily at supervising demand for immigrant workers. There was obviously a new situation now, according to the subdivision head for foreign employment in the renamed Ministry of Labour and Welfare, in which immigration in the Austrian labour market had become supply-driven.[29] Therefore important new measures needed to be taken. At that time, 1991, a campaign by the trade unions to shift the locus of control from the factory gate to the national border had already been under way since April 1990. At first they eloquently opposed the employers' attempts to introduce a seasonal worker status, distanced themselves from 'a vague humanitarian-liberal' as well as from a 'social-liberal position', and suggested 'the formulation of a comprehensive immigration concept'.[30] Its overall objective was to maintain 'an orderly labour market', as the Federation's president said in a press release in April 1990.[31] Its aims were going to be a clearer differentiation of already resident foreign workers from new arrivals, in order to protect the former against the latter, and efficient measures against unregistered employment. In 1990 the trade unions planned a four-pronged reform attack on the Foreigners Employment Law:[32]

1. They were going to imbue the old quota with a completely new meaning by setting an annual quota of first-time employment permits, which would be based on expected demand and on nationally available supply, with no easy way of exceeding it. A place in the quota could only be obtained by application from outside Austria. The quota would be broken down by province, and employers and unions would have a hand in setting it, although formally it would be set by the Minister of Labour and Welfare.
2. For all foreigners with twelve more-or-less consecutive months of employment, a newly created Work Permit would become available. They would be entitled to it and it would be issued to them rather

than to the employer, as the Employment Permit. The Licence of Release[33] would become available after five instead of eight years.
3. Employers should be severely punished for employing foreigners illegally.
4. As a transitory measure, legalisation of existing illegal employment would be offered.

Points two and four were realised as proposed. On point three the unions' offensive faltered. The maximum penalty was raised considerably, but in the courts employers tended to keep getting away with small fines. But the important point was the first one, and here the trade unions in 1990 had to settle for a compromise they did not favour. Instead of a quota and compulsory applications before entering Austria, they obtained only a legal ceiling for the size of the foreign labour force set at 10 per cent of the total labour force. The Minister of Labour and Welfare was given the power to lower the ceiling by decree. In summer 1993 the order was reversed. The ceiling was set at 8 per cent and the Minister was given the power to lift it to a maximum of 10 per cent.[34] In this way the ominous 10 per cent argument of 1975 became a legal reality in the 1990s. Trade unions have long memories.

But the trade union orthodoxy wanted the closer regulation of new entries, and if it could not be had by way of the Foreigners Employment Law, there were other means. They shifted their efforts to realise 'a comprehensive immigration concept' to the Ministry of the Interior. This had two advantages. Since the war it had always been headed by a Social Democrat except between 1966 and 1970, and it was much further removed from formal employer and trade union influence than the Ministry of Labour and Welfare. Thus Social Democrat Party discipline could be brought to bear on it. In 1991 the Ministry pledged to overhaul immigration law comprehensively.[35] In a legislative blitz, the new Asylum Law that had taken effect in 1991 was replaced by a still newer one as of June 1992.[36] On 1 January 1993, a new Foreigners Law (*Fremdengesetz*) came into effect, supplanting the previous Foreigners Police Law. On 1 July 1993, the so-called Residence Law (*Aufenthaltsgesetz*) took effect, supplanting all the sections in the Passport Law (*Paßgesetz*) pertaining to foreign citizens. The latter was the centre-piece of reform. In §2 the Residence Law states as one of its main objectives the maintenance of an 'orderly development of the labour market'. To this end it introduced a quota for immigration to be set annually by the government in consultation with the provincial governors and other bodies. Applications for a place in the quota, save one special case, cannot be made inside Austria, and they cannot be granted unless the Public Employment Service agrees. The immigration quotas set since then have been between 20,000 and 30,000 per year, including foreign students, children born to foreign citizens in the country, family reunion, and labour immigration. A quota of about 20,000 was mentioned as early as May 1990 in the editorial page of the Chamber of Labour's monthly magazine.[37] Belatedly, the trade unions were able to realise their 1990 goals in full.

When the Social Democrats did badly in the 1994 national elections, a new Minister of the Interior was appointed. Very quickly work began to change the new laws. The goal was to put a limit to the state's power to remove foreign nationals from the country, and to facilitate family reunion. After five years of continuous residence, it was suggested, economic reasons should no longer be sufficient to force people to leave, and after eight years a serious criminal offence should be necessary to give the state the power to decide the fate of a foreign national. The children of immigrants should generally be safe from deportation. A further goal was to adapt the Asylum Law in response to sustained criticism by the UNHCR and human rights groups.

The first draft of these reforms – dubbed the 'integration package' – was presented in September 1995. It faltered because the coalition partners felt they had not been sufficiently involved. Therefore negotiations with the coalition partners were started, and a second draft was presented jointly in May 1996. As prescribed by law, comments were solicited from relevant organisations, among them the ÖGB and the Chamber of Labour. Their statements turned out to be in close accord. As regards asylum, they proved to be largely hostile to any changes, fearing that a back door would be opened to economically motivated immigration. They were basically positive about enhancing the residence rights of settled immigrants but objected to the automatism the draft proposed. Instead, they urged that such rights be granted only discretionally.[38] In other words, they wanted to remain able to influence the state to deny such rights, in case they themselves felt at some future time that a reduced number of immigrants resident in Austria would be desirable. Their critical voice, together with opposition from conservative provincial governments and from the Ministry of Labour, was decisive in stopping the reform in its tracks.[39] It is unclear at the time of writing whether a third draft will ever be forthcoming.

Refugees

After the Second World War the Austrian government was hardly inclined to accept German displaced persons as permanent settlers. For this reason the 1951 Geneva Convention was only partially ratified.

Austria took exception to Article 17, sections 1 and 2a. The former provides refugees with access to jobs on the most liberal terms available to any group of foreign citizens in the country, and the latter gives labour market access on a par with that available to citizens, after three years of residence. During the 1961 World Refugee Year the UNHCR proposed that Austria withdraw its reservations. The Ministry of Foreign Affairs supported the move but the trade unions did so only partially. They consented to Article 17, section 1, but continued to oppose section 2a, citing labour market concerns as the reason.[40]

The trade unions opposed the automatism of the three-year rule in Article 17, section 2a. The Austrian practice at the time was to change annually the date before which refugees granted asylum must have taken up residence in Austria in order to be exempt from the permit requirement in accordance with the three-year rule. The trade unions agreed to this every year, but never without justifying it in terms of the small number of people concerned. The reservation was finally abolished in 1975. When the new Foreigners Employment Law was created, refugees granted asylum and given unlimited leave to stay were summarily excepted from its reach. Thereby their access to jobs became equal to nationals. No three-year clause was introduced.

'Equal Wages for Equal Work': Positioning Resident Immigrants

The trade unions, as one of their two Executive Secretaries insisted at a public lecture in November 1993, had always pursued a policy of integration. What he meant was that there had always been a declared policy of equal wages for equal work, expressed in complete equality in collective bargaining agreements. At the same time it is the ÖGB's stated policy to narrow the legal differences between Austrian and foreign employees in small steps. 'Deliberately small steps' was also how the legal reforms of 1988 and 1990 were explained.[41] For the most part the incremental overall improvements arrived through the extension of exemptions and favours, at various times, to persons with particular labour market permits or durations of residence. Only foreign nationals are the object of policy. Naturalised immigrants never received any particular consideration.

The ÖGB is unable to say how many of its members are citizens of other countries.[42] A survey at the end of 1983 found 55.7 per cent of foreign workers to be union members, a percentage very similar to the general level of membership at the time. Among Turkish citizens membership was 60 per cent, among women, who were mostly Yugoslav, it was 50.8 per cent.[43] The degree of unionisation matters little, given the fact that nationals of other countries are severely and legally handicapped in employment relations. This results from a combination of various legal discriminations.[44] The trade unions, as will be shown below, have been playing an important role, partly in creating and partly in not abolishing that legal discrimination.

The Politics of Exclusion from Works Councils

The key labour law regulating employment relations is the Employment Constitution Law (*Arbeitsverfassungsgesetz*). Among many other things it defines who may become a member of a works council. Close relatives of the employer are excluded, as are home workers and, in most industries, persons employed for less than six months. Persons who are not eligible to vote in parliamentary elections cannot stand for election as works council members unless they are citizens of EEA member countries. This excludes all third-country foreign citizens. The works council is the stepping stone into the trade-union hierarchy, and consequently there is not a single exception to the rule that union officials are Austrian.[45]

However, the law does not entirely rule out works council membership for foreign nationals. An election's validity depends only on following the prescribed procedures, *not* on the eligibility of the candidates. If, by one means or another, a foreign national gets elected, the election will be valid. The candidate, who was not entitled to stand, then becomes a duly elected member of the works council, and his or her actions in the works council are legal. Once an ineligible candidate has been elected the only remedy is a court action. It can only legally be initiated by the employer, by individual members of the works council, or by the works council as a whole. No time limit is set on when the court action can or must be started, and anything done by the works council and all its members before the court reaches a conclusion remains valid thereafter.

Given this precarious position of foreign nationals on works councils, it is not likely to be prudent politics for a workforce to elect a foreign national. Nonetheless in a few cases it was done. Significantly, all except one were associations rather than businesses. In the one case of a private enterprise, the need for a foreign national on the works council arose from one plant's internal arrangements. There the legal loophole was not used at first. Instead, the Turkish citizen was coopted to the council and through a special arrangement with management the prerogatives of a works council member were secured for him. This solution was in fact superior to the option offered by the law.[46]

Given these options the unions could have pursued a strategy of fielding non-Austrian candidates. They could even have sought a collective agreement with employers enabling foreign nationals to become works council members. This was not done, and, it would seem, was never even considered.[47] Neither were any efforts made to change the law. When it had to be changed in 1993 in the course of implementing the treaty leading to the European Economic Area (EEA), works council membership became legally possible for citizens of member states of the EEA but the exclusion of all others was upheld. The trade-union leadership in the negotiations did actually suggest that works council membership should be opened to all, but when the employers made it clear they wanted some favour in return, the point was dropped. Thus well over 90 per cent of the foreign workforce, including refugees granted asylum, remain excluded from works council membership. The remainder are citizens of member states of the European Economic Area.

A positive though inconsequential step was taken by the trade unions in 1970. In the Collective Agreement of 17 December 1970, trade unions and employers laid down, among other things, that, if the works council invited a foreign employee who was an acknowledged spokesperson for the foreign employees to sit with the works council, this worker's wage had to be paid for the time it took to deliberate on the problems of foreign workers.[48] This amounts to the formal institution of an advisory role for a worker without specifying a procedure for this worker's election or appointment and without extending a works council member's protection from dismissal to him or her. The advisory role was to the works council and only at the works council's invitation. The agreement was implemented in many places but had little practical effect.

Another attempt to change the situation was made in 1986. When the Employment Constitution Law was going to be revised, the then Minister of Social Administration and chairman of the Union of Salaried Employees, a Social Democrat, suggested a list of thirty changes. The Social Democrat de facto caucus in the Trade Union Federation thought them over and removed only one: the right of foreigners to be elected to works councils.[49]

Employers rarely took a stance on the works council issue. The unions protected them by objecting themselves. But the trade unions are not homogeneous, and a struggle has been going on within the ÖGB about this issue. The opponents are not ranged against each other along party lines. It is easy to identify the camp in support of change, and its motivation. As the chairman of the Union of Hotel, Restaurant and Personal Services waged workers (HGPD) remarked, his union operates in an industry in which it is not uncommon for businesses to have 70 or 80 per cent foreign nationals in their workforce, with all the Austrians in management and white-collar positions. In such a situation, if there is a works council at all, it is composed of the superiors of most of the employees, and therefore has little meaning. He also said,

> 'I would like to note that for a social movement such as the ÖGB it is necessary to undergo self-critique. It is necessary to broaden the co-determination rights of foreigners considerably because here the instruments of co-determination are largely absent, especially concerning works councils'.[50]

But the HGPD contributes only 3.3 per cent of the ÖGB's members. The support it receives is feeble. The executive council of the Union of Salaried Workers (GPA) passed a resolution in favour in January 1992. Although the GPA is the largest individual trade union and has been presiding over both the Viennese and the national Chamber of Labour, it is in a defensive position. The waged worker unions are holding it in line by hinting at the possibility of breaking up the GPA and merging the parts with various waged worker unions. Further support comes from Green and Communist unionists in the ÖGB.[51]

The opposition is much more diffuse and much harder to pin down. It seems to originate mainly from the Union of Building and Timber Workers and the Union of Metals, Mining and Energy Workers (MBE). Together they contribute about one quarter of the ÖGB's members. The chairman of the MBE is a vice-president of the ÖGB and would be the likely choice of president were the current president to leave for another office.[52] In a less outspoken way the Union of Textile and Garment Workers also opposes works council membership. All three of them operate in industries absorbing a large proportion of the immigrant labour force.

At different levels of the trade-union movement there seem to exist different reasons for opposing immigrants on works councils. Incumbent works-council members seem to fear being replaced by ethnically selected candidates. They tend to point to the spectre of a mass exodus from the trade unions if the national leadership were to push seriously for a change in the law.

The national leadership itself is very much at the heart of the state. It frequently ends up pursuing policies it deems beneficial to economic growth or to the minimisation of unemployment. These are often against the short-run interests of workers in employment, since they are, for instance, more interested in larger pay checks than in fewer working hours. The leadership relies on the works councils to educate the workers on the usefulness of the policies and therefore does not wish to antagonise them. If it did, its own ability to shape macro-economic policy-making through compromises and bargains would be diminished. By comparison, the issue of foreigners on the works councils is clearly less important for the leadership. There is also a concern over sovereignty. Trade union careers could take foreign nationals from works council membership to local, provincial and national union and chamber leadership. With corporatism this is a trajectory into the heart of the Austrian state, a position from which every effort is made to bar foreign nationals, including citizens of EU member states.[53]

The irony of it all is that at the ÖGB's twelfth General Assembly in October 1991, packaged into a broader social policy resolution, the board proposed to the delegates that they should demand the right of foreign nationals to join works councils. The resolution was passed. It was a dead letter. A similar resolution was tabled and passed at the thirteenth GA in October 1995. Again, no action followed.

The ÖGB executive councils of the three westernmost provinces – Salzburg, Tyrol, and Vorarlberg – are members of the Association of Alpine Trade Unions. In October 1992 in Milan, at its ninth General Assembly, the Association *unanimously* passed a comprehensive resolution committing its members to work towards the realisation of full participatory rights not only in works councils but in local elections as well. In a separate document presented in Milan the three executive councils welcomed the 10 per cent ceiling on foreign employment introduced in 1990 but denounced the restrictive Asylum Law and facile linkages made between immigration and unemployment.[54] They unambiguously demanded the right for foreign workers to stand for election to works councils and to the Chamber of Labour, for equality regarding benefits of unemployment insurance, and for equal access to housing benefit and to public and subsidised housing after two years of residence. Furthermore they remarked, 'there cannot be a reasonable policy "for" foreign colleagues', and suggested the creation of an official platform or working group of foreign members within the ÖGB's policy-making bodies.[55] Subsequently one other provincial chairman of the ÖGB expressed his solidarity with the western chairmen and provincial secretaries, bringing the number up to four provinces out of nine.

There are efforts underway to remedy the situation. There were elections to the Chamber of Labour in October 1994. As a rule the Social Democrat Party in the Chamber of Labour has made promises to foreign workers to secure their vote. This time, however, in a couple of provinces in the east, a party called Democracy for All was constituted by naturalised and EEA immigrants campaigning on the sole issue of access to works councils and of representation on the Chamber's assembly. Other small parties also fielded naturalised immigrants. Furthermore, legal action was initiated by a works council with a non-EEA foreign national member, with the aim of taking the action to the European Court of Human Rights or possibly to EU bodies. The legal action is being brought by an individual works council member. He sought the financial support of the local Union of Salaried Employees. They said they would cover the costs, if the Federation's provincial executive agreed. The executive in turn made a decision dependent on agreement by the national presidency. When, after one and a half years, the Federation's President still had not made a decision, the regional and in turn the local executive decided to support the legal action on their own responsibility.[56] By August 1996 this action had reached the European Court of Human Rights in Strasbourg.

Unemployment Benefits: Equal Duty, Unequal Rights

While the works council issue and the trade unions' involvement in it enjoys a degree of publicity, other areas of law making with crucial trade union input do not. This is partly due to the more technical nature of the laws themselves. One of them is the Unemployment Insurance Law. Chiefly, there are two kinds of benefits it provides for: unemployment benefit and distress relief (income support). Unemployment benefit is paid for specified maximum periods, depending on the previous duration of employment. Once expired, people able and willing to work have access to distress relief. Again payments are made for a specified period – and at between 92 and 95 per cent of unemployment benefit – but it can be renewed, if need be until retirement. The law guarantees equal access to unemployment money for all but excludes all foreign citizens from distress relief.[57] Though they have to pay the full insurance contribution, benefits are thus severely curtailed.

In the 1960s unemployment benefit for foreign citizens was normally restricted to twelve or twenty weeks. If they found no new job during that period and thus ended up without income or support, they became deportable. This made them subject to considerable pressure to accept any terms of employment. The same law empowered the Minister of Social Administration to exempt certain groups from the exclusion, if the persons concerned had been employed in Austria for at least three of the last five years, and if unions and employers did not oppose the measure. Refugees who had been granted asylum were early (though limited) beneficiaries of the Minister's largesse. They were exempted from the exclusion in 1958 for two years, and every other year the exemption was renewed. At the end of October 1966, sixteen persons were benefiting from it. The small number was the chief reason the trade unions saw for not opposing the exemption.[58]

The reform of the Unemployment Insurance Law in 1977, under the supervision of trade unions and employers, retained the restrictive regulations. In the revisions in 1989 and 1992 gradual steps towards equality were introduced. As of 1 August 1989, distress relief became accessible to refugees granted asylum and to holders of a licence of release, although only for a maximum of thirty-nine weeks. The three-year clause no longer applied and the trade unions and employers gave up their right to object. In 1992 this period was extended to fifty-two weeks for licence holders and made indefinite for refugees granted asylum. In these revisions between 1989 and 1992 the Chamber of Labour had an important and positive role, and did indeed facilitate small steps towards the greater integration of immigrants. Its role in subsequent years became more cautious again. Further changes towards equality came through international treaties and through the courts, not by way of political initiatives. With the coming of the European Economic Area in 1994, the citizens of its member states also gained equal access to benefits.

When Austria joined the EU in 1995, Turkish workers also became eligible, although substantial resistance was put up by government departments to recognising the Association Treaty. As a result about 30 per cent of the total foreign workforce at the time of writing have equal access to distress relief, a further 38 per cent have access of limited duration, and roughly one third are excluded from any access to distress relief. That third is under attack from a ruling issued by the European Court of Human Rights in September 1996 which states the incompatibility of the unequal treatment with the European Convention on Human Rights (and therefore with the Austrian Constitution). Thus, in comparison to the state of affairs at the end of 1993, when nearly two thirds of the foreign workforce had no access at all, and almost all of the remainder had only limited access, the situation is now almost diametrically reversed.

Trade-union gradualism on closing legal gaps between Austrian and foreign workers was crucial to the old state of affairs. It was only partly motivated by a desire not to be seen as acting too much in the interests of foreigners. Denying or curtailing distress relief (income support) was the chief means of making sure that foreigners, once unemployed, would eventually become deportable, or removable from the labour market, when benefit payments ceased. Finally, the trade unions are among those charged with running the public insurance system, and national unemployment insurance, between 1989 and 1995 alone, has profited by about 760 million Austrian Shillings from the imbalance between the rights and obligations of foreign workers.[59] Since national unemployment insurance does not make a profit overall, the conclusion can only be that this surplus was used for payments to Austrians. Thus funds were extracted from the poorer part of the resident population and transferred to the richer part.

Residence Rights: The Trade Unions' (Almost) Invisible Hand in Action

The trade unions were centrally concerned with making sure supply in the labour market would remain tight, even if they agreed to the employment of foreign citizens. This entailed looking upon foreign workers as a completely elastic supply element, available when there was demand over and above local supply and disappearing when demand slackened. Such disappearance could not be taken for granted. It had to be engineered. Since existing law provided for a mechanism whereby residence rights lapsed in the case of inadequate income, the ingeniously simple solution was to focus the incidence of unemployment on foreign nationals and to cut short unemployment benefits. If unemployed beyond a certain period of time, they would automatically lose the right to remain in the country. For the focusing of incidence the market could partly be relied upon, but the trade unions wanted to make sure. Among the eight points they made the employers sign in January 1962 was a commitment to lay off foreigners first, and to pay their journey to the border if they had to be made to leave the country. The lay-off clause was incorporated into the Foreigners Employment Law in 1975. Trade unionists like to maintain the clause is a dead letter because in reality firms never have a real choice between Austrian nationals and foreigners when it comes down to firing. This is certainly true, but it does not remove the fact of the clause still being law, and nobody in the unions has ever dared to propose it should not be there. It is, of course, living evidence of the fact that the trade unions are much less concerned with protecting all workers equally in employment relations and the labour market than with attempts to protect national workers against international ones.[60]

Conclusion: Small Steps to Nowhere

The trade unions feel there are certain shared interests between employers and immigrant workers, and they continue to make every effort to protect indigenous workers against this perceived coalition. In Austria, for the trade unions and trade unionists, there never was a question of 'equality versus support' for immigrants. On the contrary, equality to this day remains self-evidently undesirable, impossible, unthinkable. The discussion revolves entirely around the areas, the form, and the degree of legal discrimination. Outside the trade unions, among people considered by trade unionists to be not simply utopians but genuine enemies of the worker, a discussion about anti-discrimination laws and about positive discrimination began in the 1990s. It has not yet moved into trade union circles. It is quite conceivable that the trade unions will eventually come round to the idea of anti-discrimination legislation. But if they do, they would certainly want to add it to existing legislation while leaving the latter untouched, rather than removing the discrimination embodied in existing laws. They could use anti-discrimination laws to blame on employers the effects of the discrimination which in reality stem from the labour market, employment and foreigners legislation. It would be wrong to think they would do so maliciously. It is just that the 'necessity' to discriminate against foreign workers is so deeply engrained in them and seems so self-evident that they cannot and do not want to see the negative effects it has on all workers. For them the only conceivable culprit is the employer.

The trade unions never accepted that immigrants might have a right to remain in the country. They always insisted that Austria is not an immigration country, and consequently they insisted that the authorities must have the right to terminate the residence of foreign nationals no longer needed in employment, and of their dependants. Josef Hesoun, then both the President of the Union of Building and Timber Workers and the Minister of Labour and Welfare, made a subtle but programmatic distinction when he told parliament that Austria was not an *Einwanderungsland* but a *Zuwanderungsland* (i.e., it is a country experiencing immigration, but not immigration for permanent settlement).

This denial of immigrant settlement is part and parcel of a strategy to deny foreign nationals the right to decide for themselves whether and when they wish to leave the country again. The result is that in addition to a highly restrictive immigration policy the trade unions have also, in deed if not in word, pursued a strictly discriminatory policy against immigrants settled in the country. Not surprisingly, when the so-called Pro-Austria Referendum, with twelve anti-immigration and anti-immigrant points, was pursued by the right-wing populists between October 1992 and January 1993, the Prime Minister could tell the press that he could not see why the referendum was being introduced, since all those points which were not merely rhetorical had already been fulfilled by the government.

Trade-union officials, at their best, tend to make a three-way differentiation between Austrian nationals, settled foreign workers and foreign newcomers. In practice the distinction has few positive effects for settled immigrants. The unions conceded to them easier access to the Licence of Release, lengthened its duration, and increased the value of the licence by gradually adding fifty-two weeks of unemployment benefits and by establishing the formal precedence of licence holders over other non-asylum foreigners in the labour market. For workers with one year of employment they created the Work Permit which, with all its limitations, appears to be a step towards abolishing the Employment Permit. But that is as far as it goes. In spite of the rhetoric they have stubbornly refused to grant the right to form works councils, and they have maintained the critical inequality in the duration of unemployment benefits. They have also played a key role in putting legislation in place and keeping it unchanged which, crucially, has added to the insecurity of residence of foreign workers and their families. There are four fundamental areas of legal discrimination (as well as a host of minor ones):

1. exclusion of settled immigrants from access to the labour market;
2. weakened employment relations;
3. unequal duration of unemployment benefits;
4. threat of expulsion on expiry of benefits.

This is the durable core of trade-union policies on immigration and immigrants. Only very gradually have trade unionists in Austria seemed to learn the difference between policies on immigration and policies on immigrants. In so far as this is now happening, there appears to be a certain willingness to make resident foreign nationals legally more equal to Austrian nationals.

Reforms in the air at the time of writing seem to be heading towards greater security of residence for the children of immigrants and perhaps also for longer-term foreign residents. That the trade unions might support this tendency is perhaps indicated by a decision in April 1996 by the ÖGB to locate responsibility for 'integration' in all nine provincial executives, and to appoint a national coordinator. But there is still a very strong opinion within the trade union movement that all immigrants, for the good of Austrian workers, should in principle remain deportable. At the same time the trade unions remain fiercely opposed to any new immigration, even of immediate family members, and want asylum and temporary protection procedures to be applied restrictively.

NOTES

1. Österreichischer Gewerkschaftsbund.
2. Bundeswirtschaftskammer. In December 1993 the name was changed to Wirtschaftskammer Österreich, WKÖ, but the historically correct name is retained throughout this chapter.
3. August Gächter, *Preventing Racism at the Workplace in Austria: Report to the European Foundation for the Improvement of Living and Working Conditions*, Vienna, 1995.
4. Paritätische Kommission für Lohn- und Preisfragen.
5. ÖGB (Austrian Trade Union Federation) *Tätigkeitsbericht 1961*, Vienna, 1962, Vol. III, 67f.
6. The then President, Franz Olah, was himself a former chairman of the Building and Timber Workers Union.
7. August Gächter, 'Forced Complementarity: The Attempt to Protect Native Austrian Workers from Immigrants', *New Community* 21, no. 3 (1955): 379–98.
8. ÖGB (Austrian Trade Union Federation), *Tätigkeitsbericht 1962,* Vienna, 1963, vol. 1, 67.
9. AK (Chamber of Labour), *Jahrbuch 1969,* Vienna, 1970, 171.
10. BWK (Chamber of Employers), *Jahrbuch der österreichischen Wirtschaft 1972*, Vienna, 1973, 120.
11. BWK (Chamber of Employers), *Jahrbuch der österreichischen Wirtschaft 1973.* Vienna, 1974, 91; BWK (Chamber of Employers), *Jahrbuch der österreichischen Wirtschaft 1974*, Vienna, 1975, 93.
12. BWK (Chamber of Employers), *Jahrbuch der österreichischen Wirtschaft 1973.* Vienna, 1973, 90.
13. These were marked with an 'A', a practice abolished only in 1988.
14. Erich Neurath and Günther Steinbach, *Ausländerbeschäftigungsgesetz*, Vienna, 1976, 8.
15. BWK (Chamber of Employers), *Jahrbuch der österreichischen Wirtschaft 1975*, Vienna, 1976, 89.
16. Ulrike Davy and August Gächter, 'Zuwanderungsrecht und Zuwanderungspolitik in Österreich', *Journal für Rechtspolitik* 1, no. 3 (1993): 155–74; 1, no. 4 (1993): 257–81; August Gächter, 'Forced Complementarity: The Attempt to Protect Native Austrian Workers from Immigrants', *New Community* 21, no. 3 (1995): 379–98; Neurath and Steinbach, *Ausländerbeschäftigungsgesetz*, 11.
17. AK (Chamber of Labour), *Jahrbuch 1963*, Vienna, 1964, 166f.
18. Cf. Sylvia Pelz, *Ausländerbeschränkungen Österreichs in der Zwischenkriegszeit*, Diplomarbeit Universität Salzburg, 1994.
19. Neurath and Steinbach, *Ausländerbeschäftigungsgesetz*, Vienna, 1976, 123–34.
20. Ibid., 17.
21. Ibid., 13f.
22. Ibid., 14f.
23. Union orthodoxy repeated this argument in 1990 against an alleged 'social-liberal position of important representatives of the Social Democrat Party in Vienna' (Josef Wallner and Georg Ziniel (1990), 'Ausländerpolitik in Österreich', *Arbeit und Wirtschaft* 44, no. 7–8 (1990): 27. In 1975 it was said to be the housing problem in particular which would lead to 'an activation of latently existing rejection of fundamentally different [*andersartig*] minorities, if foreigners, differing from the indigenous population in language and custom, were forced to live in large numbers in small spaces under conditions inferior to what was usual in the country' (Neurath and Steinbach *Ausländerbeschäftigungsgesetz*, 16, translation AG.); Ibid., p. 15f.

24. Beirat für Wirtschafts- und Sozialfragen, *Möglichkeiten und Grenzen des Einsatzes ausländischer Arbeitskraft*, Vienna, 1976, 73–7; Felix Butschek and Ewald Walterskirchen, '*Aspekte der Ausländerbeschäftigung*', *WIFO Monatsberichte* 47, no. 4 (1976): 214–24.
25. Franz Danimann, 'Das neue Ausländerbeschäftigungsgesetz', *Arbeit & Wirtschaft* 30, no. 2 (1976): 16–19.
26. August Gächter, *Ein Arbeitsmarkt unter Druck: Über die Wirkung von Zugangsbeschränkungen zum Arbeitsmarkt*, Unpublished manuscript, 1996.
27. In the 1974–75 crisis there was also unsubstantiated trade union talk of unregistered employment on a scale of 40,000 (Helga Matuschek, 'Ausländerpolitik in Österreich 1962–1985: Der Kampf um und gegen die Arbeitskraft', *Journal für Sozialforschung* 25, no. 2 (1985): 185–98.); Kurt Horak, 'Ausländer raus oder rein?', *Arbeit & Wirtschaft* 44, no. 3 (1990a): 2; Kurt Horak, 'Ausländerbeschäftigung: Was wir wollen', *Arbeit & Wirtschaft* 44, no. 5 (1990b): 2; Richard Leutner, 'Sozialpartnerschaft und Ausländerbeschäftigung', *Kurswechsel*, no. 1 (1990): 46f; Ingrid Nowotny, 'Ausländerbeschäftigung in Österreich: Die Gesamtproblematik und aktuelle Situation', *WISO* 14, no. 1 (1991): 40.
28. Gudrun Biffl, *SOPEMI-Report on Labour Migration 1995–96*, Vienna, 1996; BMAS (Ministry of Labour and Welfare), *Bericht über die soziale Lage 1990*, Vienna, 1991, pp. 52 and 58; BMAS (Ministry of Labour and Welfare), *Arbeitsmarktvorschau 1992*, Vienna, 1992, 35; Felix Butschek and Norbert Geldner, *Kurzfristige Arbeitsmarktvorschau 1992*, Revidierte Fassung, Vienna, 1991, 6; Karl Pichelmann and Ewald Walterskirchen, *East/West Integration and its Impact on Workers: The Austrian Example.* Paper presented at the OECD conference on 'Regional Integration and Globalisation: Implications for Human Resources', Vienna, January 1994; Redaktion 'Angebotsschock am Arbeitsmarkt', *Wirtschaft und Gesellschaft* 17, no. 2 (1991): 131–39.
29. Ingrid Nowotny, 'Ausländerbeschäftigung in Österreich: Die Gesamtproblematik und aktuelle Situation', 39.
30. Josef Wallner and Georg Ziniel, 'Ausländerpolitik in Österreich', *Arbeit und Wirtschaft*, 44, nos. 7–8, (1990): 27.
31. Gerhard Hetfleisch, 'Rotation statt Integration?: AusländerInnengesetze in Österreich und AusländerInnenbeschäftigungspolitik am Beispiele Tirols', in Gesellschaft für politische Aufklärung & Verein zur Betreuung und Beratung von AusländerInnen in Tirol (eds), *AusländerInnen: Integration oder Assimilierung?*, Innsbruck, 1991, 44.
32. Richard Leutner, 'Sozialpartnerschaft und Ausländerbeschäftigung', *Kurswechsel*, no. 1 (1990): 42–8; Josef Wallner and Georg Ziniel, 'Ausländerpolitik in Österreich', 28.
33. This is a literal translation of *Befreiungsschein*; other translations are 'extended work permit' (Biffl, *SOPEMI-Report on Labour Migration 1995–96*, Vienna, 1996) or 'exemption permit' (Rainer Bauböck, *Immigration Control in Austria.* Second draft, unpublished manuscript, 1996). In addition to the Employment Permit and the Work Permit this is a third type of labour market permit. It enables its bearer to be employed in any occupation without geographical or industrial restrictions. Before 1976 it was issued to workers with at least ten consecutive years of employment, and then until September 1990 to those with at least eight years of consecutive employment. Since then it has been issued after five years of employment within the last eight years. Until 1988 it was valid for up to two years, then up to three years, and since October 1990 five years. It is renewable. Until the end of 1993 this was also the permit issued to spouses of Austrians. Since 1988 there has been a version of the Licence which is issued to the children of immigrants on the basis not of employment duration but of residence duration.

34. In April 1995 the limit of the Minister's discretion was lowered to 9 per cent. This is where the ceiling stands at the time of writing.
35. This is not to deny that the Ministry had its own objectives in doing so as well, such as seeking to quell cross-border crime, keeping tabs on the resident population, and tending to border security concerns. It was quite clear, though, that the new legislation could only contribute to the second one of the three and neither to the first nor the last. On these two other points there has been a remarkable lack of decisive action. The border patrol issue, for instance, was still completely unresolved five years after coming on to the political agenda, in spite of German pressure. During 1996 substantial progress was made on this question, because Austria intended to implement the Schengen agreements in 1997.
36. 'There is also the question of whether the right of asylum should be used as an instrument of labour market and immigration policy. We think not' (Josef Wallner and Georg Ziniel, 'Ausländerpolitik in Österreich', 26).
37. Kurt Horak, 'Ausländerbeschäftigung: Was wir wollen', *Arbeit & Wirtschaft* 44, no. 5 (1990): 2.
38. AK (Chamber of Labour) *Fremdenrechtsänderungsgesetz*. Unpublished manuscript, 3 June 1996; ÖGB (Austrian Trade Union Federation) *Entwurf eines Bundesgesetzes, mit dem das Fremdengesetz, das Asylgesetz und das Bundesbetreuungsgesetz geändert werden sowie das Aufenthaltsgesetz 1996 erlassen wird* (Fremdenrechtsänderungsgesetz/FRÄG). Unpublished manuscript, 4 June 1996.
39. The similarity in argument is sometimes uncanny. The self-consciously conservative Deputy Governor of Austria's westernmost province was quoted as warning against the 'deeply dishonest humanism' displayed in attempts to ease family reunion while the labour market did not offer the conditions for absorbing them (*Kurier*, 7 August 1996). The very same words were employed by the labour organisations in their comments.
40. AK (Chamber of Labour), *Jahrbuch 1962*, Vienna, 1962, 201.
41. Ingrid Nowotny, 'Ausländerbeschäftigung in Österreich: Die Gesamtproblematik und aktuelle Situation', 37–64.
42. Rudolf Kaske, 'Keine Apartheid in den Betrieben!', in Österreichische Hochschülerschaft (ed.), *Zwischen Mit- und Selbstbestimmung*, Vienna, 1993, 48–50.
43. Hannes Wimmer, 'Die Arbeitswelt der ausländischen Arbeitnehmer', in Hannes Wimmer (ed.), *Ausländische Arbeitskräfte in Österreich*, Frankfurt, 1986, 263.
44. August Gächter, 'Forced Complementarity: The Attempt to Protect Native Austrian Workers from Immigrants', *New Community* 21, no. 3 (1995): 379–98.
45. It has also been pointed out that unionists are one of the three common sources of political leadership for immigrant communities, the other two being priests and ethnic employers. Depriving immigrants of a say in the trade unions may also have deprived them of a chance for an effective route into Austrian politics on a broader scale. This could explain why Austria lags so far behind in the creation of local and regional consultative councils of foreign nationals (*Ausländerbeiräte*) (Eugene Sensenig, 'Interkulturelle Mitbestimmung vor Ort', *Die Alternative*, no. 9 (1994): 6–7. At the time of writing efforts had been made in about twenty towns to create such councils, but only one had come into being.
46. The lack of foreign workers on works councils is certainly not due to a lack of willingness on their part. At the end of 1983 only 14 per cent of foreign workers felt they were being represented appropriately by their works council. Among those who said not, three reasons were given in roughly equal shares: the works council represents the interests of management only; it represents the interests of Austrian nationals only; it doesn't know about the problems of foreign workers. 18

per cent of foreign workers were basically willing to be candidates and a further 16 per cent under certain circumstances (Hannes Wimmer, 'Die Arbeitswelt der ausländischen Arbeitnehmer', 241–80; August Gächter, *Preventing Racism at the Workplace in Austria: Report to the European Foundation for the Improvement of Living and Working Conditions*, Vienna, 1995.

47. This seems all the more probable since one of the Chamber of Labour's (and thereby implicitly of the trade unions') experts involved in immigration policy-making for well over ten years, on 5 May 1994, in a private conversation, flatly denied that the law had any such provisions as outlined here. Confronted with the text of the law he withdrew to the position that a works council with a majority of foreigners would not be legal (fax message from Georg Ziniel, 26 July 1994). If there is a basis for such a position at all, it must be outside the Employment Constitution Law. Other trade unionists are equally negative on the existing means of making foreign nationals members of works councils.
48. Erich Neurath and Günther Steinbach, *Ausländerbeschäftigungsgesetz.* Vienna, 1976, 101f.
49. Rainer Bauböck, 'Kein Kurswechsel des ÖGB in der Ausländerpolitik', *Kurswechsel* 90, no. 1 (1990): 50.
50. Rudolf Kaske, 'Einleitungsstatement', in Plattform gegen Fremdenhaß (ed.), *Gegen Rassismus und Ausländerfeindlichkeit*, Vienna, 1992, 1ff., translation AG.
51. Karl Öllinger, 'Der ÖGB und "seine" AusländerInnen', *Die Alternative*, no. 4 (1994): 9–16.
52. He is also the most vocal proponent of breaking up the Union of Salaried Employees. At the ÖGB's 13th General Assembly in October 1995 it was agreed to implement gradually a new structure in which there would be only three individual unions: one for manufacturing, one for service industries, and one for the civil service.
53. Only grudgingly were citizens of the European Economic Area granted the right to be elected to the Chamber of Labour, since, as some argued, the Chamber also has sovereign responsibilities.
54. Unsurprisingly, in Austria there is a close negative correlation across provinces between the unemployment rate and the share of foreign workers in the labour force.
55. ÖGB Landesexekutive Vorarlberg/Tirol/Salzburg, *Leitlinien gewerkschaftlicher Ausländerpolitik.* Vorgelegt bei der ARGE-Alp Sitzung am 15–16 Oktober in Mailand. Salzburg, 1992.
56. August Gächter, *Preventing Racism at the Workplace in Austria.*
57. Due to bilateral treaties, citizens of the Federal Republic of Germany, of the UK, and later also of Sweden did have equal access.
58. AK (Chamber of Labour), *Jahrbuch 1966*, Vienna, 1967, 188.
59. August Gächter, *Gleicher Zugang zur Notstandshilfe: Eine Folgenabschätzung.* Unpublished manuscript, 1996; Peter Wandaller, *Daten und Fakten: Ausländer in Salzburg: Finanzielle Beiträge der Ausländer zum österreichischen Sozialstaat.* Unpublished manuscript, Salzburg, 1993.
60. Foreign workers got the message. At the end of 1983, after two years of employment reduction, fully 97 per cent of those sampled in a representative survey indicated they did not plan to stay in Austria for good (Rainer Bauböck, 'Demographische und soziale Struktur der jugoslawischen und türkischen Wohnbevölkerung in Österreich', in: Hannes Wimmer (ed.), *Ausländische Arbeitskräfte in Österreich*, Frankfurt, 1986, 233).
61. Cf. Ulrike Davy, 'Stimmungsmache zuerst: Jörg Haiders Forderungskatalog ist juristisch obsolet – Was begehrt er wirklich?', *Der Standard*, 2 November 1992.

Chapter 5

Dutch Trade Unions, Immigrants and Immigration: Myopic Politics of Equality

Judith Roosblad

Introduction: Postwar Immigration in the Netherlands

From 1870 till the end of the 1950s the Netherlands always had a high emigration rate. That, however, did not mean that there was no immigration, for several immigrant groups arrived in this early period, for example in the mining industry,[1] but these were relatively small. Because the Netherlands considered itself to be mainly an emigration country, no special structures were set up to coordinate immigration or to receive immigrants in this period.

After the Second World War a number of immigrants settled in the country. In the first place there was immigration from the colonies and former colonies. Between 1945 and 1962 there was a substantial inflow of 'repatriates' from the former Dutch East Indies, most of them of mixed descent (Eurasians). They were actively incorporated into Dutch society, and the government regarded their integration as completed at the end of the 1960s.[2] In 1951 a group of Moluccan immigrants arrived in the Netherlands.[3] Considerable immigration from the Dutch overseas territories of Surinam and the Dutch Antilles started later, in the 1970s.[4] The immigration from these countries was not a consequence of recruitment, but caused by political and economic factors. Most of the colonial immigrants had

Dutch nationality and therefore a solid legal status in Dutch society. The protection of their interests, social guidance, and integration in Dutch society were mainly matters for the government and private welfare organisations. The trade unions did not perceive this as being any special concern of theirs. In some cases, in fact, trade unions showed openly that they were more concerned about the threat of competition from colonial workers with their 'own' indigenous workers, than with protecting the interests of colonial migrants. There are cases (especially in the 1950s) in which trade unions tried to keep colonial migrants from participating in the labour market,[5] and others in which they stipulated that the employment of colonial immigrants should not be at the expense of indigenous workers.[6]

Matters were quite different with the immigrants who came to the Netherlands mainly for work, the so-called 'guest workers'. Some of these came to the Netherlands as contract workers recruited from the Mediterranean area, while others arrived by spontaneous migration.[7] The employment of foreign workers must be understood in the light of the rapid economic reconstruction after the Second World War. This national reconstruction effort was so successful that even in the 1950s a shortage of labour emerged in some sectors of industry, such as mining and textiles. The recruitment of foreign labour was seen as a temporary measure: when foreign workers were not needed any more for Dutch economy, they would return home. The Dutch government and trade unions were very much concerned with this foreign labour, and wanted to have some control over the recruitment and employment of foreign workers. Accordingly, in order to regulate it properly, in 1960 the Dutch government launched the official recruitment of foreign workers under its supervision.[8] In a tripartite consultative body, in which the Ministry of Social Affairs and Employment, the employers' organisations, and the trade unions were represented, agreements were made on the principles of recruitment, and on the actual process of the recruitment and employment of foreign workers.[9]

Dutch Labour Relations

That a consultative structure was set up to regulate the recruitment of foreign labour is typical of Dutch labour relations, of which one of the features is a strong element of corporatism. After the Second World War, old corporatist structures were partly restored and partly revised. During the period of reconstruction in particular, government, employers, and trade unions worked closely together to rebuild the Dutch economy. In order to achieve that aim, a strict wage policy was pursued. The trade unions during that time put the national interest above workers' interests, and they moderated the wage claims of their members.

In order to participate in the national corporatist system, the internal centralisation of the trade unions was of great importance. Especially in the early years after the Second World War, there was a strong perception within the trade-union movement that the federations were better placed to be objective, and so were in a better position than the member unions to take decisions in socio-economic matters. To the affiliated unions fell the task of carrying out the centrally formulated policies in their respective sectors.[10] In the 1960s and the 1970s, however, the affiliated unions grew in importance vis-à-vis the trade-union confederations. This was due to several factors: the end of the reconstruction period; the general democratisation of society (which meant that the policies of the confederations were no longer automatically accepted), the widespread introduction of decentralised bargaining, a more flexible wage policy which enhanced the importance of the negotiating unions, and a growing emphasis on the well-being of individuals in the workplace.[11] Although this has led to situations in which the trade-union confederations and member unions have held diametrically opposite points of view, the centralisation of the unions is still an important feature.

The Dutch trade unions are historically divided along religious or ideological lines.[12] A limited number of organisations of employers and workers, recognised officially by the government, participate in the institutionalised consultative system. The 'recognised' trade-union federations have been the Social Democrat-oriented Dutch Federation of Trade Unions (NVV), the Dutch Catholic Trade Union Federation (NKV), and the Protestant Dutch Christian Trade Union Federation (CNV). Since 1986 the federation of white-collar trade unions, VMHP,[13] has also become a recognised trade-union federation. In 1976 the NVV and the NKV merged into the Federation of Dutch Trade Unions (FNV), which is the largest federation, in 1993 representing 60 per cent of all trade-union members. The CNV is smaller, with 18 per cent of union members in 1993. The VMHP follows with 8 per cent, and the ACV[14] represents 6 per cent of all union members. The remaining 8 per cent of union members are organised in non-affiliated unions.[15] Although the Dutch trade-union movement is ideologically fragmented, the trade-union federations often cooperate closely in consultative bodies.

There are two important bodies in which consultation at national level takes place. The first one is the Social Economic Council (SER), in which independent experts appointed by the government are represented alongside trade unions and employers' organisations. The SER is the official advisory council of the government for socio-economic matters. It is required by law that the government asks advice of the SER about policy measures in the socio-economic domain. Thus the SER plays an important role in the field of labour relations. For trade unions it is an important instrument through which to influence socio-economic decisions. The second body is the Joint Industrial Labour Council (Stichting van de Arbeid), in which employers' organisations and trade unions come to agreements about socio-economic policies. This Council may also advise the government in socio-economic matters.

The influence of Dutch trade unions in the national socio-economic decision-making process can be measured from a number of indicators. Not only do they have a firm position in socio-economic decision making through the SER and the Joint Industrial Labour Council, but they are also represented on the boards of various other important national councils like the Dutch National Health Service Council and the National Social Insurance Council. Another indicator for the position of power enjoyed by the trade unions is the link with political parties, and especially with those in power. The FNV has links with the Social Democrat Labour Party PvdA,[16] and the CNV has links with the Christian Democrat Party CDA. Particularly from 1973 to 1977, when the Social Democrats and the Christian Democrats were in power, trade unions saw a number of their demands fulfilled, including a modest convergence of incomes, an increase in purchasing power, and measures to improve the income of those on the minimum wage.

However, because of the economic recession, intensified by the oil crisis of 1973, the government was forced to bring in austerity measures, which were continued by the succeeding government of Christian Democrats and Liberals, which came to power in 1977. The socio-economic policies of the centre-right government were severely criticised by the trade unions, not least because according to them the austerity measures were at the expense of employment, but the trade unions had little success in pressing their demands with the government. Thus the shift from a centre-left government in 1973–77 to predominantly centre-right administrations from 1977 to 1989 certainly caused a change in socio-economic policies. However, that political shift had hardly any effect on policies regarding immigrants and immigration, due to the fact that migration issues were depoliticised. There were no really marked differences of opinion between the major political parties regarding these issues and there was a great deal of consensus about the way immigrants should be integrated into Dutch society.[17] As a result of this, migrant policies were dealt with in a pragmatic, almost technocratic way. A third indicator is the membership density in the trade-union movement. The Dutch trade unions have never enjoyed a high degree of organisation. But the fact that they represented only 40 per cent of the working population at their peak in the mid-1950s, falling to 24 per cent at their nadir in the second half of the 1980s,[18] has never kept them from playing an important role in the socio-economic decision-making process.

Trade Unions Positions on the Recruitment of Foreign Labour

The attitude of the Dutch trade union federations towards recruiting and employing foreign workers was quite positive in the first half of the 1960s. Like the government and employers, they took the view that the recruitment of foreign workers was necessary in order to maintain maximum production, especially in the industrial sector.[19] However, they were also concerned with the direct material interests of Dutch workers. Trade unions feared that employers would be more pleased with foreign workers, because they would be more flexible and more eager to earn as much money as possible, and therefore more willing to work overtime. In addition, the abundant supply of foreign workers might depress wages.[20]

In order to minimise ‘unfair competition’ between Dutch and foreign workers, and in order to improve the squalid conditions under which foreigners had to live, trade unions advocated the equal treatment of foreigners and Dutchmen. However, at the same time they used this equality policy as a tool to limit recruitment, because it made the employment of foreign workers more expensive and more difficult. For example, it was the employers’ duty to provide accommodation. If employers had trouble with finding good accommodation in times of housing shortage, they would not be able to recruit foreigners.[21]

In the mid-1960s the initially positive attitude of the trade unions towards recruitment changed because of the great influx of foreigners. When in 1965 the employers’ federations pressed the government to continue the recruitment of foreigners alongside the spontaneous flow of foreign workers, the trade unions opposed the proposals. They urged the government to come up with well balanced and well controlled policies regarding the recruitment and admission of foreign workers, and the coordination of policies regarding their housing and integration in society.[22]

During the short economic recession of 1966–67 the recruitment of foreign workers was temporarily stopped. The mini-crisis appeared to have little effect on unemployment among foreign workers. On the one hand this was due to the fact that they were needed for special types of labour (mostly dirty and heavy), even in times of temporary recession. On the other hand a number of foreign workers returned to their home countries. As soon as the economic recession was over, the recruitment of workers from the Mediterranean area increased again. In the period 1968–71 more foreign workers were employed, whereas the unemployment percentage in the Netherlands was higher than during the period 1966–68. This was proof of the fact that certain unskilled work had been taken over by foreigners.[23] During the economic crisis of 1972–74 too, a number of foreign workers were recruited, and so apparently they were needed even when unemployment was increasing.[24]

However, the reactions of indigenous workers to this recession and the mass redundancies that followed made clear that not all Dutch workers were willing to accept the presence of foreign labour.[25] In order to satisfy the Dutch workers the union federations pleaded for the abolition of some of the special facilities enjoyed by foreign workers. On the other hand they pressured the government to use consistent policies in recruitment, employment, housing and integration. Trade unions themselves, however, protected virtually none of the interests of foreign workers, and no attempts at integration policies were made at that time. Social assistance and social welfare took place mostly through religious institutions and welfare organisations.[26] Trade unions' demands for restrictive recruitment policies and the limitation of the immigrant population increased after the early 1970s. In the Action Programme 1971–75 of the Joint Consultation Committee of the NVV, NKV and CNV (Overlegorgaan VV-NKV-CNV), three important points of departure for general policies were stated. First, a restrictive admission policy was an absolute necessity. Secondly, wherever possible, foreign workers should be encouraged to return to their countries of origin. Thirdly, foreign workers already present in the Netherlands should have the same rights and obligations as Dutch workers.

With regard to the first policy, rules for the admission of those of foreign nationality had been laid down in the Aliens Act *(Vreemdelingenwet)* of 1965 and in the administrative orders based on the act. These rules were initially meant to regulate rather than to restrict or limit immigration, which was generally considered a temporary phenomenon, not only by the government but also by many of the immigrants themselves. During the years that followed, however, the government gradually introduced a series of measures that made it more difficult for foreign workers to enter the country without prior permission. During the 1973 oil crisis the government spoke openly for the first time of 'the need to limit the number of foreigners employed in the country to a ceiling in line with economic conditions'.[27] Trade unions supported these restrictive recruitment policies of the government. Within the

Social Economic Council (SER) as well, trade unions used their influence to limit the number of foreign workers.

In 1974 the SER advised on the recruitment and employment of foreign workers, and recommended that the government restructure its labour market policies in such a way that the recruitment of foreign workers would hardly be necessary. The overpopulation of the Netherlands, and the related environmental problems and 'social climate', were given as major arguments. From then on the recruitment of foreign workers virtually came to a halt, but the immigration of non-workers continued on quite a large scale within the framework of family reunion.[28]

A second way of reducing the number of foreign workers in the country was to make sure that foreign workers would return to their home country after the expiry of their contracts. When in 1974 the government promoted the idea of a 'return bonus' for those foreign workers who wanted to return to their home country, the unions stressed the importance of 'return projects' as part of foreign aid. The idea was to bring the jobs to the people rather than taking the people to the jobs. In cooperation with the Ministry of Development Cooperation and the governments of the countries of origin, trade unions helped returning migrants to set up small businesses.[29] These policies for return migration were criticised. Since the economic crisis of 1966–67, a discussion had arisen about the importance of foreign labour to the Dutch economy.

On the one hand it performed a buffer function. In periods of economic expansion, foreign workers could easily be recruited through the official channels, or through foreign workers already in employment. In times of economic recession, recruitment could be stopped and a number of foreign workers would return to their home country, because they could not find employment and their legal rights as unemployed foreign workers were limited. On the other hand the economic crisis of 1966–67 made clear that foreigners were needed even in times of recession. So although government, employers and trade unions kept claiming that the employment of foreign workers was a temporary measure, from as early as 1967 there were reasons to believe that the so-called 'guest labour' was taking on a more permanent character.[30]

From within the trade unions as well, the return policy was criticised. An official of the NKV stated that it was unfair to buy off workers with a return bonus as a way of limiting the number of foreign workers, simply because they were not needed any longer for the Dutch economy.[31] Although the trade unions focused on limiting the number of foreigners in Dutch society, they also emphasised the need to integrate those foreign workers already present into

Dutch society. They stated that foreign workers should have the same rights and obligations as Dutch workers.

Using such equality-based arguments, they opposed bills proposed by the government which violated the rights of foreign workers, such as the Foreign Workers Employment Bill (*Wet Arbeid Buitenlandse Werknemers*, WABW) of November 1975. It stipulated that an employer had to have a work permit for a foreign worker before he could employ that particular foreigner.

Furthermore, it also set a limit to the number of foreign workers whom firms were allowed to employ, which meant that foreign workers could only be employed by companies which had not yet reached their limit. The limits, set by the government, were a new instrument to control and reduce the number of foreign workers. The bill was severely criticised because its provisions were considered discriminatory. In a combined statement, the FNV and the CNV pointed to the 'unacceptable consequences' of the proposed regulations, because they felt that foreign workers, once they had been admitted to the Netherlands, should have the same chances and entitlements to employment opportunities as Dutch workers.[32] For the unions, the principle of equal rights for all those present in the country evidently overruled the principle of limitation, which clearly should be attained by admission policies and not by employment regulations. However, despite the severe criticisms, the bill was enacted in 1979, and the trade-union federations resigned themselves to that fact.

Protection of Foreigners' Interests

In the 1970s the immediate protection of the interests of foreign workers was still done mainly by welfare organisations for foreigners. Even though union leaders were on the boards of some of these organisations, there often was a controversy between the two types of institutions. The numerous action groups of and for foreigners, which came into being at the beginning of the 1970s, became more and more important.[33] They drew the attention of the unions to their responsibilities towards foreigners. The federations answered that they were indeed concerning themselves with the specific interests of their foreign members. According to them they promoted the interests of foreigners within the SER, the Joint Industrial Labour Council, and in numerous committees. Furthermore they were establishing separate consultation times, laying on courses for foreigners, publishing the important documents in different languages (like forms, information packs on legislation, strike calls), and creating special advisory committees. To coordinate these activities on behalf of foreign members the CNV set up a Foreign Workers Committee in 1971, and in 1979 it instituted a Secretariat for Foreign Workers. In 1972 the NVV followed with the creation of its Secretariat for Foreign Workers and the Contact Committee for Foreign Workers. The NKV never had such a committee or a secretariat for foreign workers. The promotion of the interests of that group was the responsibility of one of the union officials.[34] From 1975 on, after the NVV and NKV had merged in the FNV, the Secretariat for Foreign Workers and the Contact Committee Foreign Workers became part of the FNV.

These measures, however, were not able essentially to improve the position of foreign workers,[35] and in spite of such efforts, the level of organisation of foreign employees remained low. In 1973 less than 15 per cent of foreign employees were union members, compared to about 36 per cent of indigenous workers. According to the unions this was due to language problems, the temporary nature of the stay, bad experiences with trade unions in the country of origin, and the problems of collecting union dues from people who often changed their address.[36] According to some of the foreign workers the secretariats and activities of the trade union at federation level served as an excuse for some of the member unions to make no real effort to protect foreigners' interests, but to leave it to the secretariats.

In labour conflicts as well, the interests of foreign workers appeared to have low priority. There is relatively scarce evidence, but a study by Van de Velde and Van Velzen of participation by foreign workers in a nation-wide strike in 1977 shows that the unions made little effort to inform foreigners and involve them in their actions.[37] According to this study, the organisers of the strike, the Industrial Unions NVV and NKV, hardly ever involved foreigners in the decision-making process, even though in some plants foreigners made up 20 per cent of the workforce.

The First Attempt to Formulate Minorities Policies

Towards the end of the 1970s the impact of the economic crisis manifested itself more and more in society. In 1979 the government expressed in its Memorandum on Aliens Policy (*Notitie Vreemdelingenbeleid*) the need for even more restrictive policies, and its scope was extended to all foreigners. High population density was presented as a major argument for restrictions. In addition, however, it was argued that 'the Dutch tradition of hospitality should no longer be manifested in admitting larger quantities of foreigners', but rather 'by setting up immigrant policies of good quality for those who are in the country already'.[38] In other words, curtailing immigration was considered a prerequisite for the development of a sound immigrant policy.

The long-standing official denial that the Netherlands was a country of immigration had prevented the development of clear immigrant policies. The need for coherent policies was publicly recognised in 1979 when the Scientific Council for Government Policy,[39] a high-level advisory body to the government, recommended the government to proceed on the assumption that foreign workers and other immigrant groups were going to be a permanent part of society. After this report the government hesitatingly came to realise that some immigrants had settled permanently and that policies should be directed at overcoming their disadvantaged position. In the Memorandum on Minorities (*Minderhedennota*) the government finally recognised the fact that the Netherlands was an immigration country,[40] and that special immigrant policies were needed, irrespective of the nationality of the immigrants and their reasons for immigration.[41] The new government policies focused predominantly on removing disadvantages suffered by ethnic minorities,[42] as well as creating a multicultural society. In practice employment, education, housing and welfare were the dominant policy areas.

After the report of the Scientific Council for Government Policy the trade unions also accepted the fact that the Netherlands was indeed an immigration country and that immigrants were going to be a permanent element of the labour market. The alteration in the official attitudes of the FNV on return migration was typical of this change of direction. The initiation of remigration projects, as advocated previously, was abandoned as having proved to be unproductive. An important result of the minorities policies of the government and the acceptance of the fact that the Netherlands was an immigration country was that trade unions too, following the government, focussed on all ethnic minorities (at least verbally), instead of concentrating solely on the category of foreign workers, which did not include the colonial and other categories of minorities. This was expressed within the FNV by changing the name of the secretariat. Previously it had been called the Secretariat for Foreign Workers; from 1985 it was referred to as the Secretariat Workers' Interests Ethnic Minorities.

Following the national policies of the government, the CNV and the FNV gradually began to formulate minorities policies. In 1980 the CNV produced the brochure, *The Alien within the Gate*, which was meant to inform the Dutch rank and file about their foreign colleagues, but also to convince foreign workers that the CNV was serious about promoting their interests and that they should join the CNV. The CNV had already amended its articles of association in order to create the possibility for workers of other (non-Christian) religions to join CNV unions. It also recognised the importance of foreigners having their own organisations, and the federation was prepared to cooperate with them.

Within the FNV the basis for minorities policies was laid down in the 1982 memorandum, *Together rather than Separate*,[43] the aim of which was to stimulate a discussion among the member unions in order to formulate more detailed minorities policies. Only in the second place was it meant to create a basis for these policies among the rank and file. The memorandum concentrated on problems such as housing, education, and the integration of foreign workers. Remarkably enough, it did not say very much about ways of improving the labour market position of minorities. It was rather brief on what the member unions themselves could do to improve the position of foreign workers.

Despite the moderate tone of the memorandum, it was the target of much criticism from member unions and from the Dutch rank and file. They felt that it was too much in favour of foreign workers, and did not sufficiently take into account the interests of Dutch workers. The indigenous members of the FNV only wanted to show solidarity with foreigners as long as these foreigners had the same rights and duties as Dutch workers, and as long as there was no 'affirmative action' in favour of foreign workers. Moreover, Dutch FNV members seemed to have the idea that foreign workers were in a preferential position; for example, they were supposed to have longer vacations. According to the rank and file, foreigners had to adapt to Dutch society in exchange for solidarity.[44]

In society at large, the trade-union federations seemed to become more aware of the importance of their task of protecting the social interests of minorities, and stood up for them in political debates. For example, in the SER in 1983, the federations opposed the 'country-of-residence' principle, according to which foreigners would receive lower child allowances for children who were still in the country of origin. The action against this plan, taken in cooperation with other organisations, was successful, and the government withdrew its proposals. The price for this show of solidarity was a general, though minor, lowering of child benefits.[45] The unions also presented themselves as a social movement in the struggle against racism. When in the general elections of 1982 the extreme right-wing Centre Democrats party won a seat in parliament, the trade unions publicly raised their voice against racism and right-wing extremism. The FNV, together with the CNV and organisations of and for foreigners, initiated the 'Anti-Discrimination Consultative Body', and as a consequence of these consultations, the federal council of the FNV decided that union members who were members of or openly sympathised with racist organisations should be expelled. The

CNV also stated that within their organisation there was no place for members of extreme-right parties.

During the general elections of 1994, once more the trade unions spoke out strongly against such parties, especially when a survey had shown that a significant number of FNV members (56,000, or 2.8 per cent of the membership) were voting for the Centre Democrats. It implied that one fifth of Centre Democrat supporters were members of the FNV. At the elections of 1994, the FNV issued a negative voting recommendation, calling on its members not to vote for an extreme-right party. Unions proceeded to put into effect the decision to expel members of and open sympathizers with such parties. The FNV produced a practical manual how on to fight racism,[46] in order to counter racism within its own ranks, and one was also produced especially for staff members charged with education and training. These manuals were distributed among the unions.

Nevertheless, as far as the position of minorities on the labour market was concerned, little had changed. The minorities policies of the government did not succeed in improving the social position of minorities, and indeed that position had deteriorated greatly between 1976 and 1983, as measured by such standards as unemployment and its duration. Neither did the minorities policies of the trade unions seem to have much effect. On the labour market in particular, minorities found themselves in a deprived position. Studies had shown that the disproportionate unemployment rate among ethnic minorities was largely to be explained by direct and indirect discrimination against them in recruitment and selection by employers, and by overrepresentation of ethnic minorities when it came to redundancies. In 1986, the government's Advisory Committee on Minorities Policy (ACOM) therefore recommended affirmative action, as had been implemented in the United States and the United Kingdom.[47]

However, these recommendations from the ACOM were not well received. Although the SER, in its advice of 1987, proposed a number of measures in the area of training of ethnic minorities and common action by employers and trade unions to improve the position of minorities, it categorically rejected any form of obligatory affirmative action.

Efforts to Improve the Labour Market Position of Minorities

The government, as an employer, decided in 1986 to implement a weak form of affirmative action within its own ranks, because in government service the proportion of minorities was also very low.

However, the government refrained from intervening in the private sector, and left it to the social partners to come up with a solution. When at the end of the 1980s it became clear to the government that its reserved attitude towards the private sector had been unproductive, it urged the social partners to reach solid agreements; otherwise, it threatened to take legislative measures. This threat resulted in an agreement between the employers and trade unions in the Joint Industrial Labour Council in 1990,[48] on how to reduce unemployment among minorities. The aim was to reduce it to the level current among the indigenous population within five years.[49] In order to attain that objective, 60,000 additional jobs for minorities would have to be created; however, within two years it was evident that this agreement was not being taken seriously, either by employers or trade unions. Employers' organisations did not even bother to inform their members; in the process of collective bargaining, trade unions gave the agreements on ethnic minorities a lower priority than wage claims and other primary conditions of employment.

The disappointing results of this agreement led the government, but also the opposition, to prepare for legislation. In 1994 the Employment Equity Act (the WBEAA), an opposition initiative, was passed.[50] The act obliges firms with more than thirty-five employees to report on the ethnic composition of their workforce; to develop a recruitment policy for minorities; to register migrant employees; and to make an annual public report on the efforts made to employ ethnic minorities, and the results of those efforts. They were bound to set up a plan of action, indicating how they intended to implement the recruitment of employees from minority groups.

The act is not a fully binding one: the only penalty in the law is for not reporting. As could be expected, the act was severely criticised by employers. They threatened they would no longer cooperate under the agreement made in the Joint Industrial Labour Council if it became an additional obligation under the law. The threat was hardly realistic, for the act was a reaction to the fact that in practice the agreement had yielded no results. It was remarkable that the trade-union federations did not lobby to get the legislation passed, but kept a low profile. They had committed themselves to the agreement they had made with the employers, and were obviously not in favour of additional legislation. This led to a somewhat irritated reaction from Rosenmöller, one of the MPs for the Green Left Party, who had taken the initiative for the bill:

> 'The unions do a great deal of talking about what should be done in politics. When we do something that is not in accordance with their agreements with employers, they do not approve'.[51]

In 1996 the trade unions and employers renewed their commitment to reducing unemployment among minorities. In this new agreement there are no fixed target figures and there is no fixed time limit within which proportionate unemployment has to be achieved. At the same time as renewing the agreement, they have negotiated a revision of the Employment Equity Act, which undermines this impotent legislation even further.

The Position of Minorities Within the Trade Unions

The STAR Agreement made clear to the trade unions that within their own organisation the percentage of minority employees generally, and the percentage in staff positions, were very low.[52] Minorities inside and outside the trade unions also pointed to the fact that within the trade unions far too little was being done on behalf of minorities. In addition to the secretariats, both the CNV and the FNV had installed advisory bodies for minorities, but they had hardly any influence and only an advisory function. The real decisions were taken at board level, and the advisory bodies had a hard time trying to get their issues onto the boards' agenda.

Within the FNV, the Secretariat Workers' Interests Ethnic Minorities recognised the fact that the minorities policies of the FNV, up to that point at least, were mainly paper policies.[53] It stated that in practice little had happened to improve either the labour-market position of minorities, or their position within the trade unions. In order to do something about this, the FNV and its member unions formulated a 'non-discrimination code' in 1993. The code was meant as a step in order to overcome the disadvantaged position of migrant workers, both on the labour market and within the trade unions. The main measures proposed were affirmative action to alleviate the disproportionate representation of minorities in employment, and the improvement of selection procedures, including screening them for direct and indirect discrimination. But again the practical implementation of the proposed policies remained rather vague. Given the severe criticism by some of the member unions, especially the mighty Industrial Union FNV, of the proposed measures and of affirmative action in particular, it remains to be seen what will come of this code.[54]

Conclusion

In the early phase of official recruitment, the trade unions had been quite positive as far as the recruitment and employment of foreign labour was concerned. By the mid-1960s this attitude was changing. After a short economic recession in 1966–67, trade unions began to demand restricted recruitment policies. During the period from 1968 to 1972 the government introduced a series of measures that made it more difficult for foreign workers to enter the country without prior permission. Especially after the oil crisis of 1973 the government complied with trade union demands for restricted recruitment policies. During the following years the recruitment of foreign workers virtually ceased, but in a framework of family reunion, the immigration of non-workers continued on quite a large scale.

As far as inclusion or exclusion of migrants is concerned, there never has been any formal exclusion of immigrant workers. Therefore in this chapter the inclusion or exclusion of immigrants is seen principally as the extent to which trade unions have protected immigrants' interests. From the very beginning of the recruitment and employment of foreign workers, trade unions demanded equal treatment for foreign and indigenous workers. This was done not only out of concern for the rights of foreign workers, but also to minimise competition between indigenous and foreign workers. According to Marshall-Goldschwartz,[55] this policy of equal treatment was used as a tool to limit recruitment, because it made the employment of foreign workers more expensive. During the 1970s, trade unions engaged in a number of activities to improve the protection of foreigners' interests, such as special consultation times, special courses, and special advisory committees for foreign workers. However, the immediate promotion of foreign workers' interests was still carried out mainly by welfare organisations.

It was not until the beginning of the 1980s that trade unions started to formulate minorities policies. It was the recognition by the Dutch government that foreign labour was not a temporary phenomenon, and that special policies were necessary to integrate migrants into Dutch society, which generated these policies in the trade unions.

Three areas can be distinguished in which trade unions can protect the interests of minorities: in society as a whole; in the labour market; and in their own organisations. First, the trade unions strove for an improvement of the social position of minorities in Dutch society at large. In this domain the unions took a firm stand: for example they opposed several laws that undermined the social rights of foreign workers, like the Foreign Workers Employment Bill and the 'country-of-residence' principle; they spoke out against racism, discrimination and right-wing extremism; and they campaigned for good housing and education for minorities. In these activities they manifested themselves as part of a social movement.

With regard to the labour market, however, the policies of the trade union federations have been rather vague. Unemployment among minorities is very high. In the 1982 FNV minorities policies, and in the CNV document of 1980, no serious proposals were made to address this situation. Also in this respect the impact of government policies on trade-unions actions is striking. When in 1990 employers and trade unions made an agreement to reduce the relatively high unemployment among minorities, this was done under threat of legislation by the government. For that matter, the agreements only postponed legislation. When it became clear that the agreements were not yielding results after all, the Employment Equity Act was introduced in 1994. This example illustrates that, as far as the labour market is concerned, trade unions are more inclined to cooperate with the social partners within the institutionalised consultative structures.

On the inclusion of minorities within the trade unions as well, it is clear that although the trade unions created special facilities for minorities in order to include them within the trade-union organisation – such as special advisory bodies – there is still an under-representation of minorities, not only in membership but also at board level and in other influential positions. The trade unions have not so far substantiated their claims of inclusion in this area by introducing consistent measures to improve the position of minorities within the trade unions.

NOTES

1. P. Brassé and W. van Schelven, *Assimilatie van vooroorlogse migranten: Drie generaties Polen, Slovenen en Italianen in Heerlen*, The Hague, 1980.
2. In 1992 the number of people of Eurasian descent was about 442,000 (Statistics Netherlands, *Monthly bulletin of population statistics* 43 no. 7 (1995): 11; H. van Amersfoort, *Immigration and the formation of minority groups: The Dutch experience 1945–1975*, Cambridge, 1982.
3. In 1994 the number of Moluccans in the Netherlands was approximately 37,500 (H. Smeets and J. Veenman, 'Steeds meer "thuis" in Nederland: Tien jaar ontwikkelingen in de Molukse bevolkingsgroep', in H. Vermeulen & R. Penninx (eds), *Het democratisch ongeduld: De emancipatie en integratie van zes doelgroepen van het minderhedenbeleid*, Amsterdam, 1994, 15–43; J.H. Kraak, P. Ploeger and F.O.J. Kho, *De repatriëring uit Indonesië: Een onderzoek naar de integratie van de gerepatriëerden in de Nederlandse samenleving*, The Hague, 1957; F. Steijlen, *RMS: van ideaal tot symbool: Moluks nationalisme in Nederland 1951–1994*, Amsterdam, 1996.
4. In 1992 some 350,000 people of Surinamese and Dutch Antillean descent were living in the Netherlands (Statistics Netherlands, *Monthly Bulletin of Population Statistics* 43 no. 7 (1995): 11).
5. In the case of Moluccan migrants, see Commissie Verwey-Jonker, *Ambonezen in Nederland: Rapport van het Minsiterie van Maatschappelijk Werk uitgebracht door de daartoe ingestelde commissie onder voorzitterschap van Mevr. Dr. H. Verwey-*

Jonker, The Hague, 1959; and J.H. Kraak, P. Ploeger and F.O.J. Kho, *De repatriëring uit Indonesië: Een onderzoek naar de integratie van de gerepatriëerden in de Nederlandse samenleving*, The Hague, 1957.

6. For instance in 1951 the Railway Unions stipulated that the employment of Eurasians must not be at the expense of 'already employed' (read, indigenous) personnel. Annual report of the Joint Council of the Railway Unions (*Jaarverslag van de Personeelsraad*, 1951, 54).
7. The largest groups of former 'guest workers' in Dutch society are Turks and Moroccans. In 1992 the number of people of Turkish descent was 239,000, and the number of people of Moroccan descent was 193,000 (Statistics Netherlands, *Monthly Bulletin of Population Statistics* 43, no. 7 (1995): 11).
8. Official recruitment began with an agreement between the Dutch and Italian government in 1960. Soon after that, agreements with other Mediterranean countries like Spain, Portugal, Turkey (1964), Greece (1966), Morocco (1969), Yugoslavia, and Tunisia followed (P. Schumacher, *De minderheden: 700.000 migranten minder gelijk*, Amsterdam, 1987).
9. J.W. Janssen, 'Opvattingen en beleid van de werkgevers- en werknemersorganisaties', in R. Wentholt et al., *Buitenlandse arbeiders in Nederland*, Leiden, 1967, 39.
10. J.P. Windmuller, C. de Galan and A.F. van Zweden, *Arbeidsverhoudingen in Nederland*, Derde herziene druk, Utrecht, 1979.
11. W. van Voorden, 'The Netherlands', in Joan Campbell (ed.), *European Labor Unions*, Westport/London, 1992.
12. Not only the trade unions in Dutch society were divided along religious lines; until the mid-1960s Dutch society as a whole was a pillarised one in which Catholics, Protestants, Socialists and Liberals lived more or less segregated lives. They had their own separate institutions, like schools, churches, leisure organisations and political parties. On the government and management level the leaders cooperated in national (and local) institutions and organisations (Lijphart, *The Politics of Accommodation: Pluralism and Democracy in the Netherlands*, Berkeley, CA, 1975; Stuurman, *Het onstaan van der verzuiling in Nederland*, Amsterdam, 1981).
13. Vakcentrale voor Middelbaar en Hoger Personeel (Federation for Middle and Senior Management).
14. Algemene Vakcentrale (General Trade Union Federation).
15. B. Klandermans and J. Visser, *De vakbeweging na de welvaartstaat*, Assen, 1995, 31–2.
16. The present Prime Minister Kok is the former chairman of the FNV.
17. This has changed in the 1990s. From 1991, the leader of the Liberal Party (VVD), Bolkestein, has made repeated attempts to politicise minorities issues, to the great dissatisfaction of the other major political parties.
18. B. Klandermans and J. Visser, *De vakbeweging na de welvaartstaat*, Assen, 1995; J. Visser and B. Ebbinghaus, 'Een halve eeuw verandering: Verklaringen voor convergentie en diversiteit van werknemersorganisatie in West-Europa', in Jelle Visser (ed.), *De vakbeweging op de eeuwgrens: Vijf sociologische studies over de vakbeweging*, Amsterdam, 1996, 24.
19. J.W. Janssen, 'Opvattingen en beleid van de werkgevers- en werknemersorganisaties', in R. Wentholt et al., *Buitenlandse arbeiders in Nederland*, Leiden, 1967, 33–56.
20. J.A.M. Heijke, *Sociaal-economische aspecten van gastarbeid*, Rotterdam, 1979.
21. A.J. Marshall-Goldschwartz, *The Import of Labour: The Case of the Netherlands*, Rotterdam, 1973, 63–70.
22. Janssen, 'Opvattingen en beleid van de werkgevers- en werknemersorganisaties', 33–56.

23. P. Schumacher, *De minderheden: 700.000 migranten minder gelijk*, Amsterdam, 1987.
24. Ibid. The number of foreign workers from the Mediterranean area had risen from 7,000 in 1960 to 25,000 in 1964, 64,000 in 1968, 140,000 in 1972 and 190,000 in 1976 (J.A.M. Heijke, *Sociaal-economische aspecten van gastarbeid*, Rotterdam, 1979, 1).
25. A. Zwinkels, 'Buitenlandse arbeiders en vakbonden', *Informatiebulletin werkgroepen buitenlandse arbeiders*, no. 3 (1972): 71–9.
26. K. van Twist, *Gastarbeid ongewenst: De gevestigde organisaties en buitenlandse arbeiders in Nederland*, Baarn, 1977. 100; WRR *Ethnic minorities*, The Hague, 1979, 116.
27. WRR, *Ethnic Minorities*, 127.
28. H. Entzinger, 'Netherlands', in T. Hammar (ed.), *European Immigration Policy: A Comparative Study*, Cambridge, 1985, 50–88; WRR *Ethnic Minorities.*
29. R. Penninx and H. van Renselaar, *A Fortune in Small Change: A Study of Migrant Workers' Attempts to Invest Savings Productively through Joint Stock Corporations and Village Development Cooperatives in Turkye*, The Hague, 1978.
30. R. Penninx and L. van Velzen, *Internationale arbeidsmigratie: Uitstoting uit 'thuislanden' en maatschappelijke integratie in 'gastlanden' van buitenlandse arbeiders*, Nijmegen, 1977.
31. The union official Cees Commandeur said this in an article in *Richting* (the newspaper of the Transport Union NKV), 23 July 1974.
32. R. Penninx and L. van Velzen, *Internationale arbeidsmigratie*, 38–40.
33. A.J.F. Köbben, *De zaakwaarnemer: Inaugurele Rede Erasmus Universiteit Rotterdam*, Deventer, 1983, 12–13; WRR *Ethnic Minorities*, 121.
34. Cees Commandeur.
35. A. Slob, *De buitenlandse werknemers en de Nederlandse vakbeweging*. Unpublished manuscript, Vakgroep Sociologie, Faculteit der Economische Wetenschappen, Erasmus Universiteit Rotterdam, 1982, 80–1.
36. *Handboek Buitenlandse Werknemers*, Alphen aan den Rijn, 1973.
37. B. van de Velde and J. van Velzen, 'De Nederlandse vakbonden, internationale solidariteit en buitenlandse werknemers: Ideologie en werkgelegenheid', in F. Bovenkerk (ed.), *Omdat zij anders zijn: Patronen van rasdiscriminatie in Nederland*, Amsterdam/Meppel, 1978, 166– 88.
38. Notitie Vreemdelingenbeleid, 1979, 8.
39. Wetenschappelijke Raad voor het Regeringsbeleid (WRR).
40. Ministerie van Binnenlandse Zaken, *Minderhedennota*, The Hague, 1983.
41. H. Entzinger, 'The Netherlands', in T. Hammar (ed.), *European Immigration Policy: A Comparative Study*, Cambridge, 1985, 50–88.
42. The target groups of these policies were foreign workers from the Mediterranean area, the Surinamese, Dutch Antilleans, Moluccans, gypsies, caravan dwellers, and refugees.
43. FNV, *Samen, beter dan apart: De FNV en de buitenlandse werknemers*, Amsterdam, 1982; see also R. de Jongh, M van der Laan and J. Rath, *FNV'ers aan het woord over buitenlandse werknemers*, Uitgave 16, Leiden, 1984.
44. Ibid.
45. Ibid.; G. Ritsema, *De participatie van Turkse werknemers in de FNV*, Amsterdam, 1993.
46. FNV, *Non-discriminatie code voor FNV en bonden: Richtlijnen voor de vereniging en werkorganisatie*, Amsterdam, 1993.
47. F. Bovenkerk, *Een eerlijke kans: Over de toepasbaarheid van buitenlandse ervaringen met positieve actie voor etnische minderheden op de arbeidsmarkt in Nederland*, The Hague, 1986.

48. This so-called STAR Agreement was titled *More Work for Minorities* (Stichting van de Arbeid, *Méér werk voor minderheden*. Publication no. 6/90, The Hague, 1990).
49. In 1990 the unemployment rate among minorities was 23 per cent, compared to 8 per cent of the indigenous working population (R. Wolff and R. Penninx, 'Donkere wolken boven de arbeidsmarkt', *Migrantenstudies* 10, no. 1 (1994): 1–18).
50. The WBEAA (*Wet Bevordering Evenredige Arbeidsparticipatie Allochtonen*) act is strongly influenced by the Canadian Employment Equity Act.
51. H. Stokman, *De toegankelijkheid van de FNV voor allochtonen*, Amsterdam, 1995.
52. In the Netherlands there are no reliable national figures for the membership density of minorities. The problem with estimating the density is the way in which the unions register their members: if they register the 'ethnic background' at all, it is attached to the criterion 'nationality', not 'country of birth'. This means that immigrants with Dutch nationality remain invisible. Various unions are now developing a registration system which also registers 'ethnicity'. This, however, is done on a voluntary basis: those who do not want to be labelled as part of an 'ethnic minority' are not registered as such, which gives an incomplete picture. Not only do the estimates diverge widely; neither do the results of research offer much clarification. From data in Rotterdam it appears that there is considerable variety in the degrees of organisation of the various ethnic groups: 58 per cent of Spaniards, 13 per cent of Turks, and 15 per cent of Surinamese are members of a trade union, while 21 per cent of the indigenous workers in Rotterdam are organised (De Jongh et al., 8). However, according to Reubsaet et al. (T.J.M. Reubsaet, J.A. Kropman and L.M. van Mulier, *Surinaamse migranten in Nederland, deel 2: De positie van Surinamers in de Nederlandse samenleving*, Nijmegen, 1982, 222) only 4 per cent of Surinamese workers are members of a union. Furthermore, membership density varies for each branch of industry. From an inquiry at the National Railways in 1976, for instance, it appeared that 80 per cent of Turks were members of a union (Vervoersbond CNV, *Leven en werken in Nederland: Een sociologisch onderzoek onder Turkse werknemers in dienst van de N.S.*, Utrecht, 1976.
53. FNV, *'Onder ons gezegd, maar niet meer gezwegen': Naar een implementatie van anti-discriminatiebeleid bij FNV en bonden*, Amsterdam, 1992.
54. H. Stokman, *De toegankelijkheid van de FNV voor allochtonen*, Amsterdam, 1995.
55. A.J. Marshall-Goldschwartz, *The Import of Labour: The Case of the Netherlands*, Rotterdam, 1973.

Chapter 6

Trade Unions and Immigrants in France: From Assimilation to Antiracist Networking

Cathie Lloyd

Introduction

A historical approach is crucial to understanding the long involvement between immigrant workers and the labour movement in France. In the past, trade unions were seen as having played a key role in the assimilation of (mainly European) immigrant workers. The main structures and ideological approaches developed by trade unions to work with immigrants were laid down before 1960 according to a paradigm of the 'assimilable immigrant worker'. Three more recent phases of mainly non-European immigration provide the main focus for this chapter: the period of postwar reconstruction, the ending of primary immigration and the beginning of settlement of those already in France in the period after 1974, and the most recent period in which immigrants have demanded and gained new rights. This last period has seen a fundamental shift in the position of the immigrant worker, situating ethnic minority populations in a broader space of political, welfare, and human rights.[1] Developments since the 1980s have required trade unions to rethink their approach to immigrant workers, which has not always been successful.

The general framework of trade-union attitudes towards immigrant workers is influenced by the way in which all political discourse in France is linked to myths of legitimation of the Republic, which focus on different interpretations of the French Revolution and the ideas of 'Equality, Liberty and Fraternity'. This tradition has emphasised universalist discourses of human rights rather than community-based ideas of rights.[2] The ideas of 'universalism' and 'particularism', however, are present in complex and ambiguous forms. Thus trade unions insist that immigrants should be treated as equal to all other workers while often remaining insensitive to structural aspects of inequality. Despite criticising the idea of 'communities', unions have recognised different categories of immigrant workers. There is a great deal of rhetoric with which we need to engage in order to assess trade-unions' attitudes towards immigrants and ethnic minorities. It is also important to bear in mind the different local circumstances and attitudes.

We shall look briefly first at some basic information about migration to France and the structure of trade unions, before posing four related questions: what is the attitude of trade unions towards immigration? Are immigrants included or excluded by unions? What are unions' policies on immigrant workers? And what are their roles in the struggle against discrimination and racism?

Immigrant workers have been an important part of the French workforce for most of this century. After the First World War the loss of manpower coupled with a demographic deficit pushed French industry to recruit abroad. Demographers consider that immigrant labour will continue to be essential to the French economy into the twenty-first century.[3] Today there are 4.2 million immigrants in France (excluding seasonal workers and other temporary residents) and they constitute approximately 7 per cent of the working population.[4] The largest group of immigrants is from North and Francophone West Africa (45 per cent of the total) and 12 per cent are from the Asian Far East. The older 'immigrants' and their descendants originate from Portugal, Italy, Spain, and Poland. However, the 'second generation' with French nationality does not appear in official statistics.[5] Today, immigrants are over-represented in vulnerable intermediary unskilled employment with fixed short-term contracts.

The second generation has been particularly badly affected by the economic recession, experiencing high levels of unemployment. Non-nationals have rates of unemployment about twice that of the indigenous French, with levels of about 17 per cent compared with 9 per cent of the population as a whole in 1990. Youth unemployment is very high: it reaches levels of over 50 per cent for those under twenty-five, compared with 20 per cent for French youth.[6]

Immigrants in France are not regarded as guest workers although there always have been important numbers of contract workers. The model that developed up to 1939 was that of an assimilable European-origin workforce that would eventually settle in France, taking French nationality. The Nationality Code was based on the idea of *jus soli*, so that the children of immigrants born in France were automatically French. Although xenophobia appeared particularly at times of recession, or when immigrants were deployed to take French workers' jobs or break strikes, the notion of assimilation, whereby the individual was incorporated into full citizenship rights and duties, meant that separate provision for minorities was not regarded as necessary or desirable.

As immigration came from further afield, particularly from France's ex-colonies, the government attempted to introduce limitations in the late 1960s.[7] Their rights depended on where and when a person had been born. The idea of the *jus soli* was not seriously questioned until the mid-1980s, when proposals for changes in the Nationality Code were debated. They were initially defeated by massive popular mobilisations, but enacted in 1993. However, despite new limitations on access to nationality, numbers of young people have continued to opt for French nationality, and the model will, it seems, have a continued existence.[8]

Participation in trade unions has been open to immigrants in a way that other forms of political activity is not to non-citizens. French unions are divided along political lines into confederations with their own specialist federations concentrated in different sectors. In the recent economic crisis, union membership has fallen dramatically. Industrial sectors where membership was strong (mines, metallurgy, automobile manufacture, public services) have declined and areas of weak union organisation (catering, services, part-time employment) have proliferated. Immigrant workers' membership reflects this general picture.

This chapter focuses on the two main confederations, the General Confederation of Labour (CGT) and the French Democratic Confederation of Labour (CFDT), which together command more than 59 per cent of trade union support in workplace ballots.[9] French unions organise about 10 per cent of the economically active population. Union membership tends to be activist and concentrated in particular industrial sectors so that figures do not reflect mobilising capacity. The largest is the CGT, with membership of around 650,000. The CFDT is a little smaller at about 570,000.[10] Estimates for workplace council elections in 1987 showed support for the CGT at about 36 per cent and the CFDT 23 per cent of all union voters. Government measures for direct workplace participation during the 1980s, known as the Auroux laws, further eroded the position of unions in the workplace.[11]

Given the weakened support for trade unions, the CGT and the CFDT have attempted to overcome their political divisions and build a united front on several occasions over the years. The 'Common Programme' between the parties of the left in the 1970s opened up a temporary perspective for cooperation. Both the CGT and the CFDT campaigned for the introduction of works councils in the 1970s together with an extension of the local franchise to non-citizens.[12] Cooperation was hindered by the abandonment of the Common Programme, and further weakened when the Socialists were elected to power in 1981. The CGT resolved to maintain a critical distance, while the CFDT was more inclined to support the Socialists. After 1981 initial consultations took place on a wide range of issues, including economic planning, industrial policy, immigration, health and transport, but this was never consolidated.[13] The return of the right to power in 1993 forced the unions into a more defensive position. Unions do not find it easy either to impose solutions to industrial conflicts or to control strategy.[14]

It is difficult to obtain data on immigrant membership of unions, given that in France it is illegal to keep records of named individuals' ethnic or religious background.[15] Attendance at union national congresses is a rough guide to levels of participation, which show an increase of immigrant delegates to CGT congresses from 2.5 per cent in 1965 to 6.3 per cent in 1985.[16] These figures are based on members who do not have French nationality, so that numbers of ethnic minorities attending conferences and participating in union activities should be higher.

Analysis of representation at the seventh CGT Immigrants Conference in 1992 showed twenty-one nationalities present, the majority (67.63 per cent) were skilled manual workers.[17] The largest occupations represented were cleaning, construction, the steel and chemical industries, commerce, and railway workers. The CGT has a general aim that at least 7 per cent of Congress delegates should be 'immigrants'. Some industries would have higher numbers than others; for instance, representation in public service unions would be low because employment depends on having French nationality.[18] Figures for CFDT congresses show a slightly lower level of immigrant representation.

The Attitude of French Trade Unions towards Immigration

Unions experience a major contradiction between their roles of defending the national labour force and promoting international labour solidarity. In the postwar period, three views about immigration have been articulated in French trade union circles that illustrate this contradiction. Firstly there is a concern that immigrants' cheap labour will undermine the position won by French workers. Concern about labour competition is more important than ideas of physical difference between different 'racial' groups, and focuses particularly on 'illegal' immigrants. Secondly there is a belief that immigrants are part of the same class, which should not be divided. This idea is linked to a denial that the working class is racist, and an assertion that any racism is part of the capitalist tactic to increase the rate of exploitation. Thirdly there is the idea of international labour solidarity, which should lead unions to defend the rights of people to work wherever they want with equal rights.

Four periods or contexts can be identified, within which to understand the changing trade union approaches to immigration. First there is the early twentieth century, during which unions attempted to adjust to immigration as part of the supply mechanism for the labour market. The second is the interwar period of severe economic and political crisis, of refugees joining other immigrants, and of increased xenophobia in France. Thirdly there is the postwar period, in which immigrants played a key part in reconstruction, and fourthly the period after 1974, in which new immigration largely ceased and there was a move towards settlement, particularly of the immigrants from North Africa.

In the period leading up to 1914, the *laissez-faire* view was dominant, immigration being seen as an extension of rural-urban migration. Xenophobia against Italian, Polish, and Belgian immigrants was common wherever they settled. Trade unions were no exception: they moved to exclude immigrants as a threat to living standards and security. The first immigration restrictions were introduced in the 1890s, and it was stressed that those who came should be capable of easy assimilation into French society. However, unions did attempt to bring immigrants 'into the fold' and to support their rights. The CGT's 1918 programme argued for

> the right of all workers whatever their nationality to have the right to work where they can. Each worker should have the right to all the guarantees of union membership, especially the right to participate personally in the administration of his trade union.[19]

During the interwar period immigration was from Spain, Portugal, and the French colonies, in particular North Africa and Indo-China, and in the form of refugees fleeing anti-Semitism in Eastern Europe. Government surveillance and control of immigrants increased. Unions tended only to condone immigration at times of low levels of unemployment, although in the 1920s the Unitary General Confederation of Labour (CGTU),[20] the product of a temporary split in the CGT, supported the free operation of migration, even when the crisis encouraged 'French first', and opposed deportations (which were often aimed at its most politically active foreign members). While xenophobia and nationalism affected the working class, congresses of the period adopted resolutions in solidarity with foreign workers and the colonial labour force, especially Algerians.[21]

However, in the context of the deepening economic and political crisis of the 1930s, the CGTU changed its emphasis to stressing its primary duty to protect the national labour force. The CGT opposed employers recruitment of foreign workers at times of high unemployment, pressing for rational immigration procedures. They argued that immigration was being used by the employers against the national workforce. This analysis often took a patronising tone as it emphasised how immigration was manipulated:

> From the beginning the immigrant is wronged. Big promises of high wages! [...] Everything to import manpower to create wealth at a low cost, men who don't know the language, customs, rights and gains won in the advanced struggle of French workers. No! these workers don't come to France freely; the bosses import them for their own benefit, buying them as cheaply as possible.[22]

The CGT seemed unaware of the problems it was creating by simultaneously presenting immigrants as the victims of capitalism and encouraging working class solidarity. These debates rarely referred to the ethnic origins of the immigrants concerned: one can find similar statements at different times about Italian, Belgian, Polish, Spanish, Portuguese, Algerian or African workers.

Immigration from North Africa increased during the period 1968–74 by approximately 270,000 each year.[23] Despite their divisions, union confederations shared a restrictive attitude to immigration. They called for planned immigration with guaranteed equal rights with French workers, and supported the creation of a National Office of Immigration (ONI) in 1945. This had a administrative council of twenty-four members, composed of trade unions, employers and government representatives. Although initially it curbed immigration, employers increasingly by-passed it and recruited labour abroad themselves. Furthermore, Algerian immigration did not come under its remit until after independence in 1962. Under De Gaulle after 1958, the trade unions lost influence in the ONI and its main task became retrospective regularisation, applied to 70–80 per cent of all immigrants. From the late 1960s trade unions regained some influence, but the ONI remained uninfluential. Georges Pompidou explained the advantages of uncontrolled immigration in September 1963: 'Immigration is a means of establishing a certain flexibility in the labour market and resisting social pressure'.[24]

While the CGT emphasised its vocation as a union of mass class struggle, the French Confederation of Christian Workers (CFTC)[25] presented itself as being based on Christian moral values, which meant that its strength was among East European immigrant workers. After the 1964 split, the newly formed CFDT substituted references to *morale sociale chrétienne* for *la solidarité humaine*:[26] an immigrant worker is a comrade who must be trained to be aware of solidarity and the international fraternity of the labour movement .[27] It emphasised the enormous debt owed to immigrant workers for the postwar growth of French industry: 'Without the foreign workers there would be no expansion, which means that there would be less employment than there is at present, and the situation for young people would be worse'.[28]

Attempts by the CFDT to recruit North African members focused on their need for employment promotion and training.[29] Both union confederations stressed this educational and training role, providing literacy and language classes at the grassroots.[30]

Thus, in the immediate postwar period both main trade union confederations regarded immigrant workers as an important section of the working class, who should be included in their struggles against the employers' divisive tactics. They stressed that trade-union delegates had to explain to French workers why the immigrant worker was there, how they came to France, and some of the economic reasons forcing them to leave their native country. Immigrant workers needed sympathy, understanding, fraternity and human warmth.[31] The approach was rational: if the French worker understood the situation of immigrants there would be no problem with racism. Unions wanted to encourage a spirit of responsibility towards the more vulnerable and exploited immigrant workers but this often came across as patronising.

Until the 1970s unions followed public opinion in assuming that many immigrants were in France temporarily. By the early 1970s with immigration controls, there was greater awareness of immigrant family reunion and the settlement of immigrants in France. In 1946 women and children had comprised only 0.72 per cent, but by 1973 this had risen to 14 per cent of all immigrants.[32] In 1971 a joint CGT-CFDT programme against racism and xenophobia called for equal union rights, and equal wages for equal work. They demanded adequate housing, and the teaching of the mother tongue.[33] They did not refer to problems of cultural cohabitation, and minimised the problem of racism in the everyday interaction between French and immigrant workers. The focus was on the position of immigrants in the production process, attempting to prevent their insecure position being exploited by management.[34]

An important turning point came in the early 1970s when immigrant workers played a key role in industrial disputes at Penarroya mines, the Renault-Flins, and Gennevilliers (Cables de Lyon).[35] Other disputes at Citroen-Aulnay (1982) and Talbot-Poissy (1983–84) involved violent conflict between riot police, a right-wing 'management' union, the Confédération des Syndicats Libres (CSL), and a mainly Moroccan workforce resisting redundancies. During the Talbot-Poissy dispute the unions were divided on how to respond to a surprising demand by immigrants for a repatriation package.

In 1981 a Charter of Demands was adopted at the CGT's fifth National Immigrants Conference calling for a 'real choice' for immigrants about whether they wanted to remain in France as foreigners with guaranteed respect for their culture and social and professional rights, to become fully integrated as French, or to return to their country of origin after receiving useful training.[36] The Charter emphasised that immigrants and French workers formed a community of interest, and that discrimination damaged not only the immediate victims but the whole working class. The surest way to counter capitalist-induced divisions between workers was to work against discrimination and for equal rights [37].

Today, unions oppose increasing primary immigration and instead focus on the need to accept immigrants who now live in France. The CFDT has a slogan, 'The world moves and so do people'. Union interest in the impact of new immigration focuses on qualified labour from Eastern Europe, which may undercut both settled immigrants and French labour. They have joined a campaign to enable Algerians to come to France on a short-term basis to secure respite from the civil war. Both unions have campaigned recently against the increase of checks on identification papers within a 'Fortress Europe'. They also press for equal access to social welfare benefits (stressing industrial health and safety) for European and 'third-country nationals'.

Inclusion or Exclusion?

Having established that trade unions accept immigrants as a more or less permanent part of the workforce, it becomes possible to understand how they include immigrants in their activities. From an early stage their international and anticolonial analysis had included foreign and colonial workers. Structures which were set up to organise immigrant workers from the second decade of the twentieth century onwards were adapted and extended to new groups. Thus the dilemma of separate organisation versus inclusion in general structures was confronted early on in France in a context of European immigration. This did not prevent xenophobic outbursts against European immigrants. Within this structure, unions were frequently torn between a universalist 'proletarian internationalism' and the particularist desire to protect the national workforce from competition.[38]

The CGT called for the right of non-citizens to belong to professional unions as early as 1883, and in 1913 its journal, *La Vie Ouvrière*, campaigned for greater autonomy for trade unions in Algeria.[39] French trade unionists helped to set up unions in French colonies, including a Bourse de Travail in Algiers in 1893.[40] During the split in the CGT between 1922 and 1936, the radical CGTU unsuccessfully attempted to involve French unions with the anti-colonial struggle in a series of strikes.[41]

Trade-union structures for immigrant workers were established early on in France. In particular, the CGT/CGTU developed specific workplace national and language groups organised hierarchically. Their regional and national committees gave immigrant workers an informal voice, to formulate specific demands and become involved in the trade union. These committees were a training ground for future trade-union leaders. The CGT's Immigration Section was formed in 1919, based on the militant Casquettiers Union de Paris.[42] It supported the right of immigrants to work and to participate in their union. The CGT had a Confederal Bulletin for Overseas Territories, and the CFTC organised foreign workers through its international department. These structures for integrating immigrant workers developed an antifascist role in the 1930s and during the period of the Resistance .[43]

After the period of illegality during the war, the CGT established a National Committee of Immigrant Labour meeting monthly at Confederal level. Its role was to monitor migration, examine the problems of immigrant workers at national level, and to define the kinds of action needed to meet their demands. They worked closely with the editors of the foreign language journals. At departmental, union and local levels, the CGT established immigrant labour committees considering housing, working conditions and social legislation. It was also responsible for formulating immigrants' demands, and producing posters and leaflets in different languages. Thus unions took responsibility for raising a broad range of immigrant workers' demands, reaching beyond immediate workplace concerns.

Immigrant labour committees comprised four types of members: immigrants representing the main national groups; representatives of the main sectors of industry; union officials from companies and workplaces where immigrants were strongly represented; and at departmental level the of social security and family benefits administrator who was responsible for immigrant labour. These committees were intended to enhance union presence among immigrant workers and provide coordination between the grass roots and the union leadership.

Workplace language groups decentralised the CGT's activity among immigrant workers. The experience of the tight-knit Polish language group illustrated the difficulties of this approach: they could be singled out for victimisation, other workers found it difficult to know what was going on and to support them, and the Polish workers were isolated from the main union activities.

The tension between particularism (organisation in language groups) and universalism (incorporation in the main body of the union) was never far below the surface. Some union leaders could see no need for language groups, and insisted that they treated immigrants equally. This ignored the need to articulate specific demands. The committees were criticised as unstable and as having low levels of participation, and there were indeed problems arising from immigrants' high levels of mobility which made them difficult to organise.

Today, the CGT has a 'Migration Section' with a small staff based in the Confederation Offices at Montreuil with similar arrangements in the member federations. A bi-monthly journal, *La Tribune de l'Immigration*, is produced and articles on racism and immigration appear regularly in the main union magazine *La Vie Ouvrière*. In the 1990s translations are no longer used, because most readers know French, and it was limiting the *Tribune*'s content and readership. The new emphasis ensures that immigrants' concerns are an integral part of the union's work.

The Migration Section has a national collective which meets monthly, composed of twelve elected delegates from the main industries with high concentrations of immigrant workers. In 1990 the collective comprised a Portuguese member (Construction), a West African (Ports and Docks cleaners), a Moroccan, and an Algerian (Talbot and Renault automobile workforces). A National Commission comprising between twenty and thirty members, with responsibility for equal rights, meets three times a year, with similar structures at federal, regional and departmental levels. The CGT has held seven national conferences on Immigration. At a recent one in December 1992, nearly 400 delegates attended, representing twenty-one nationalities. Debates ranged over racism, insertion, residence rights, deportation, union rights and solidarity work according to *La Tribune de l'Immigration*, November/December 1987.

The other union confederations developed similar structures. Before 1939 the CFTC did little for immigrant workers, apart from providing an affiliation structure for small groups of Polish and Russian Christian workers. In 1950 thirteen different foreign sections were affiliated to the CFTC: Ukrainian, Byelorussian, Russian, Lithuanian, Latvian,

Polish, Bulgarian, Croatian, Rumanian, Slovakian, Czech, Hungarian and Italian. These sections were responsible for material socio-legal assistance and cultural activities. But the central trade union structures retained control over employment matters.

The Foreign Workers' Section of the CFTC was strongly anti-Marxist, and focussed on the situation in Eastern Europe. This broadened after March 1966 when the newly reformed CFDT held its first National Conference for Immigrant Workers. The Confederation thenceforth aimed to integrate workers of all nationalities in its life. It emphasised that the immigrants should be responsible for orienting the union towards their demands, which were essential for success in the general objectives of the union. Activists should be identified at workplace level to make contact with the different nationalities, and distribute literature. In 1966 it recommended that each level (workplace section, department, and confederation) should establish Immigrant Worker Committees, to maintain links between foreign workers and the union. A permanent official was sited in the Departmental Union office. An informal structure of people responsible for immigration now exists in the CFDT, with a Confederal Secretary at the apex.

Much union work on immigration operates through public consultative organisations. The most important of these is the Social Action Fund (FAS), which has seventeen regional offices, and funds urban policies and immigrant associations. Its current priorities are to support recent arrivals, the unemployed and young people having problems with integration, and to provide information services about immigrants' rights.[44] All the union confederations have four delegates on the FAS regional and national committees, at least half of whom are immigrants. These are important positions of responsibility for union members with a good record of union activity.[45] Unions are also represented on the national Economic and Social Committee, which is a consultative body with limited impact.[46] Trade unions relate closely to immigrant and antiracist organisations. They have participated in nationally co-ordinated campaigns such as a major mobilisation against reform of the Nationality Code in 1986–87,[47] and more recently against the Pasqua Immigration Law and Nationality Law reform, and in support of 'undocumented' immigrants. Both confederations join collectives to organise demonstrations and circulate antiracist literature.

Trade Union Policies on Immigrant Workers

The tension between the dominant universalist model of integration and particularist forms of organisation of immigrant workers makes it difficult to distinguish between different immigrant groups in France. In the past, as we have seen, unions organised immigrant workers in separate language groups, while aiming for their eventual incorporation into the union.

In the period since 1960, unions have responded to new distinctions between groups. The dominant factor has been animosity towards Algerians, which in turn affects all North Africans. This gives rise to many acts of racist violence from extreme-right groups, but also daily harassment.[48] Newly emerging groups of immigrants with particular needs are workers from Eastern Europe and refugees, particularly from the former Yugoslavia. Another group which has emerged with its distinct problems are West African families, who in recent years have been struggling for decent housing and stable residence rights.

Racist violence and riots on suburban housing estates became a particular problem after 1983. Trade unions link the current animosity towards 'young Maghrebins' to old conflicts over Algerian independence. They are aware that hatred towards North Africans is based on physical perceptions, and that racists do not stop to enquire whether a person has a French identity card in his or her pocket.[49] Trade unions distinguish between different demands made by 'North Africans': there are those of the older immigrant workers, those of their children who do not accept the low-paid degrading work their parents undertook, despite unemployment, and the demands arising from their Muslim identity.

Early primary labour migrants from North Africa were concerned with immediate working and living conditions. They were involved in their own national liberation and the great industrial and housing movements of the 1970s. Today they have been affected by changing immigration laws and limits on the right of family reunion. Their sons and daughters were born in France, have French nationality and have disappeared from the official statistics. The *mouvement beur* of the 1980s, with massive mobilisations and active publicised associations, campaigned against racist and police violence and against the 'double punishment' (whereby young people who did not have French nationality risked deportation if convicted of a criminal offence). They secured a ten-year residence and work permit in 1984. Trade unions have difficulties in addressing this 'second generation', whose circumstances range from the upwardly mobile, employed in new technology and the media, to those being heavily exploited in the service sector and the disaffected unemployed. The third category, 'Muslims', comprises many people who have come to value their religious identity in an inhospitable environment.[50]

Trade unions were made aware of the specific demands of Muslim workers during the 1970s disputes. A study of how unions have begun to respond to the specific demands of immigrant workers at Renault-Billancourt in 1984–86 showed a growing recognition by the CGT of Muslim workers' demands for mosques and working hours to accommodate prayer times. The CGT adopted a strategy of 'working with' specific currents, on the principle of 'if you can't beat them join them'. Incongruously, Marxist secular officials supported demands for prayer rooms. One CGT shop steward explained,

> We had two CGT members who were Muslim believers. But we feared the Muslim fundamentalists would use the prayer room for propaganda. Once it was presented differently, most members could support it. We had a dramatic event: one lad was praying and was nearly crushed. It would have been an outrage to human dignity. The prayer room was a legitimate demand, linking health and safety to human dignity.[51]

Trade unionists everywhere would recognise the demand once it was made in terms which were recognisable within the framework of union discourse, such as 'health and safety'. As such it could be supported. This denotes both the possibilities and the limitations of such gains, but suggests a significant step forward in accepting Muslim workers in the labour force. This situation, however, varies from one local union branch to the next.

Trade unionists found it difficult to resolve the problems arising from the 'Muslim headscarf affair', which flared up in autumn 1989. Here the issue of identity has been raised in a way which is particularly problematic for French secular institutions, which make a specific distinction between the public and the private sphere. The CFDT argued that while secular principles require tolerance and the recognition of difference, the wearing of religious symbols such as headscarves in school is unacceptable. This issue is posing a continuing problem for union members in schools and colleges, and marks the limits of what is tolerated.

Trade Unions in the Struggle against Discrimination and Racism

Trade unions use a pedagogical approach to discrimination and racism among their members, and lobby with antiracist and human rights associations against racist practices. Antiracist actions often escalate into general political confrontations, involving a wide range of issues. Unions have been involved in important struggles for antiracist legislation, for immigrants' rights to better housing, and against new restrictions on immigration and nationality. The most overt political involvement was the solidarity with immigrant workers during decolonisation, especially during the Algerian war from 1954 to 1962.

While police and right-wing violence towards North African workers during this period was traumatic, the CGT's fourth Conference of North African Workers in December 1950 supported the Movement for Democratic Liberties (MTLD) led by Messali Hadj. Unions participated in solidarity campaigns with Algerians and protested after the killing of seven Algerians during demonstrations in Paris on 14 July 1953. Conflicts over which Algerian trade union structures to support were resolved after 1962, when Algeria established the General Amicale of Algerian Workers in France (AGTA), which encouraged affiliation to French trade unions. Both union confederations participated in a general strike against the right-wing colonists' uprising in Algiers on 1 February 1960, and on 8 February 1962 the CGT and CFDT were involved in the demonstration for peace in Algeria, which ended in eight deaths at the hands of riot police at Charonne metro station.

In July 1971 and February 1972 in a context of rising racist violence which echoed the Algerian war, unions united in a campaign for equal rights for immigrants.[52] A CGT-CFDT joint declaration stated,

> The CFDT, CGT, aware of the dramatic situation faced by immigrant workers and the use to which this is made by the employers, intend to develop their actions at every level for equal rights for French and foreign workers and for the solution to the specific problems which the latter face in France. The two organisations intend to struggle energetically against racism in all its forms, especially to inform workers and to mobilise them as a class.[53]

The campaign for antiracist legislation was supported by the CGT and the CFDT.[54] They assisted in lobbying deputies from all parties to support the legislation, enacted in 1972 and extended in 1990.[55] A campaign followed to inform union members of the new law in workplaces and other locations. The key position of trade unionists at the centre of a web of other workplace and neighbourhood organisations gives them considerable scope for this kind of activity.

Unions working with antiracist organisations attempted to challenge the relegation to an inferior status which flowed from the idea of a subordinate immigrant underclass, generated to cushion indigenous workers.[56] The unions insisted on the universalist discourses of fraternity and equality:

> The most solid mark of fraternity, the constant and tenacious defence of the demands of the Algerian workers, firstly through equal work through equal status, the defence of family rights, conditions of living and housing.[57]

This sort of campaign attempted to acknowledge that the working class could be divided by racism, understanding this as 'false consciousness'. CGT leader Henri Krasucki (himself of Polish origin) addressed the problems of working class racism:

> It is true that the working class of our country has a profound international spirit and great traditions. But is this true "as a block", as a class? We should not naively idealise things and imagine that everyone is spontaneous. The working class is continuously renewed, it is composed of different strata. Nothing is gained once and for ever. This is the role of the CGT and the most advanced layers of the working class, to instruct, to educate the whole, to combat chauvinism, prejudice, suspicion, and feelings of superiority. Our role is to constantly explain to French workers the reasons for immigration, the direction of the policies of the employers, and to show them their interest together with their internationalist duty.[58]

Unions campaigned against government measures such as the Fontanet-Marcellin circulars (1972), which made residence conditional on full-time employment and attempted to encourage repatriation.[59] In the mid-1970s the SONACOTRA housing dispute challenged the accepted picture of immigrant workers in France. At its height this dispute involved 20,000 foreign (mainly Algerian) workers, major clashes with the police and debates in the National Assembly.[60] Housing for immigrants in France has been a major issue since 1945. Many lived in austere, frequently hazardous hostels for single males run on semi-military lines.[61] Increasing numbers inhabited *bidonvilles* or 'transit cities' on the outskirts of major cities.

While the SONACOTRA housing company was funded by immigrants, contributions to the FAS, they had no say in the running of the hostels. A major rent rise precipitated a protest which became a highly politicised campaign against discrimination, protesting against immigrants' lack of control over their own lives. The rent strike escalated in the Hauts de Seine, where two rival committees attempted to co-ordinate the strike: a departmental committee comprising the CGT, the French Communist Party (PCF) and the Amicale des Algeriens en Europe (AAE), and a more militant coordinating committee insisting on a 'global' and autonomous approach to the workers' grievances rather than a hostel-by-hostel settlement. The Mouvement des Travailleurs Arabes (MTA) played an important role in this committee. They argued for direct representation to prevent betrayal by external organisations, challenging the CGT's claim to represent the immigrant worker as part of the French working class, and rejecting more orthodox modes of struggle (demonstrations, petitions, or negotiation between established organisations).

The rent strike became a *cause célèbre*, particularly after sixteen coordinating committee delegates were arrested and deported (for 'illegal actions which could threaten public order'), sending others underground. The government's over-reaction mobilised antiracist associations to support protest meetings and demonstrations. This was under the auspices of the CFDT, whose Paris office (more left-wing than the national leadership) became a base for the Co-ordinating Committee. During this crucial battle, immigrant workers articulated new demands for autonomy, and the two main union confederations were on opposing sides. The CGT saw the dispute as beyond the bounds of 'respectable' struggle, suggesting that it was controlled by 'gauchistes' and influenced by police infiltrators.[62]

The SONACOTRA dispute caused trade unions to pause for thought, especially the CGT, who found themselves 'out of step' on an popular issue. Immigrant workers emerged from the dispute as a significant political force, gaining in self-confidence as political activists who mobilised against racist and police violence in the late 1970s.

Other industrial disputes, at the Renault-Billancourt works in 1982 and Talbot-Poissy in 1983–84, involved workers and unions in violent confrontations with a right-wing union, the Confederation of Free Unions (CSL),[63] and riot police. The dispute raised issues of public order, risking deportations. Immigrant workers' participation in industrial disputes, such as at the Longwy steel works, helped to shift attitudes towards them.[64] Union officials had criticised their reluctance to become involved in trade union activity, without realising that many demands were irrelevant to them, like the demand for retirement at sixty, or national elections when they could not vote. Threatened with deportation under the Bonnet-Stoléru law of the late 1970s, immigrant workers were reluctant to risk dismissal through union activity. For many, the most significant development during the strike at Longwy was the use of free radio which enabled them to speak directly to one another and to the French public. This helped to challenge racial stereotypes and build mutual respect.

These disputes of the 1970s and 1980s signalled that unions needed to accept the relative autonomy of newer 'immigrant communities'. The idea of a multicultural working class was first developed in a CFDT Resolution of 1973. A terminological shift from 'multinational' to 'pluri-cultural' denoted acceptance of a settled immigrant population. The 1985 Congress called for the defence of victims of racism, xenophobia and insecurity, but also immigrants, to obtain supervisory jobs and fuller political participation (including local voting rights). They pressed for forms of recognition and insertion at all levels to be devised, together with local actions in schools with the support of representative organisations.

The CGT also reformulated its approach, emphasising 'insertion' rather than 'integration', signalling a new sensitivity to particularities.

It saw integration as easily confused with 'assimilation', which implies that some people are culturally and religiously incapable of becoming part of French society. 'Insertion' focused on basic rights, and left the cultural aspects of adjustment to individual choice.[65] It meant ensuring that immigrants had equal access to rights, training, education and housing: objective factors.

The issue of housing remains a continuing concern, given restrictions on social housing allocations to immigrant families. Protesting against unsatisfactory housing, Malien families formed a 'tent city' outside the Chateau de Vincennes in 1992. Women played an important role in this campaign, both in the initial stages and in maintaining the infrastructure of the protest, while the men were at work (mainly as street cleaners in central Paris). The local CGT office lent material support (especially office accommodation) when local café's refused the families access even to water supplies. The unions also raised broad questions of international solidarity such as that of Third World Debt in protests against the GATT summit held during the bicentennial celebrations of the French Revolution of 1789. This was used to open debate about immigration and the North/South divide. French unions have urged the ratification and implementation of international agreements.

The CGT's most recent documents stress the concept of the 'insertion' of immigrant workers on the basis of the recognition of equal rights and access to material benefits. A letter to the government in 1990 argued for more effective action against racist violence, the repeal of repressive immigration and asylum laws, and for equal opportunity in education and training. It emphasised the need for third-country nationals to have equal rights with nationals of the European Community.

Trade unions have been fairly reluctant, however, to tackle the question of racism within their own ranks. Terms of abuse, including the terms 'yellow' and 'saracens', have been applied to strike-breakers, and echo earlier concerns that foreign workers might erode hard-won rights.[66] While their focus on global developments to explain the causes of immigration is important, they find it difficult to transform rather abstract notions into immediate messages. A recent CFDT initiative is attempting to challenge current ideas about 'illegal' immigrants, and both confederations have joined campaigns to allow hospital treatment to foreigners who are seriously ill and who are in danger of deportation. Union action is also supporting trade unionists working in public administration to thwart instructions to examine people's residence permits when they apply for benefits. They aim to collate information about cases, in order to support members in taking action against the Pasqua legislation which seeks to encourage 'informers'.

Conclusion: The Equal-versus-Special-Treatment Dilemma

This chapter has examined how unions approach the specific interests of immigrants. Such interests have long been latent because 'In France [...] it was long assumed that foreigners would become citizens. Thus there was not the [...] conception of a formal problem of political participation and representation engendered by migration'.[67] This was the case for European immigrants who came in the pre-1914 and interwar periods. Given the emergence of racism based on the physical identification of people as arabs, unions acknowledge that immigrants will face a continuing problem of racism whatever their nationality.[68] This became evident in campaigns during the 1970s against police and racist violence. Unions are aware of cumulative disadvantages involving their legal status, qualifications, language ability, and education, but also racist attitudes and practices in everyday life.

In France trade unions now operate in a context established by national antiracist organisations. Since the upturn in mobilisation following the liberalisation of the regulation of foreigners' right to form associations in 1981, there has been considerable debate about the role of these organisations. Some were seen as operating in rather traditional channels, focussing on the 'immigrant worker', and directing their campaigns to a small audience, largely ignored by the media. The phenomenal success of SOS-Racisme in the 1980s was criticised as focussing too much on its media image, with massive rock concerts, mobilising a very young audience with anodyne antiracist slogans which addressed racist attitudes but not the underlying causes.

This heterogeneous antiracist movement has spearheaded a number of important mobilisations, working increasingly in a 'transversal' way through collectives.[69] They often receive trade union support, assistance with premises for meetings and congresses, publicity and common declarations. As traditional forms of political participation have declined, the membership of parties and trade unions has fallen. However, there have been important antiracist mobilisations, operating in the sphere of civil society. In the 1950s unions were the main organisations with substantial contact with immigrant workers, but today there is a proliferation of associations articulating different demands. This means that unions have to shift their mode of functioning from that of a dominant labour movement to one among many social movements. However, this development has provided a new way out of the old problem of steering between particularist and universalist concerns, expressed recently as 'new citizenship', including all members of society on the basis of residence rather than nationality. Trade unions have responded to this new development by forming an important part of these new networks.

NOTES

1. Sais Bouamama et al., *La Citoyenneté dans tous ses etats: De l'immigration à la nouvelle citoyenneté*, Paris, 1992.
2. Claude Nicolet, *L'idée républicaine en France: Essai d'histoire critique*, Paris, 1982.
3. Didier Blanchet and Olivier Marchand, 'Au-delà de l'an 2000, s'adapter à une pénurie de main-d'oeuvre, *Economique et Statistique*, no. 243 1991.
4. In 1931 foreign workers in France represented 6.6 per cent of the population, so this figure has remained quite stable.
5. INSEE, *Les Étrangers en France*. Collection Contours et Caractères, 1994.
6. Haut Conseil à l'Intégration, La Connaissance de l'Immigration et de l'Integration, Paris, 1991; INSEE, *Les Étrangers en France*; *Tribune de l'Immigration,* April 1992.
7. Max Silverman, *Deconstructing the Nation: Immigration, Racism and Citizenship in Modern France*, London, 1992, 48.
8. The new nationality law does not seem yet to have deterred people from applying, with 24,583 people registering their applications in the six months from January 1994, and 18,298 fully registered. About 25 per cent of these applicants were born in France (*Le Monde*, 16 September 1994).
9. The Confédération Générale du Travail (CGT) is closest in its politics to the Parti Communiste Française (PCF), while the Confédération Française Démocratique du Travail (CFDT) has links to the Parti Socialiste (PS). The Force Ouvrière (FO) split from the CGT in 1947 moving to the right, and the Confedération Française Chrétien du Travail (CFTC) was the product of a split from the CFDT in 1964.
10. Dominique Labbe, 'Trade Unionism in France since the Second World War', *West-European Politics* 17, no. 1 (1994): 148.
11. W. Rand-Smith, 'Towards Autogestion in Socialist France', *West European Politics* 10, no.1 (1987).
12. The law of 11 July 1975 (M. Bonnechère, 'La condition juridique des travailleurs immigrés et la crise en France', *Questions de l'Immigration et Syndicalisme, Etudes et documents économiques*, February (CGT), Paris, 1981, 37.
13. Jeff Bridgeford and Peter Morris, 'Labour Confederations and Socialist Governments in France 1981–86' in W. Brierly (ed.), *Trade Unions and the Economic Crisis of the 1980s*, Aldershot, 1987.
14. Ibid.
15. Paul Webster, *Petain's Crime*, London, 1990.
16. René Mouriaux and Francoise Subileau, *Approche quantitative du syndicalisme francais 1945– 1986*, Paris, 1987.
17. The nationalities represented were: 42 per cent French, 15 per cent Algerian, 10 per cent Portuguese, 7.5 per cent Moroccan, 6.25 per cent Malian, 4.9 per cent Senegalese, 14.8 per cent others.
18. Interview with Jean Bellanger, secretary of the Immigration Section of the CGT, March 1990. Interview with Gerard Chemouie, Secretary for Migration Sector, CGT, August 1994.
19. All translations from the French are my own; Confédération Générale du Travail, *La CGT et le mouvement syndicale*. (Paris, 1925.), 170.
20. Confédération Générale du Travail Unitaire.

21. Léon Gani, *L'attitude des syndicats ouvriers à l'egard de l'immigration en France 1945–1968*, Thèse de Doctorat, Paris, 1969.
22. *Le Guide du Mettalurgiste*, April 1965, cited by Léon Gani, *L'attitude des syndicats ouvriers à l'egard de l'immigration en France 1945–1968*, Thèse de Doctorat, Paris, 1969.
23. James F. Hollifield, 'l'Etat Français et l'Immigration', *Revue Française de Science Politique*, no. 1 (1993) 953; James F. Hollifield and George Ross, *Searching for the New France*, London, 1991, 120.
24. Cathérine Wihtol de Wenden, *Les Immigrés et la politique*, Paris, 1988, 87.
25. See note 9.
26. *Syndicalisme*, 27 February 1965.
27. *Formation*, March-April 1967.
28. *Syndicalisme*, 26 February 1966.
29. CFTC, 26th Congres National, 12–14 May 1951, Rapport moral, 136–8.
30. Ralph Grillo, *Ideologies and Institutions in Modern France*, Cambridge, 1985.
31. *Le Peuple*, May 1965.
32. Hollifield, *Searching for the New France*, 120.
33. Confédération Générale du Travail, *Pour une politique de l'immigration conforme aux intérets des travailleurs francais et immigrés mémoire remis au Premier Ministre le 21 Mai 1970*, Paris, 1971.)
34. Maryse Tripier, 'Syndicats, Ouvriers Français, Immigration et Crises', *Pluriel*, no. 21, (1980): 43–44.
35. *Guardian Weekly*, 26 December 1982.
36. M. Bonnechère, M. 'La condition juridique des travailleurs immigrés et la crise en France', *Questions de l'Immigration et Syndicalisme, Etudes et documents économiques*, February (CGT), Paris, 1981, 54.
37. Maryse Tripier, 'Français et Immigrés', *Questions de l'Immigration et Syndicalisme, Etudes et documents économiques*, February (CGT), Paris, 1981, 54.
38. Maryse Tripier, 'Concurrence et différence: Les problèmes posés au syndicalisme ouvrier par les travailleurs immigrés', *Sociologie de Travail*, July 1972.
39. Jacques Capdeville and René Mouriaux, 'Conflit Social et Immigration: Le cas de la Cellophane', *Projet*, 22 February, Paris, 1968, 170–8.
40. René Leveau, Cathérine Wihtol de Wenden and Gilles Kepel, 'Syndicalisme Française et Islam', *Revue Française de Science Politique*, 37, December, Paris, 1987; René Mouriaux and Cathérine Wihtol de Wenden, 'Syndicalisme Française et Islam', *Revue Française de Science Politique*, 37, December, Paris, 1987.
41. Emilien Carassus, *Les grèves imaginaires*, Paris, 1982.
42. Interview with Jean Bellanger, March 1990.
43. Stéphane Courtois and Gilles Kepel, 'Musulmanes et Prolétaires', *Revue Française de Science Politique* 37, no. 6 (1987): 789.
44. Fonds d'Action Sociale, *Circulaire d'information sur la procédure de dépot des dossiers*, Campagne 1995 Juillet, Paris, 1994.
45. Interviews with François Srotzynski, Secretaire Confederale des Immigrés of the CFDT, 27 July and 13 October 1994.
46. Anne Stevens, *The Government and Politics of France*, London, 1996, 44.
47. Sarah Wayland, 'Mobilising to defend nationality law in France', *New Community* 20, no.1 (1993).
48. Amnesty International, *France: Shootings, Killings and Alleged Ill-treatment by Law Enforcement Officers*, AI Index Eur. 21/02/94, London, 1994; Guidice Fausto, *Arabacides: Une chronique française 1970–1991*, Paris, 1992; Cathie Lloyd, 'Racist Violence and Antiracist Reactions: A View of France', in R. Witte and T. Bjørgo (eds), *Racist Violence in Europe*, New York, 1993, 207–20.

49. Interview with Gerard Chemouil, Secretary of the Migration Section of the CGT, 1 September 1994.
50. Leveau et al., 'Syndicalisme Française et Islam'.
51. Mouriaux and de Wenden, 'Syndicalisme Française et Islam'.
52. Cathie Lloyd, 'Universalism and Difference: The crisis of anti-racism in Britain and France', in A. Rattansi and S. Westwood (eds), *On the Western Front: Studies in Racism, Modernity and Identity*, Cambridge, 1994.
53. Confédération Française Démocratique du Travail, *Textes de base*, Paris, 1974.
54. Mouvement Contre le Racisme et Pour l'Amitié Entre les Peuples (MRAP), *Chronique du flagrant racisme*, Paris, 1984.
55. The law of 1972 deals with direct discrimination in employment, housing, and the provision of services, but in practice tends to emphasise action against racist publications and statements.
56. F.A. Maucorps, A. Memmi and H.-F. Held, *Les Français et le racisme*, Paris, 1965.
57. Léon Gani, *L'attitude des syndicats ouvriers à l'egard de l'immigration en France 1945–1968*, Thèse de Doctorat, Paris, 1969, 240.
58. *Le Peuple*, March 1963.
59. Bonnechère, 'La condition juridique des travailleurs immigrés et la crise en France'.
60. M. Miller, *The Problem of Foreign Worker Participation and Representation in France, Switzerland and the Federal Republic of Germany*. PhD thesis, University of Wisconsin, USA, 1978.
61. Peter Jones, 'Race, Discourse and Power in Institutional Housing: The Case of Immigrant Workers Hostels in Lyons', in M. Silverman (ed.), *Race, Discourse and Power in France*, Aldershot, 1991.
62. André Gorz and P. Gavi, 'La Bataille d'Ivry', *Les Temps Modernes*, March, Paris, 1970.
63. La Confédération des Syndicats Libres.
64. Gerard Noiriel, *Vivre et Lutter à Longwy*, Paris, 1986.
65. Interview with Gerard Chemouill.
66. Mouriaux and de Wenden, 'Syndicalisme Française et Islam'; Maurice Tournier, 'Les Jaunes: Un mot-fantasme à la fin du 19e siècle', *Mots*, no. 8 (1984): 125–46.
67. Miller, *The Problem of Foreign Worker Participation and Representation*, 416.
68. Cathie Lloyd, 'Racist Violence and Anti-racist reactions: A view of France', in R. Witte and T. Bjørgo (eds), *Racist Violence in Europe*, New York, 1993, 207–20.
69. Interview with Mouloud Aounit, General Secretary of MRAP, December 1990; on the idea of transversality see M. Yuval-Davis, 'Women, Ethnicity and Empowerment', in K.-K. Bhavanani and A. Phoenix (eds), *Shifting Identities, Shifting Racisms*, London, 1994.

Chapter 7

British Unions and Racism: Organisational Dilemmas in an Unsympathetic Climate

John Wrench[1]

A Different Background of Immigration in the UK and Its Consequences

Postwar immigration into the United Kingdom has followed a rather different pattern from that of most continental European countries. In the period following the Second World War a number of industries in Britain also began to experience a shortage of labour. The context and the pattern of response, however, were different.

Initially, Britain recruited Polish ex-servicemen and then 'European Voluntary Workers' (EVWs) from refugee camps and from Italy. This was motivated to a significant extent by the need for their labour power; thus this early part of the postwar period was the only time when the state was active in using immigration policy in reponse to labour market pressures.[2] It was also the only time when trade unions were involved in immigration policy. The Trades Union Congress (TUC), and the miners' union in particular, insisted on strict conditions: where EVWs were to be employed, it should be where no British labour was available; in the event of redundancy, EVWs should be the first to go; EVWs should join the appropriate trade union, and should receive the same wages and conditions as other workers.

After this short period immediately after the Second World War, however, labour migration came from ex-colonies, primarily the

Caribbean, India and Pakistan, to find employment in foundries in the Midlands, textile mills in the North, transport industries in major cities, and the health service. Unlike many other European countries, this labour migration was not officially organised; these workers had the legal right to enter the country through their Commonwealth citizenship. Until 1962 they had the right to live and work in Britain without restriction. In contrast to the earlier direct government encouragement of European Voluntary Workers, both the Conservative and Labour governments quietly attempted to use administrative measures to discourage Commonwealth immigrants from coming.

Because of their former colonial status most of the postwar migrants to Britain were different from the 'guest workers' found in many other European countries. They had the same political and legal rights as the indigenous population, including voting rights in both local and national elections. Coming from former colonies they had a knowledge of the language and culture of their new home. Relatively quickly they ceased to be 'immigrants' and became settled ethnic minorities[3], preparing the ground for their spouses and children to join them at a later date. Something else which contrasts with the experience of many other European host countries is that in Britain, postwar migrant workers have had an above-average propensity to join trade unions.

Although these migrant workers held the same rights in theory, in practice they occupied a subordinate position in employment compared to white British workers. Despite the need for their labour, their presence aroused widespread hostility from many levels of the trade union movement. Over time, the racism and discrimination encountered by these workers ensured that they remained in a relatively restricted spectrum of occupational areas, over-represented in low-paid and insecure jobs, working unsocial hours in unhealthy or dangerous environments. Research has more recently confirmed that the descendants of these workers, who were born and educated in the UK, still suffer discrimination and are more likely than their equivalently qualified white peers to be unemployed, or employed beneath their qualification level.[4]

The various dilemmas facing unions in terms of their response to migrant workers have been categorised in a threefold manner by Penninx and Roosblad in this volume. The first is whether to resist immigration or cooperate with and try to influence state immigration policies; the second is whether to include migrant workers as trade union members once they have arrived; and the third is, once they have been recruited, whether special union policies should be established for migrant and minority ethnic members alongside general policies for all members.

Trade Union Responses to Immigration and Migrant Labour

In Britain, there was variation in these stages at different levels. For example, in the immediate postwar years of immigration, many at the TUC level were relatively sympathetic to migrants from ex-colonies. Some sections of the British political leadership felt that the former colonial power had some sort of 'duty' towards these migrants, and this was also true among the leaders of the trade-union movement in the TUC. TUC leaders in the 1950s had some sympathy for migrants whom they saw as having been forced to come as a result of colonial exploitation, and were strongly opposed to discriminatory treatment against them.[5] However, opposition in principle did not necessarily mean doing much in practice, and the TUC was initially firmly opposed to government plans to introduce anti-discrimination legislation in Britain, arguing that conciliation was better than the law, and that industrial relations might suffer.[6]

However, the TUC did give support to the immigration legislation of both the Conservative and Labour governments. Although the TUC General Council declared that it was opposed to any form of immigration control that was racially biased, it failed to oppose the Commonwealth Immigrants Act of 1968 and the Immigration Act of 1971, even though a motion of opposition to the 1971 Act was passed at the 1973 Congress.[7] The combined effect of these acts was to keep out non-white citizens from the New Commonwealth while leaving it possible for white colonial citizens to 'return' to Britain.

Trade union and TUC hostility to immigration from the New Commonwealth was mainly on social rather than economic grounds because in the 1950s and 1960s immigrant workers did not constitute a threat to the jobs of British workers.[8] Thus opposition tended to be framed in terms of arguments that immigrants were failing to 'integrate' properly. Sometimes spurious labour market arguments were drawn upon – for example, that the emerging 'technological revolution' and the ending of conscription meant the end of the demand for labour – but in reality the labour shortage in some sectors of work meant that Commonwealth immigrants were still required. To keep the price of labour from falling, trade unions have traditionally tried to do two things: to limit the labour supply, and to improve and equalise wages and conditions. If the first strategy – limiting the labour supply – had not been possible, then the second – organising these new workers and demanding equal pay and conditions – should have been given some priority. In reality this second strategy proved to be embraced less rapidly than it might have been, and this is where the variable of racism enters the equation. Although racism can be mobilised as part of union attempts to restrict the labour supply, it runs counter to the principle of equalising wages and conditions.

In Britain, racism had been drawn upon in the fight to keep out immigrants, and between and after the two world wars there were many examples of this.[9] In the 1950s transport workers banned overtime and staged strikes in protest against the employment of black labour, and others sent motions to annual conferences asking for black workers to be excluded from their sectors.[10] There was a 'determined effort' by the National Union of Seamen to keep black seamen off British ships after the war.[11] However, with the postwar permanent settlement of new migrant-based communities in Britain, racism interfered with the second strategy – the need to get migrant workers organised and defended. In practice, despite being union members, migrant workers received different and inferior treatment, were given the worst jobs and shifts, and often were given lower wages for the same work as white workers. There were often understandings between management and white trade unionists that the principle of 'last in first out' at a time of redundancy would not apply if this was to mean that white workers would lose their jobs before blacks.

Once in the union, black workers often had to fight to secure equal treatment and their membership rights. For example, in the 1965 dispute at Courtaulds' Red Scar Mill, Preston, white workers and the union had collaborated with management in an attempt to force Asian workers to work more machines for proportionately less pay, and later that year a strike by Asian workers at the Woolf Rubber Company was lost through lack of official union backing.[12] Partly as a result of such experiences, minority ethnic workers tended to organise themselves outside the factory walls, making such organisations more 'community-based' than 'work-based', and in subsequent industrial disputes they would draw upon such groups. In the late 1960s and early 1970s there occurred a number of strikes characterised by strong support of Asian workers by local community associations and an equally noticeable lack of support by a local trade union. In particular, three notorious disputes were those at the Coneygre Foundry in Tipton in 1967–8, Mansfield Hosiery in Loughborough in 1972, and Imperial Typewriters in Leicester in 1974. All three were precipitated by management and union collusion in discriminatory practices, such as paying Asian workers lower wages, barring them from promotion, or selectively making them redundant. In each case the strikers benefited substantially through the support of local community organisations and political groups, and Asian workers from other factories.[13]

As mentioned earlier, in Britain (in contrast with many other European migrant-receiving countries) postwar black migrant workers had an above-average propensity to join trade unions. For example, a Policy Studies Institute (PSI) survey showed that in 1982, 56 per cent of Asian and West Indian employees were union members, compared with 47 per cent of white employees.[14] Although some of this difference is due to the fact that black workers are over-represented in those industrial sectors where trade union membership rates are higher for all workers, the PSI study reports that the greater inclination for black migrant workers to join unions holds true even when allowing for the differences in occupational concentration. This reflects a generally greater ideological commitment to the principles of unionism by black migrant workers in the UK. This was no doubt partly due to the fact that trade unions based on the British model had earlier been formed in the colonies to deal with workers' grievances, and these attempts to form trade unions had received support through resolutions and letters of encouragement from unions and trades councils in Britain. 'Now that the ravages of colonial poverty led colonial workers to seek jobs in Britain it seemed natural that they should join the trade union movement'.[15]

The most recent PSI study showed that employees from certain ethnic groups in the early 1990s still have higher rates of unionisation than white employees: Afro-Caribbean and Indian employees had 44 per cent and 38 per cent respectively, compared to 35 per cent of white employees. On the other hand, Pakistani and African-Asian employees had slightly lower rates than whites (33 per cent and 28 per cent) and Bangladeshi employees significantly lower (14 per cent).[16]

Equal versus Special Treatment

With the inclusion of migrant workers into unions, and the transformation of migrant workers into ethnic-minority British workers, the third dilemma began to take precedence over the previous two: that of equal versus special treatment. Should a trade union concern itself only with issues common to white and ethnic-minority members or should it in addition operate special policies relating to the specific interests of the latter? If ethnic-minority workers suffer disadvantages not experienced by white workers then 'equal treatment' will allow these disadvantages to remain. However, as Penninx and Roosblad argue in this volume, if a union devotes extra resources to issues specifically concerning ethnic-minority members, this may cause resentment and resistance on the part of white workers who see ethnic-minority members as getting favourable treatment.

With regard to this 'third dilemma' there was initially a *de facto* consensus at all levels of the trade-union movement in Britain. Until the end of the 1960s the standard trade-union position on this was exemplified by the TUC view that to institute any special policies would be to discriminate against the white membership. As one TUC official put it in 1966: 'There are no differences between an immigrant worker and an English worker. We believe that all workers should have the same rights and don't require any different or special consideration.'[17] In 1970, Vic Feather, TUC General Secretary, argued: 'The trade union movement is concerned with a man or woman as a worker. The colour of a man's skin has no relevance whatever to his work'.[18]

However, in the early 1970s the TUC began to adopt special policies against racism. This shift came about for a number of reasons. Firstly, there was the increasing organisation on the issue by black and white trade union activists. In the 1970s many locally based committees were set up in union branches in London, the Midlands and the North of England to combat discrimination and to attempt to change the policy of their respective unions and the TUC. Local Trades Councils organised conferences and campaigns, expressing concerns about racist ideology and racial discrimination within the Labour movement. 'Thus within the trade union movement there existed a small but concerned minority of trade unionists who desired a more positive policy from the TUC.'[19] Secondly, there were the above-mentioned industrial disputes in the late 1960s and early 1970s which had highlighted union racism towards striking black members. And thirdly, there was the growth of extreme right-wing groups such as the National Front, who played on the divisions between black and white workers and gave open support to the white trade unionists in some of these disputes.[20] Thus the TUC, having first dropped its opposition to race relations legislation, now started active campaigns against racism in the movement.

In the late 1970s and early 1980s the TUC began to produce educational and training materials on equal opportunities for use in trade union education courses. In 1979 the TUC sent out a circular to all its affiliated unions recommending that they should adopt a policy on racism. In 1981 the TUC published *Black Workers: A TUC Charter for Equal Opportunity*, encouraging unions to be more active on the issue. The Charter's main points included:

- the need to remove barriers which prevent black workers from reaching union office;
- the need for vigorous action on employment grievances concerning racial discrimination;
- a commitment to countering racialist propaganda;
- an emphasis on personnel procedures for recruitment and promotion being clearly laid down;

- the production of union material in relevant ethnic minority languages when necessary, and
- the inclusion of equal opportunity clauses in collective agreements.

Seven years later the TUC reissued the Charter. The TUC also worked with the Commission for Racial Equality (CRE) in the production of a 'Code of Practice', and has encouraged unions to make use of this code. In recent years in the wider European forum the TUC has lobbied the European Trade Union Confederation to take on board issues of migrants' rights and racial equality, drawing attention to the UK experience of the important role of legislation in combating discrimination.

Increasingly in the UK, individual unions have set up separate committees or structures to deal with race relations and/or equal opportunities issues, and have adopted equal opportunity policies and anti-racist statements. Many have installed national officers to take responsibility for issues affecting black members, for encouraging the participation of black members and for furthering equal opportunities. A survey carried out in 1988 found that about half of the twenty-four unions surveyed had instituted such changes.[21]

Combating Racism within the Unions

There are two main areas where the debate about special policies are seen to be most relevant. The first of these concerns the problem of racism and how to tackle it, and the second concerns the level of ethnic minority participation in union activities and structures. For example, the above-mentioned 1988 survey found little evidence of adoption by unions of rules against racist behaviour, and little change in the numbers of black officials at higher levels in union structures. Black members still argue that unions are slow to act against the racism and discrimination they experience, both in wider employment and within the movement itself. One black shop steward told researchers, 'White stewards are blind to the impact of racism on black workers because they have never experienced it.' Another said, 'Even those white people that want to take these issues on are too frightened [...] they just leave it to me'.[22]

British unions operate in the context of more than twenty-five years of race-relations legislation. Legislation against racial discrimination was strengthened and extended by the (third) Race Relations Act of 1976, when the Commission for Racial Equality (CRE) was created. Under the Race Relations Act individuals who feel that they have been the victims of racial discrimination may institute proceedings, and employment cases are heard by Industrial Tribunals. In practice the success rate of applications to Industrial Tribunals alleging unlawful discrimination is very small. Experience shows, however, that the likelihood of success of applicants increases if they are supported at the Tribunal by their union. However, research published in 1992 showed that black workers still have little faith in trade unions taking up grievances over discrimination and harassment. Instead, fearing a lack of sympathy from their own union, they prefer to seek the support of the Commission for Racial Equality.[23] Trade-union officials have argued that they are reluctant to take racial discrimination cases to Industrial Tribunals because of the poor record of success in such cases. The Commission for Racial Equality is trying to encourage more unions to get involved with their members who have complaints in such cases, and argues that if trade unions give greater priority to cases of racial discrimination at Industrial Tribunals, then the success rate will improve.

Participation within Unions

Although the density of union membership is higher among the black population than for white workers, the participation in union positions remains much lower, particularly at the senior level. (The most noticeable exception is the case of Bill Morris, the black General Secretary of the largest manual trade union in Britain, the Transport and General Workers Union, who was elected to that position in 1992 and re-elected in 1995.) The 1984 PSI study found that black members were much less likely to hold an elected post than white members even though they are more likely to join unions than white people, and attend meetings with about the same frequency.[24] In the early 1970s the low participation of black workers in unions was explained by factors such as 'language difficulties' and the 'lack of trade-union experience' of immigrant workers.[25] Phizacklea and Miles argued that an awareness of racial discrimination and racism at the place of work and within the union was a factor in explaining the lower level of black participation in workplace union activity. The reason there were so few black shop stewards was not because they were 'new' – they weren't – but rather because they weren't 'invited' through the usual informal processes. Furthermore, a black worker who felt that racism was a feature of the work environment would be less likely to take on a position which entailed making 'personal sacrifices for the collective good'.[26]

Black workers have reported that at union meetings they felt that their issues were being excluded because of the apathy of the white majority. This was seen as the fundamental problem of being a minority in an organisation run by majority interest. As one black trade unionist put it: 'How are you going to work within a democratic system where by the sheer virtue of a majority they can prevent progress by the minority?'[27]

This leads to the debate on whether there should be separate black structures of organisation within trade unions:

> The relative absence of blacks and minorities in positions of influence in trade unions has prompted speculation that selforganisation rather than incorporation into a race-blind union movement may be part of the answer to black and minority problems in the same way that women's groups may be part of the answer to patriarchal control.[28]

Self-organisation within Unions

Many black workers feel that the way to get their voices heard is by self-organisation within unions, in their own separate structures. This tactic tends to be regarded with suspicion by the white union hierarchy, who generally prefer what could be called the 'passive assimilation' strategy. The assumptions within this model were described in a paper on self-organisation:

> ... eventually, minorities will rise through the ranks of the union movement and provide role models for others to follow; in the meantime the unions themselves will become progressively more liberal, thereby setting up a virtuous circle to bind minorities properly into the labour movement, where their similar experience and interests as workers will transcend what differentiates them along ethnic lines.[29]

Many white British trade unionists, however, argue against separate organisation for black workers on the grounds that class-based interests as employees and workers take precedence over any other sectional interest such as race or ethnicity. The 'colour-blind' trade union approach argues that whatever problems minorities suffer from can best be resolved through a strategy that asserts from the beginning that all are equal. Autonomous organisations within the body politic, therefore, are considered as divisive and counter productive.[30] A classic expression of this position was made by a leading member of a large white-collar trade union:

> I've got personal reservations about the policy of self-organisation. The rise of self-organisation has actually diverted energy to the sidelines [...] I think the principle of self-organisation is not a way forward [...] I want a broad-based union [...] I don't want a little gay bit, a little black bit, a little disabled bit and a little women's bit. [...] The more we have of this separatism, where you say you can't come to this meeting because you're white, the more I find it abhorrent.[31]

In reply to this position, the supporters of self-organisation deny that such structures detract from the mission of the union, and argue that, on the contrary, it provides an extra means of achieving the main goals of the organisation. A black union member put it,

> It is not self-organisation for the sake of being separate. It is to ensure exactly the opposite – that black issues and rights are addressed by the trade union [to] which we belong in a way acceptable to black members. As black trade unionists we believe in the principles of solidarity and support but these can never happen if they work only for some.[32]

In the light of these debates, and the continuing centrality of trade unions to any advance in equal opportunity in employment, the CRE in the early 1990s commissioned research on the participation of black workers in unions.[33] The research included interviews with black and white members and officials in three separate unions. The research demonstrated that there is still some division among black trade unionists over the principle of self-organisation. For example, in one South London white collar union branch there was a degree of disillusionment among black activists, who still saw the main problem with the union as one of failing to tackle racism at work. As one black member put it, 'I support self-organisation […] Only we know our problems and if we can't put forward what we need to address these problems, then no-one can do it for us.' However, in a Midlands branch of the same union the mood was against self-organisation. There, both black and white interviewees argued that it might only serve to 'ghettoise' the fight against racism, leaving it to be addressed only by black members when it should be tackled by all members. The branch secretary argued, 'I don't want to see it go down the road of only black members dealing with black members' issues […] because as a union we all deal with the same issues, and it is important that we don't segregate.' He felt that it might lead to a form of stereotyping where black members would only be expected to speak out on black issues.

Only a minority of respondents in this research saw self-organisation to mean the creation of a separate black trade union. More common was the view expressed at the TUC national black workers' conference in 1992 that self-organisation meant the creation of black members' groups at all levels in a union, with an annual black workers' conference where decisions are made by black representatives on issues of specific concern to black members.

Virdee and Grint relate the issue of self-organisation to the theories of Marx and Weber. Weber claimed, in reaction to Marx, that status could exist independently of class and could be the locus of political organisation, which would be likely to be more effective because status groups were less heterogeneous than class groups. They conclude,

> As such, organisations that focus wholly upon either status or class are unlikely to maintain permanent or universal support. A critical ramification of this is that neither unions nor relatively autonomous self-organised black and minority groups are likely to be sufficient, in and

of themselves, to secure the interests of blacks and minorities: both are necessary.[34]

Virdee and Grint come to the conclusion that a strategy of self-organisation may be a viable addition, if not necessarily an alternative, to conventional policies. This is especially so where general representatives are not regarded as adequate to the task of articulating and resolving the grievances of particular interests. They conclude that the practice of non-discrimination is not guaranteed by anti-racist policies and regulations alone; there is also the need for black and minority participation at all levels in the union to increase the likelihood that such policies will be enacted.[35] Moreover, self-organisation is one strategy that can increase participation and facilitate the participation of black members into the mainstream union structures more easily.[36]

Debates continue within the British trade-union movement over the nature and extent of special measures. The TUC now has an annual black workers conference, which sees itself as a forum for debating issues of specific concern to black trade unionists before going on to campaign on these issues within the broader movement. In 1993 there was a row over the suggestion that attendance should be restricted to members from ethnic minorities, with white members admitted only as observers. The recommendation was supported by the TUC's Race Relations Advisory Committee, which has a black majority. It was opposed by Bill Morris of the TGWU, who told the congress that the move was divisive and would antagonise many unions which had not yet set up structures to encourage more black participation.[37]

Organisations External to the Unions

There are some black and ethnic minority organisations which operate externally to trade unions but which nevertheless see their role as one of influencing union policies on issues relating to black workers. In the 1980s a number of work-based black groups were set up outside trade unions. For example, one group of workers in the National Health Service formed an association to influence a number of Health Service unions; other groups formed associations within local authorities to put pressure on local Councils and relevant unions.[38] One example of an external group which has for many years operated to influence trade unions is the Indian Workers Association (IWA), which expects its members to belong to unions, and assists them in making representation at branch, district or TUC level on issues of importance to its members.

The Indian Workers Association (Great Britain), known as the IWA(GB), traces its origins back to organisations of Indians in Britain in the 1930s. These organisations were largely concerned with the independence of India, and after the political independence of India and Pakistan in 1947 went into decline. However, they became active again in the 1950s, one stimulus being the need to provide assistance to the newly arriving Indian migrants to Britain. The IWA has always had a distinctive political philosophy – it locates its work of fighting racism and discrimination within its overall mission of creating a strong and united working-class movement. The IWA believes that, because many white workers have been corrupted into racism, while black workers have at the same time become more politicised, both through their experiences of exploitation as well as by their earlier struggles against imperialism, black workers must take the initiative in workplace struggle:

> We feel unity (between black and white) will develop in struggle. This does not in any sense deny the need for black workers to have their own caucuses in every factory and place of work. We do not advocate separate black unions; that would be to play the capitalists' game of dividing the working class.[39]

The IWA has had some success in its activities, initially in forcing specific unions to accept Indian members, and then in numerous campaigns on behalf of individual victims of racism and discrimination in the workplace. IWA members see themselves not as constituting an alternative to trade-union organisation, but as strong trade unionists themselves, who welcome alliances with other multi-racial progressive groups. On principle, however, they do not involve themselves with any of the bodies set up by the British Government, such as the Commission for Racial Equality.[40]

New Problems of Organising Migrant and Minority Workers

Although the Asian and Afro-Caribbean migrants of the 1950s and 1960s were always good 'joiners' of unions, the above-average propensity of black workers to join unions now seems to be declining. This could be related to the disillusion experienced by first-generation migrant workers over their treatment by unions over the years, and the fact that the second generation cannot be relied upon to have an automatic ideological sympathy towards unions. Then there is a growing category of black or migrant workers who are under-unionised. These are the workers in the expanding sector of low-paid, unregulated, marginal work: sweatshop workers, part-time workers, cleaners, home-workers. Often they contain the most vulnerable groups, such as older Asian women who speak little English, and newer arrivals such as refugees, migrants, and undocumented workers, and these are the most difficult categories of workers to organise. Across Europe, as rules for work permits become tighter, more migrant workers become 'illegal' or unauthorised. Consequently, 'they are particularly favoured by employers because of their restricted bargaining power'.[41] Or in Sivanandan's words,

> With no rights of settlement, rarely the right to work, no right to housing or medical care, and under the constant threat of deportation, the new migrants are forced to accept wages and conditions which no indigenous worker, black or white, would accept. They have no pension rights, no social security, the employers do not have to insure them – they are illicit, illegal, replaceable.[42]

Many within British unions have realised the need to organise such workers. For example, in 1989 the Transport and General Workers Union (TGWU) attempted to organise sweatshop workers – including Kurdish refugees and undocumented workers – in North London, with some success in recruiting membership and gaining compensation for unfair dismissal and payment of unpaid wages. As the chair of the local TGWU branch put it, 'This happens to illegal workers – they work for one or two weeks; when they ask for their wages the boss says "No way; if you stay here I am going to call the police."'[43]

The Complexity Illustrated by the Burnsall Dispute

The present position of the unions in relation to these workers is characterised by a combination of complicating factors: the problematic position of these vulnerable workers – often women – themselves, difficulties of the unions in organising them and protecting their rights adequately, the oppressive new governmental policies relating to industrial action, and, finally, the complex relations between unions, self-organisation and the communities of these workers. The complexity can be illustrated by one case – the Burnsall dispute – where a manual trade union attempted to organise a group of workers who were mainly ethnic minority women.[44]

The example concerns the attempts of the GMB union to organise a group of mainly South Asian women sweatshop workers employed at Burnsall Ltd., a small metal finishing company in Smethwick, the West Midlands, in 1992–3. Work was hard and intensive, carried out in stuffy conditions, with long hours, imposed overtime and arbitrary docking of wages. The main catalyst for the strike was the health and safety issue. Workers complained of inadequate protection from the chemicals with which they worked; they reported developing skin rashes and dizziness from the tanks of heated chemicals, and that safety clothing such as gloves would not be replaced when damaged. The management ignored the request of a pregnant woman who lifted metal pieces out of a degreasing tank to be moved to lighter tasks. In May 1992, when three months pregnant, she was rushed to hospital and suffered a miscarriage. The doctor who attended her said that the cause of her miscarriage was consistent with the lifting work she had been doing.

In the three months before the strike, the union made many approaches to secure recognition. A secret ballot of twenty-six of the twenty-nine workers who had joined the union took place and on 15 June 1992 the strike began. The objective was union recognition to combat low and unequal pay, imposed overtime and a hazardous environment.

There were twenty-six strikers, mostly Punjabi women who spoke little English. In the fifty-four weeks of the strike there was a daily picket, with at least one full-time union officer spending at least some time on the picket line each day. The strike was intermittently featured in newspaper articles and television news and documentary programmes, and attracted considerable public support. A London support group was formed, and later a local Birmingham support group too. Marches of solidarity were held, and concerts and social events organised to raise money for the strike fund.

Despite the general public sympathy, the strike failed. Legal restrictions on picketing and secondary action limited the impact of the strike on the company, which found it relatively easy to recruit blackleg replacement labour. The majority of Burnsall's customers were non-union, which made it impossible to organise boycotting of products treated by Burnsall. There were a few unionised companies which took their products, but the union had very little success in persuading these to terminate their relationship with Burnsall.

In May 1993 a blackleg worker who had been hired at Burnsall only that day attacked with a knife a young male striker on the picket, who later underwent emergency surgery for partially severed fingers. The union featured this vicious assault in a four-page leaflet calling for solidarity, distributed at all the unionised factories that do business with Burnsall. After twenty-six days without a single response to the leaflet, the union officials came to the conclusion that the strike was over. They argued that if other trade unionists were not going to take solidarity action for a fellow trade unionist mutilated on an official picket line, then they were unlikely to take action whatever further appeals were made. The union officials had no further initiatives to propose, saw no prospect of victory, and recommended calling off the strike, which had lasted for just over one year.

The strike ended in a great deal of acrimony between the union and the external support groups. The union had committed itself to an official dispute, within the law, including compliance with the law on balloting, picketing and secondary action. This policy was criticised by the support groups who favoured a wider blacking of Burnsall work, and mass picketing. This was rejected by the union for legal and practical reasons – if the GMB broke the law it would leave itself open to raids on its finances.

A leaflet issued by the London Support Group during the strike argued that it was precisely because of the new restrictive legislation that broader action was necessary:

> Historically, strikes by black workers have only been successful through the support of the community and mobilisation by black and anti-racist organisations. In the 90s, with the ban on secondary picketing and other anti-union legislation making it harder than ever to mobilise through traditional trade union structures, community action is vital.

However, in this case, community mobilisation was problematic for the GMB. In January 1993, half-way through the strike, a support group external to the union was set up in Birmingham, and a crisis was precipitated by the call for mass picketing and secondary action by the General Secretary of the IWA(GB) at a meeting of the support group, on the grounds that the strike could not be won by lawful means. The GMB felt that if this action was taken on behalf of the union in an official dispute it could place the union and its funds in extreme jeopardy. The courts and Burnsall could legally raid the union's finances. The GMB tried to get the support group to limit its role, which the support group was unwilling to do. Therefore the union issued a statement that 'the Union will not accept the involvement, in any aspect of the Burnsall dispute, by members of the Birmingham support group'.

Another problem which made the relationship between the union and the strikers difficult was the fact that many of the strikers had limited or no English language skills, and the union could not provide a full-time officer who could speak the language of the Asian strikers. The union officers therefore relied heavily upon an Asian community activist to translate for them. However, because this activist was an active member of the IWA(GB) and the support group, the full-time officers felt, rightly or wrongly, that he was misleading the strikers as to the union's position. The IWA strongly denied this allegation; either way, the union officers conceded that the union had been seriously weakened by not having a sympathetic Punjabi speaker to negotiate on their behalf.

The strike illustrates the fact that the issue of 'community support' for trade unions in disputes involving ethnic-minority workers is more problematic than many have realised, not least because of the often very different ideologies and aims of many of these groups and unions. After the strike was called off the IWA(GB) stated, 'The calling off of the strike has vindicated the IWA(GB)'s view that it was never possible for this action to succeed within the law.' For the IWA(GB), the lesson of the strike was that unions must sometimes be prepared to campaign outside the law, in order to build a mass movement and secure fundamental rights. A similar statement by the London Support Group urged that in the context of anti-union legislation, strikes such as Burnsall's can only be successful through mobilising wider community support and developing new strategies. They accused the GMB officials of being 'less interested in winning the strike than in keeping it within their control', which led ultimately to the 'bitter betrayal' of the strikers.

Much of the criticism of the union harked back to memories of the 1950s and 1960s when postwar black migrant workers experienced white trade-union racist exclusion. However, in this case the GMB's actions should not be seen as of the same order as those of the blinkered and racist union officials who abandoned and undermined black struggle at Imperial Typewriters and other industrial disputes mentioned earlier. The strike began with a genuine and determined commitment by the union to the Burnsall strikers. It devoted a great deal of union resources in time and money to the strike, and was able to generate much national sympathy through media coverage of the dispute. Indeed, media pressure forced a previously unsympathetic Health and Safety Executive to write a critical report of the factory, imposing four improvement notices, and demanding other alterations to current company practice. The union saw this as having an important effect on the morale of the strikers and the continuation of the strike. Thus, while the support groups felt the union had sold the strikers short, the union felt it had done all it was able to do, including initiating some rather innovatory tactics.

In the previously mentioned strikes of the 1960s and 1970s, community action played a significant role in support of the strikers. However, in the Burnsall case, community support was shown to be a more problematic issue. More specifically, there is a clear distinction to be made between those forms of community support which are lawful and those which are not. In the early stages of the Burnsall dispute, the union did engage the broader local community in the action, and, with the support of local groups and key religious and commercial figures, succeeded for over two months in preventing the company securing an alternative workforce. In this, the union had the support of the IWA(GB), which used its local influence to try to shame the blacklegs in their local communities:

> We've put their names up in local temples and distributed leaflets, naming them and the Indian villages they come from. Some might say it's direct humiliation. But we're saying, by crossing the picket line for a few bob, you are a disgrace to your community (IWA spokesman, *Guardian*, 7 October 1992).

Nevertheless, in this case the community support did not produce the desired outcome. Despite the local popular support for the strikers the company was able to secure a replacement workforce, including many from the local Punjabi community.

This sort of community support did not pose a challenge to the trade-union organisation of the strike: it was lawful, although ineffective. When, however, community support becomes of a different order – mass picketing and potentially unlawful secondary action, which might possibly be effective – then it poses a direct threat to the trade union concerned.

Although the other previously cited cases where industrial struggle involved community support were often quite innovative and radical by the standards of normal official and unofficial disputes at that time, they were nevertheless legal in terms of the laws of the day. One major difference in the context of similar struggles today is the undermining of workers' collective power through structural unemployment and the increasingly repressive employment legislation. In particular the legislation has made once-normal collective action much more likely to be defined as unlawful activity.

Rival Views on Organisation and Action

The evidence of the changing reaction of unions to migrants and ethnic minorities in the postwar period, along with the most recent issues exemplified by the Burnsall's case study, suggest a categorisation of five different positions regarding trade unions and black/migrant workers in Britain.

1. The first position is that of *racist exclusion*, as characterised by many trade unionists in the prewar and early postwar periods, and by some members and officials in the disputes of the 1960s and early 1970s. The preference is first to keep migrant workers out of the labour market; later, to keep them out of the union, and when in the union, to keep them excluded from the union benefits to which they were entitled.
2. The second position is one of *incorporation*, where union membership is extended to ethnic-minority workers, but where the

basis of inclusion goes no further than that consistent with a traditional trade-union class analysis. Membership unity is seen as central; thus any special measures which distinguish between types of workers are to be discouraged. The natural preference is to be 'colour blind'. The 'hard' position within this is to extend no special measures at all to migrant workers, as was the position of many unions in the 1960s. A later, more flexible, position is to encourage the adoption of some measures which take account of the different circumstances of ethnic-minority members, such as producing literature in different languages. The incorporation model forms the premise upon which most of the unions' organisational arrangements for ethnic-minority members, such as regional 'Race Advisory Committees', are currently based.

3. The third position is one of *partial autonomy*, held by many black trade unionists and some white activists, who argue that union rules, structures, and policies should change to allow for the experiences of exclusion and racism of the minority black membership, as these disadvantages are suffered over and above those suffered by the white membership. Furthermore, the fact that black members are generally in a minority within unions means that normal union structures operate to exclude their voice from being heard by the majority.[45] Thus some ethnic-minority workers feel that the only way to get their voices heard is by self-organisation within unions, in their own separate structures.
4. The fourth position is a more radical *race and class* perspective, stressing the potential of black groups for galvanising of unions into more radical and political action. By this view, British unions are reformist and non-political organisations concerned only with the immediate remuneration of their members. Black workers can offer the labour movement the opportunity to break the reformist distinction between the political and the economic.[46] Sivanandan writes,

> Trade unions, once an instrument of class struggle, have in the course of achieving legitimacy, come to act as a buffer between the classes – absorbing the impact of working class radicalism on behalf of capital in exchange for wage concessions on behalf of labour. [...] Black workers [...] have been forced by the racist ethos of British society (worker and capitalist alike) to address themselves more directly to the political dimensions of their economic exploitation. They have [...] been compelled to recognise that a purely quantitative approach to the improvement of their conditions can by itself have no bearing on the quality of their lives. Their economic struggle is at once a political struggle. And that puts them in the vanguard of working class struggle.[47]

This position is similar to that of the West Midlands based IWA(GB) involved in the Burnsall dispute. The IWA(GB) believes that because many white workers have been corrupted into racism, while black workers have at the same time become more politicised, both through their experiences of exploitation as well as by their earlier struggles against imperialism, then black workers will often find themselves taking the initiative in workplace struggle.

5. The *separatist* position states that after years of evidence of white-trade-union racism to black members and workers, black people can only be properly represented by their own organisations, including their own black trade unions. Any organisation where black workers are led by white leaders is bound to neglect black interests in favour of the white majority. The perspective of 'black separatism' is rarely found among black union members. In general, the term is over-used by white trade unionists, and is often attributed by the trade-union leadership to black activists when they begin to move beyond the normal limits of traditional trade-union activity. A study of four trade unions found no evidence of this perspective being articulated by either rank and file black workers or their representatives within the structures of the union dealing with issues of importance to black members, such as 'Race Advisory Committees'.[48]

The perspective is more likely to be held by activists external to trade unions. Activists in the London Support Group held varying positions on 'separatism': while some made pronouncements during the strike which were quite sympathetic to separate black organisation, others threatened to withdraw if the group became 'separatist'. However, for some individuals the failure of the Burnsall strike itself seemed to stimulate a 'separatist' perspective. After the strike, some of the members of the London Support Group became even more convinced of the importance of black support organisations, and were giving serious thought to the issue of separate black union organisation.[49]

Unfavourable Conditions for Solutions

The problem for unions is that the failure of campaigns such as Burnsall's could lead to a more general disillusion with unions on the part of ethnic minority workers and make further recruitment more difficult. As one of the GMB union officials recognised, 'there is no doubt that we are going to find it more difficult to recruit Asian workers in the future, because of what happened in the Burnsall strike'.[50] Many labour movement activists now argue that the trade union movement has no hope of bringing unionisation to exploited ethnic minority workers unless it works in cooperation with communities and links unionisation to broader issues such as workplace discrimination, sexual and racial harassment at the workplace, health and safety, cultural linguistic and religious rights, harassment by the police and immigration authorities, and so on:

> If the trade union movement wants to tackle the creation of low paid, racially defined ghettos in employment, it has to shift its priorities. It must encourage community initiatives rather than fearing where they might lead. It must offer resources and be willing to stick with the local and community groups when the inevitable industrial disputes arise. This means working jointly to build solidarity and, most importantly, confront anti-union legislation.[51]

However, the Burnsall case study reveals a number of difficulties inherent in such action. These stem first from the broader context of economic restructuring, recession, and structural unemployment, together with the Conservative government's employment legislation. Other difficulties were seen to stem from the legacy of suspicion held by many black groups of trade unions because of the racist exclusion of ethnic minority workers in earlier years. Still more fundamental difficulties could be seen to be inherent in the contradictory nature of trade unions in a capitalist society and the conflict within the labour movement over the strategies and values they should adopt.

One of the key differences between a radical and a reformist position is the readiness in the former to take action outside the law, when that law is seen as unjust and representing the narrow interests of the ruling elite. However, unions by their very nature are not easily radical organisations in this sense. Much has been argued as to the radical or conservative potential of unions in social transformation.[52] Many have argued since the times of Lenin and Gramsci that trade unions are basically defensive organisations operating within the confines laid down by capitalist society, are essentially competitive, and are unlikely to be the instrument of a radical transformation of society.[53]

The problems of organising ethnic minority workers within 'poor work' sectors means that broader forms of action are likely to be necessary to achieve success. This includes allying the trade union with broader based community groups which can assist in organising such difficult sectors of workers. At the same time, the increasingly restrictive legislation in the UK means that broader action with these groups, such as mass picketing, is vulnerable to being defined as unlawful. However, it has been argued that black workers and their communities, due to the politicising nature of their life and work experiences, are far more ready to embrace a political and radical dimension to economic struggles and struggles of union recognition.

They are therefore more ready to involve themselves in potentially unlawful actions in order to remedy a greater injustice. This sets them against trade unions who are concerned to remain within the law to protect their own assets. The combination of all these factors means that when unions embark upon similar campaigns to assist highly exploited groups of workers in poor and unhealthy work they are more likely to find themselves addressing broader questions outside the remit of conventional trade union action. By this analysis the tensions which arose during the Burnsall dispute are understandable, and are likely to arise again in future union attempts to organise ethnic minority workers in 'poor work' sectors.

In Conclusion

There are still many vigorous debates going on within the British trade-union movement regarding the specific forms of its relationship with migrant and ethnic minority workers. There is now a broad acceptance of the desirability of special equal opportunities and anti-racist measures, not only at TUC level but also within many individual unions. Nevertheless, although the old forms of open racist exclusion have gone, there remain serious issues of racism and discrimination in employment and in the trade-union movement itself. Many of the current arguments on the nature and extent of 'special measures' stem from the conviction of black trade unionists that the movement still drags it feet in fighting the racism they experience. In particular, many of the current debates on self-organisation within unions are rooted in this concern. More broadly, there are new problems and dilemmas facing unions over the need to recruit and organise the expanding cohorts of more severely exploited migrant and ethnic minority workers, in the context of an unfriendly political and economic climate. There are many who believe that unions need to change their approaches, become more flexible and move away still further from traditional ideas and practices of trade unionism before they will be able to attract and retain the new generations of ethnic-minority workers.

NOTES

1. I would like to thank Peter Fairbrother for his help with information for this article.
2. D. Kay and R. Miles, 'Migration, Racism and the Labour Market in Britain 1946–1951', in M. van der Linden and J. Lucassen (eds), *Racism and the Labour Market: Historical Studies*, Bern, 1995, 563–80.
3. The 1991 Census was the first to collect information on the ethnic composition of the British population, and found the ethnic minority population to be just

over 3 million, or 5.5 per cent of the population (D. Owen, *The Location of Ethnic Minorities in Great Britain.* National Ethnic Minority Data Archive, 1991 Census Factsheet no. 1, 1992. Warwick: Centre for Research in Ethnic Relations, University of Warwick). By far the majority of these are the postwar migrants and their descendants: they are of South Asian ethnic origin (Indian, Pakistani, or Bangladeshi) or are Black Caribbeans. Debate in the UK no longer uses the word 'migrant' to refer to these groups. Common usage refers to these groups as ethnic minorities. As the term 'black' is often also used to describe both these Asian and Caribbean groups, particularly by activists in the trade-union context, the two terms are used interchangeably in this chapter.

4. C. Brown, *Black and White Britain: The Third PSI Survey*, London, 1984; C. Brown, '"Same difference": The Persistence of Racial Disadvantage in the British Employment Market', in P. Braham, A. Rattansi and R. Skellington (eds), *Racism and Antiracism: Inequalities, Opportunities and Policies*, London, 1992; M.J. Cross, J. Wrench and S. Barnett, *Ethnic Minorities and the Careers Service: An Investigation into Processes of Assessment and Placement.* Department of Employment Research Paper no. 73, London, 1990; G. Lee, J. Wrench, *Skill Seekers: Black Youth, Apprenticeships and Disadvantage*, Leicester, 1983.
5. J. Vranken, 'Industrial rights', in Zig Layton-Henry (ed.), *The Political Rights of Migrant Workers in Western Europe.* Sage Modern Politics Series vol. 25, London, 1990, 58.
6. A. Phizacklea and R. Miles, *Labour and Racism*, London, 1980.
7. Ibid., 93.
8. R. Miles and A. Phizacklea, *The TUC, Black Workers and Immigration 1954–1973.* Working Papers on Ethnic Relations, no. 6, Birmingham, 1977.
9. P. Fryer, *Staying Power: The History of Black People in Britain*, London, 1984.
10. S. Bentley, 'Industrial Conflict, Strikes and Black Workers: Problems of Research Methodology', *New Community*, nos 1–2, Summer (1976): 135.
11. Fryer, *Staying Power*, 367.
12. A. Sivanandan, *A Different Hunger: Writings on Black Resistance*, London, 1982.
13. J. Wrench, 'Unequal Comrades: Trade Unions, Equal Opportunity and Racism', in R. Jenkins and J. Solomos (eds), *Racism and Equal Opportunity Policies in the 1980's*, Cambridge, 1987, 166–7.
14. C. Brown, *Black and White Britain: The Third PSI Survey*, London, 1984, 169.
15. R. Ramdin, *The Making of the Black Working Class in Britain*, Aldershot, 1987, 339.
16. T. Jones, *Britain's Ethnic Minorities*, London, 1993.
17. B. Radin, 'Coloured Workers and British Trade Unions', *Race* 8, no. 2 (1966): 159.
18. Quoted in J. Wrench, 'Unequal comrades', 165.
19. Phizacklea and Miles, *Labour and Racism*, 93.
20. Ibid., 93–4.
21. Labour Research, July 1988.
22. S. Virdee and K. Grint, 'Black Self Organisation in Trade Unions', *Sociological Review* 42, no. 2 (1994): 212.
23. TUC, *Involvement of Black Workers in Trade Unions*, London, 1991.
24. C. Brown, *Black and White Britain: The Third PSI Survey*, London, 1984, 170.
25. Runnymede Trust, 'Trade Unions and Immigrant Workers', *New Community* 4, no. 1 (1974): 24.
26. Phizacklea and Miles, *Labour and Racism*, 125.
27. G. Lee, *Unionism and Race: A Report to the West Midlands Regional Council of the Trades Union Congress*, Birmingham, 1984, 9.
28. Virdee and Grint, 'Black Self Organisation in Trade Unions', 206.

29. Ibid., 208.
30. Ibid.
31. Ibid., 209.
32. Ibid., 209–10.
33. CRE, *Part of the Union?: Trade Union Participation by Ethnic Minority Workers*, London, 1992; see also S. Virdee, (forthcoming), *Organised Labour and the Racialised Worker in England: Racism, 'Racial' Formation and Working Class Militancy*. PhD thesis.
34. Virdee and Grint, 'Black Self Organisation in Trade Unions', 210.
35. Ibid., 222–3.
36. Ibid., 219.
37. *Financial Times*, 7 May 1993.
38. See Wrench, 'Unequal comrades', 177.
39. Report of the General Secretary, IWA (GB), J. Joshi, 1970, 21–2, quoted in S. Josephides, 'Principles, Strategies and Anti-racist Campaigns: The case of the Indian Workers Association', in H. Goulbourne (ed.), *Black Politics in Britain*, Aldershot, 1990.
40. Ibid.
41. Labour Research, February 1989.
42. A. Sivanandan, 'Racism 1992', *Race and Class*, January-March (1989): 87.
43. Labour Research, August 1989.
44. Much of the following discussion on this case is taken from J. Wrench and S. Virdee 'Organising the Unorganised: "Race", Poor Work and Trade Unions', in P. Ackers, C. Smith and P. Smith (eds), *The New Workplace and Trade Unionism*, London, 1996,
45. G. Lee and J. Wrench, *Skill Seekers: Black Youth, Apprenticeships and Disadvantage*, Leicester, 1983.
46. S. Joshi and B. Carter, 'The Role of Labour in the Creation of a Racist Britain', *Race and Class* 15, no. 3 (1984).
47. A. Sivanandan, Editorial, *Race Today*, August 1973.
48. Virdee, *Organised Labour and the Racialised Worker in England.*
49. M. Büyüm, *The Burnsall Strike: Account of a Struggle*, MA dissertation, Department of Sociology, University of Warwick, 1993, 52.
50. Quoted in Büyüm, *The Burnsall Strike,* 37.
51. CARF, 'From Red Scar Mill to Burnsalls: Black Workers Today', *Journal of the Campaign against Racism and Fascism*, March/April 1994, 5.
52. E.g., R. Hyman, *Marxism and the Sociology of Trade Unions*, London, 1971; J. Kelly, *Trade Unions and Socialist Politics*, London, 1988.
53. See C. Harman, *Gramsci versus Reformism*, Bookmarks, 1983.

Chapter 8

Sweden: Insiders outside the Trade Union Mainstream

Wuokko Knocke

Introduction

1946 was the year in which postwar labour immigration to Sweden was initiated, and a new phase in the migratory history of the country began. Contrary to many other West European countries, Sweden had been spared from wartime devastation. The country's economic and demographic situation was marked by an ageing male population, little support for women's economic activity, and an expanding industrial sector. Sweden was faced with a severe shortage of labour, a fact that seriously worried both the representatives of Swedish capital and the government. Therefore, in 1946, after deliberations with the social partners, the government appointed a Preparatory Commission of Experts with representatives from the employers' side, the trade unions and the National Labour Market Commission (AK), to investigate the possibilities of transferring foreign workers into Sweden. Discussions started in Parliament and investigations were initiated by the employers on how to supply labour, primarily to the industrial sector.[1] The main alternatives discussed for solving the problem were the untapped indigenous reserves of women, elderly and partly disabled persons on the one hand, or the 'import of foreign workers' on the other.[2] Women's organisations and the trade unions were negative towards the immigration of labour, and spoke in favour of mobilising domestic labour reserves, especially the large number of married women. But no steps were taken by the unions to facilitate the entry of women into the labour market.

The recruitment of foreign workers was the alternative chosen by the employers and by government as the quickest way to supply workers to the industrial sector. In 1946, an investigation into the supply of labour conducted for the Swedish Industrial Institute for Economic and Social Research (IUI, an employers' institute) recommended the recruitment of 100,000 to 200,000 foreign workers over the next decade. The demand was explicitly for young, able-bodied male workers, who were expected to work in Sweden for a few years to help out with industrial bottlenecks.[3] Women as immigrants were strikingly absent from any of the discussions. Even at a later stage, government commission reports only considered male workers in relation to labour market needs. Women were initially considered as family members left behind in the home country, and later on as family members joining their economically active partners.[4]

Postwar Recruitment of Labour

Discussions about establishing a common Nordic labour market, which had started in the mid-1930s, were resumed immediately after the war.[5] A first agreement was signed in 1946 between Sweden and Denmark. Due to their particular economic circumstances, Finland and Norway were not yet prepared to lose skilled labour to Sweden. On the other hand, Nordic citizens had been entitled since 1943 to take a job without needing a work permit. Finally, the agreement of a common Nordic labour market, which gave full rights to settlement and work, was signed in 1954 and still remains in effect today.

In 1947, as a result of the work of the Preparatory Expert Committee, the first bilateral agreements for the recruitment of non-Nordic foreign labour were signed with Italy and Hungary. An agreement was also signed with Austria and the Inter-governmental Committee on Refugees to transfer 1,800 displaced Sudetan German workers to Sweden for permanent settlement. This particular agreement fell outside short-term labour market considerations. The immigration of refugees was not, and is still not, meant to be connected to labour market needs. Early postwar immigration of labour was thus arranged collectively through bilateral agreements. A whole system of recruitment was developed by the National Labour Market Board (AMS), which in 1948 replaced the Labour Market Commission. Recruitment offices with Swedish staff were set up in the foreign countries to manage the details of recruitment and the collective transfer of the workers. The number of workers to be transferred, their occupational qualifications, and the industrial sectors of employment in Sweden were stipulated in detail.

Foreign workers were, however, allowed to change jobs within the occupational sector for which they were recruited.[6] Thanks to the close cooperation between the Social Democrat government, concerned state authorities and the trade unions, an organisation clause was included in the agreements: foreign workers were to commit themselves to join the appropriate union for their profession, and to remain unionised during their entire stay in Sweden; this represented an exception to the principle of freedom of association established in the 1938 Basic Saltsjöbaden Agreement between labour and capital. No similar obligation existed for Swedish workers. The agreements also stipulated that the contracted workers should be equal to Swedish workers in working conditions and wages. They were covered by insurance against unemployment, accidents and illness, in accordance with Swedish legislation.

The influential position of the trade unions and the active intervention of the state were thus significant in rapidly placing the immigrant population, workers, and non-workers, foreigners as well as naturalised, on an equal footing with the indigenous population, in most respects legally and formally.[7] Basic freedoms and legal protection for all foreigners were written into the 1954 Aliens Act. Social protection and the right to welfare benefits, including childcare and study allowances, social assistance, and the like were introduced through a number of reforms in the 1960s.

Within the bilateral programme, more than 5,000 foreign workers were contracted up to June 1950.[8] The persistent demand for labour and the abolition of visa requirements for citizens from a number of Western European countries around 1950 led to a change in the recruitment system. Companies that wanted to recruit non-Nordic workers could place a request with the Labour Market Board. After consultations with the Regional Employment Board and after hearings with the concerned local unions, the AMS would, where there was a positive response from these consultations, assist in the recruitment process by introducing the company to the labour market officials in the country where recruitment was to take place. Simultaneously recruitment initiated by the government continued in a number of countries in Western and Southern Europe like Germany, the Netherlands, and later in the 1950s in Italy, Austria, Belgium and Greece, without any formal agreements. Nonetheless, the number of contracted non-Nordic workers who came to Sweden in the 1950s only amounted to 12,000, making up 5 per cent of the total immigration of 285,000 persons to Sweden in that decade. The overwhelming majority had come from other Nordic countries, mainly from Finland.[9]

Although the Trade Union Confederation (LO) was represented in the Preparatory Commission of Experts, they were opposed to the 'import' of foreign workers and negative towards the bilateral agreements. Apart from wanting to give priority to activating untapped domestic resources, trade-union arguments against the recruitment of foreign labour were based on fear of social problems, and on fear that social development programmes initiated by the unions would be endangered. The following arguments against foreign recruitment were more specifically voiced by the Board of the Metal Workers' Union in 1946:

- problems in relation to foreign workers who were already employed in industry;[10]
- lack of housing;
- the high costs associated with labour import.[11]

Although the LO and individual unions were negative about the bilateral agreements of the 1940s and critical of the employers' recruitment campaigns in the 1950s, they remained passive with regard to continued non-Nordic immigration on the one hand and the entrance of married women into the labour market on the other.[12] It is therefore probably more correct to define union attitudes as ambivalent, caught as they were in the conflict between trying to get domestic labour reserves trained and into the labour market, and the insight that industrial growth depended on a rapid supply of skilled workers.

What about Women in Migration?

At this point it seems indicated to locate women in the migratory process. In contrast to many other West European labour-recruiting countries, the idea of a guest-worker system never took root in Sweden and was short-lived in practice. The fundamental right of family reunion was never questioned and was accepted without any special political decision. The assumption at government level had been that foreign workers, mainly from Southern Europe, would not find it attractive to settle for good in a cold Nordic country.[13] When this proved wrong, the right to bring in wives, children and fiancées was never disputed. According to Hammar,[14] the unproblematic acceptance of family reunion is partly explained by the position of Nordic immigrants, principally the large group from Finland. Nordic immigrants made up two-thirds of the immigrant population, and according to the agreement of 1954 they had unlimited rights of settlement in Sweden together with their families. It was therefore no great matter of principle to grant the remaining third of the immigrant population the same rights. Rather, as Hammar puts it, it would have been difficult not to give them permanent rights of settlement and work.

Sweden had wanted young, able-bodied male workers.[15] But women had been coming too, both married and single women. It is clear from the statistics that the women were more numerous than the men in the early 1950s.[16] A majority of women from Finland had come independently, knowing there were jobs for them, and better women's wages than at home.[17] Women from other countries came more often, though not always, as family members or wives. Sweden did not, as did many other European countries, treat women as dependants of the male breadwinner, giving them only derived rights of residence and work. Women were considered legal subjects in their own right with access to both residence and work permits. This fact is reflected in labour-force statistics and in case studies. At the end of the 1960s, women from Finland, Italy, Yugoslavia and Greece had higher labour-force participation rates than Swedish women.[18] They were also more likely than Swedish women to be members of trade unions.

The women were present and a majority of them were in the labour force. The official discourse, however, rarely took notice of them. They remained invisible and their voice was not heard. Between 1946 and 1972, only one parliamentary debate, in 1966, made explicit reference to women.[19] In two sentences there is a mention of recruitment in Yugoslavia of some nurses, who then were attending courses to prepare for work in Sweden. Formally having the same status and rights as male immigrants did not help to put the women on the public agenda. Neither has statistical evidence of economically active immigrant women succeeded in correcting the dominant social imagery of the 'immigrant woman' as a 'problem'.[20] Instead of recognising their structural subordination and powerlessness, the socially constructed image has been that of helpless, poorly educated women, burdened by their traditional women's roles, tied to their homes by large families and oppressive husbands, in short what Aleksandra Ålund has termed in 1989 'problem ideologies'.[21] The negative images testify to the social disregard and low esteem in which women immigrants are held. They indicate the strength of the gendered and ethnically segregated Swedish social system, which has contributed to the marginalisation of women immigrants to the bottom of the hierarchy of working life and their invisibility at the level of society.[22]

Trade Unions and Immigration in the 1940s and 1950s

In the conflict between activating domestic labour reserves and accepting the immigration of foreign labour, the initially negative and thereafter passive attitude of the trade unions in the 1940s and 1950s was not due to lack of influence. In 1947, a circular letter from the Labour Market Commission (AK), the predecessor of the Labour Market Board (AMS), confirmed that local associations of employers and employees (i.e., local unions) should have the opportunity of stating their opinions with regard to each individual case of foreign recruitment. Trade-union influence was strengthened in 1951 and even more so in 1954, when a circular letter from the AMS ruled that, 'In every case of a first-time application for a work permit, it is mandatory that the concerned trade union local states its opinion.' Local employers' associations were at this point in time only given a voice if special factors were involved.[23] In 1949 the Metal Workers' Union Central had, however, demanded to be permitted to express its opinion directly to the AMS, which in practice implied a right of veto. Trade-union locals were to have consultative status with their central organisation; this model was the one adopted for a few years by the major industrial unions.

A new order was again introduced with the adoption of the 1954 Aliens Act. The AMS was made responsible for appraising the labour market situation, on which the social partners (unions and employers) were given the right to express their opinion. The decision to grant work and residence permits became the responsibility of the central aliens authorities (from 1937 to 1969 the National Office for Aliens; from 1969 the Swedish National Immigration Board). Both the employers and the unions were represented, first in the Labour Market Commission (AK), and later on in the Labour Market Board (AMS), and could therefore exert direct influence on non-Nordic labour immigration. This arrangement was in line with the Swedish corporatist model of direct union representation in major decision-making and implementing bodies, especially in the area of labour market policies,[24] a model established in the 1938 Basic Saltsjöbaden Agreement between labour and capital.

The 1960s and the Regulation of Immigration

In the context of collective recruitment, unions had had the opportunity to express their opinion before the workers came to Sweden. When companies started recruiting in the 1950s, unions could give their consent or refuse when the worker applied for a work permit.

During the period of company recruitment, it was not uncommon for a representative from the local union to join the recruitment team 'to make sure that we only took the best ones, so we wouldn't get problems when they came here'.[25] Thus, although initial trade-union influence had much of an ad hoc character, unions had a say from the start and increasingly gained a strong position in the institutional structure which was established for matters of labour immigration. But neither Sweden as a nation state nor the trade unions had as yet formulated any consistent immigration policy.

It was only in the mid-1960s, with the dramatic increase of non-Nordic immigration, that the trade-union movement felt it was losing control. Between 1964 and 1965, immigration from Yugoslavia grew eightfold, from Greece threefold, and immigration from Turkey doubled.[26] The non-Nordic immigrants of the mid-1960s constituted a large wave of spontaneous worker immigrants, who had neither been recruited through government measures nor contracted by employers. Previously only qualified workers had been admitted by the trade unions and only in sectors where no domestic supplies were available. There are numerous examples of union locals turning down requests for work permits for foreigners, either because they did not match up to qualification requirements, or because domestic workers were available.[27] The reason for accepting only qualified workers was to avoid the risk of wage pressure from unskilled workers. In the words of the Metal Workers' Union, 'Swedish workers will be the ones to suffer losses, if unskilled ones are taken in.'

Faced with the uncontrolled wave of immigration, the AMS and the trade-union movement urged the government to take responsibility for formulating an immigration policy and to regulate immigration. The other principal social partner, the Swedish Employers' Association (SAF), was not in favour of regulation. But since both the AMS and the LO insisted on more controlled inflows of labour, those in favour of regulation carried the day. In March 1967, the immigration of non-Nordic workers became regulated in that a work contract, a work permit, and housing all had to be arranged before entering the country.[28]

Sweden's need for labour had initiated immigration. Even after the regulation, until the beginning of the 1970s labour market needs were allowed to determine continued immigration. Almost simultaneously with the adoption of the regulation, bilateral agreements were signed with Yugoslavia in 1966 and with Turkey in 1967.[29] While the unions had been negative towards the 1947 agreements, this time they gave their backing. According to Nelhans,[30] trade unions accepted that industrial growth and the generation of prosperity was dependent on the labour supply, which at this point in time was not available in the country. The trade union movement was prepared to let immigration help out with bottlenecks in the production process. Their basic position, however, was that spontaneous immigration should be stopped and replaced with a controlled flow to make increasingly possible a better use of domestic labour resources, both present and potential.

The feminist historian Gunhild Kyle argues that the 1967 regulation of immigration meant that the trade union movement had finally decided to choose domestic women before foreign workers.[31] Her argument is sustainable in view of the fact that the regulation of immigration coincided with the political acceptance of the two-earner family and the beginning of a shift in employment from industry to services. The need now was for a predominantly female workforce for the rapidly growing public services sector, in health and childcare, care of the elderly, and education.[32]

It would take until 1972 before labour immigration came to a halt. Instead, the economic boom years of 1969–70 were record-breaking, with an immigration surplus of 100,000, of which 60,000 came from Finland and 30,000 from non-Nordic countries. It was only in 1971 that immigration decreased. The drop was dramatic, from a net surplus of 52,300 in 1970 (32,300 Nordic, 19,900 non-Nordic) to a net loss of 6,700 in 1972 (-8,600 Nordic, 1,900 non-Nordic) (see Table A3.1 in Appendix 3).

The LO Stops Non-Nordic Labour Immigration: 1972

From the very start of postwar labour immigration, the trade-union movement stands out as one of the most powerful actors in the institutional structure of decision-making. The influential position of the trade union movement in labour market and immigration matters derived to a large extent from its intimate link to and close cooperation with the Social Democratic Party or, as argued by Olsson,[33] it was due to

> the symbiotic relationship between the party (SAP) and the labour movement, centralised under its national body, the Swedish Confederation of Trade Unions (Landsorganisationen, or LO). The bonds between the SAP and the LO were very strong; the metaphor commonly used was that the labour movement had two branches, the political and the union.

Coincidence or not, the stop to worker immigration from non-Nordic countries came in February 1972, well before the oil crisis, in the same year that separate taxation for spouses was introduced, making it economically more profitable for women to work. Significantly, it was not by government decree but through an internal circular letter issued by the LO to affiliated unions and union locals. Tomas Hammar, who located the crucial document, comments,

> It was not a parliamentary or government decision that was taken in this important question but rather an LO decision. The Trade Union Confederation recommended that the unions henceforth should reject requests for work permits with reference to the general situation on the Swedish labour market. When thereafter the locals said no, the unions would say no and the AMS would say no: no more work permits were issued and practically all labour immigration came to an end.[34]

The entire structure and composition of immigration changed radically. Non-Nordic labour immigration, which is submitted to labour market considerations and thus union influence, soon dropped to 5 per cent of total immigration. Later years confirm that the shift was definitive. In the early 1990s non-Nordic immigration to Sweden was principally composed of family reunion cases of earlier labour immigrants and refugees (approximately 55 per cent), of political and humanitarian refugees (35–40 per cent), and small numbers of visiting students and children for adoption.[35] None of these categories, according to Swedish legislation, is supposed to be considered in terms of the labour market situation. The LO agrees with this policy and maintains the continued stop of non-Nordic labour immigration. Permits granted for labour market purposes amount now to less than 1 per cent of total permits issued each year.

Union Organisation

Hammar argues that the rejection of a guest-worker system,[36] and the right to permanent settlement, confirmed in 1967–68, were largely due to the egalitarian stand taken in relation to immigrant labour by the workers' movement. But the following quotation makes clear that equal treatment was initially pursued less out of concern for the foreigners than because of the perceived threat to Swedish workers and their wage levels:

> It has been an old trade union demand that there should be equality in wage and employment conditions between Swedish and foreign workers. Low-income foreign labour was not intended to be used for competitive purposes.[37]

To achieve equality, it was paramount for the unions that collectively transferred or otherwise recruited workers should be organised.

Therefore, and as a remarkable exception to the principle of freedom of association, codified in the 1938 Basic Saltsjöbaden Agreement, the government included a clause in the bilateral agreements with Italy and Hungary in 1947, according to which workers had to commit themselves to join the trade union of their occupational sector and remain unionised during their entire stay in Sweden.[38] The fact that the organisation clause was written into the bilateral agreements can be seen as one of the many expressions of trade union power. The organisation clause was in part an expression of the government's lack of confidence in employers' methods of labour recruitment. It was also due to the fact that foreign workers, at that time, were less organised than their Swedish counterparts, as shown in a study by the Metal Workers' Union in 1946.

The organisation clause was abolished in 1965 and replaced by an agreement between the LO and the SAF, whereby employers committed themselves to recommend that foreign workers join the union. It may not have been the best way of getting informed and interested union members, but when it came to making foreign workers join, it was a method that worked.[39] A common practice, especially in industrial workplaces, was that the worker was asked to go to the local union office even before signing the employment contract. In a workplace study conducted in the mid-1980s at four industrial plants and in two large hospitals,[40] 111 women from four countries (Finland, Yugoslavia, Greece, and Chile) were interviewed about their reasons for joining the union, among other subjects. A majority of the women in industrial work confirmed that for them becoming a union member had seemed to happen either automatically or was thought to be a precondition for getting a job in the first place:

> One had to take that paper to the union office before starting. I thought everybody had to be a member. They didn't ask anything, there was no choice. One wouldn't have got a job without joining the union (Finnish woman at an industrial plant).[41]

The study also revealed striking gender variations between male and female-dominated unions in their approach towards immigrants. While it was common for the male-dominated union locals in the Factory Workers' Union to use the 'automatic' method, local shop stewards in the female-dominated Municipal Workers' Union took time to explain basic union principles. The women were given a chance to decide whether they wanted to join – which almost all of them did.

Compared internationally, the degree of union organisation is very high in Sweden. Union density for blue-collar workers has been close to 90 per cent for many years, and 'at a record level of 86 per cent density for all employees', including white-collar and professional.[42]

Although a closed-shop system has never existed in Sweden, it has been taken more or less for granted, especially in the blue-collar sector, that working people join the union. My numerous interviews with both central and local trade-union officials confirm that the organisation of immigrant workers has never been problematic.[43] Both male and female immigrants have, with few exceptions, joined the unions to the same degree as Swedish workers. There is evidence that immigrant women, apart from having had higher economic activity rates, were also organised to a higher degree than Swedish women in the 1960s.[44]

Of the LO's total membership around 15 per cent are foreign-born and another 5 per cent have an immigrant background in that at least one parent was born outside Sweden.[45] Generally speaking, immigrant workers display the same patterns and the same degree of union organisation as Swedish workers.[46] There exist minor differences in the degree of organisation between national groups, depending on background factors such as educational level, previous experience of unions or political activity, and rural or urban origin. More important has been the concentration of certain nationality groups into 'poor job' sectors. An example are Turkish immigrants in the 1980s with a low of 40 per cent union membership. Alpay's study records minor differences in the degree of organisation between rural (36 per cent), urban (42 per cent), and well-educated (44 per cent) Turkish immigrants.[47] The main reason, though, for their relatively low union density was their employment in the hotel and catering sector, or in building maintenance and cleaning. These occupational sectors have displayed generally low degrees of organisation. Contrary to other blue-collar unions, with organisation levels at around 90 per cent, union density in the Hotel and Restaurant Workers' Union has been at approximately 60 per cent, and in the Building Maintenance Union around 40–50 per cent, irrespective of national background. Working part-time in isolated jobs, often during unsocial working hours, are factors which explain low union density for all the workers employed in these low-skilled, low-status job sectors.[48]

The combined effects of marginalising jobs and poor work environment characteristics, together with the over-representation of certain immigrant groups in these types of occupations have, therefore, been more decisive for low union membership than factors related to ethnic background as such.[49] On the contrary, industrial workers have always had high degrees of union density regardless of their position in the job hierarchy, of whether they are Swedish or immigrant workers, or of gender. High union density has been especially true of the Metal Workers' Union, which also was the union first to receive the major bulk of foreign workers. The same holds true for the Factory Workers' Union, with relatively high concentrations of immigrant workers of both sexes.[50]

For a number of reasons discussed above, Swedish trade-union strategy was from the very start of postwar immigration that foreign workers should join their ranks. But why has it been so easy to get them to join? To answer that question, it is necessary to look at several interrelated factors at different levels of explanation. As mentioned earlier, methods of recruitment at local level often gave the impression that union membership was mandatory. Becoming a union member was something that seemed to happen 'automatically', and immigrants knew no different. Besides, unorganised immigrants risked creating irritation and pressure from workmates for not being loyal to the workers' collective.[51] A number of years later, many of the women in my workplace study gave voice to their feelings of powerlessness, especially when recalling the male unionists' methods of recruitment: 'One didn't know about anything and didn't dare to question.' And further in the same vein: 'I thought it had to be this way, I had no say.' On a more positive note, none of the 111 interviewees was against being a union member. The union was seen as something to turn to when difficulties arose at the job, and also as a protection against unemployment.[52] Despite serious complaints about the disinterest of male shop stewards for their actual work situation, many of the women felt loyal to and identified with the union. 'The union is us' was one such expression.

For explanations at the more general level, we have to look at union structure and strength. First, as Schmitter argues,[53] a unitary structure and relative strength are decisive for trade union influence in political and social decision-making, including issues related to immigration and immigrants. Both union strength and union structure are important for the organisation and the contacts between immigrant populations and the host country. In terms of structure, the organisation of the Swedish trade-union movement can be characterised as unitary, with a strong Trade Union Confederation and affiliated unions organised by occupational sector. In addition, unlike the unions in France for example, Swedish trade unions have never been organisations of militant activists, but have had the character of popular mass movements.

Comparative studies conducted by the ILO[54] have shown that where trade unions are mass movements, union density for immigrant workers is generally higher than in countries with militant activist organisations. The powerful and influential agency of the Swedish trade union movement in the process of worker immigration is thus explained by several interrelated factors. Although it is hardly possible without more focused studies to point out one factor as being more decisive as any other, the following factors:

- the combined effect of a unitary structure and strength;
- the union movement's character of a popular mass movement; and
- direct representation in labour market-related decision-making bodies,

created, taken together, favourable preconditions for the organisation of immigrants.[55]

The 1970s and 1980s: Equal or Special Treatment?

Separate union organisation on ethnic grounds has never been seriously discussed in Sweden. Foreign workers were supposed to join existing unions under equal conditions with Swedish workers. Although equality was initially more an expression of concern for the Swedish than for the foreign workforce, it meant protection against over-exploitation and sub-standard wages and working conditions. Sadly, though, and although the unions insisted in the early decades on the recruitment of qualified workers, they did not prevent employers from placing skilled immigrants in unskilled jobs, and neither have the unions taken any forceful action to help immigrant workers to get away from poor job sectors.[56] A case study at the Volvo car plant in Gothenburg indicates that union representatives and foremen are often carriers of gendered prejudice on the one hand and of different sets of ethnic prejudice on the other. Only Finnish male workers received union support for advancement to better jobs, while immigrant women in general and male workers from Yugoslavia were trapped in monotonous line-work.[57] Though equal treatment at the job has been a union policy, it has only been patchily applied to work practice.

It took until the end of the 1960s before the Trade Union Confederation started to show genuine concern for the social and work situation of immigrants. The LO initiated negotiations with the SAF, which in 1970 led to an agreement, the objective of which was to facilitate the process of adaptation of immigrant workers to Swedish society and working life. Guidelines and recommendations were drawn up on how to integrate them at their place of work, and on the provision of 200 hours of Swedish language training, of which the employer had to pay the first sixty hours. The Metal Workers' Union was the only LO union to object to this provision, considering 200 hours too few. They insisted instead on 240 hours of language training to be entirely paid by the employers.[58] The Metal Workers' Union's viewpoints were taken as guidelines, when the legal right to Swedish language training during paid working hours was codified in the Act of 1973. The legal right to language training worked fairly well in large companies. At smaller workplaces, though, and in times of recession, it was difficult to make employers comply, which finally led to new legislation in 1986. The number of hours for training in basic Swedish increased to 500 hours, with an additional 300 hours for professional Swedish, if needed. Municipalities, instead of the employers, were made financially responsible for offering language training free of charge, and for informing newly arrived immigrants of their rights. For immigrants at work, the new law obliged employers to arrange time off from work after consultations with the municipality and the relevant trade-union local.

The First LO Action Programme

In the early 1970s, the LO had consultative status in all issues related to immigrant policy reforms both at the level of society at large and in the trade-union movement. But it was only at the 1976 LO congress that the decision was taken to concentrate efforts and to formulate a Programme of Action for Migrant Workers. The first Action Programme was published in 1979. It confirms that 'all non-Nordic immigration to Sweden shall be on regulated lines and take place in an organised fashion'. The Programme also recommends that Sweden should pursue an active and generous refugee policy. Concern was expressed for the linguistic, social and cultural situation of both adults and migrant children. The importance of giving children access to knowledge and training in their own language was stressed.[59]

Recommended activities inside the trade unions focused on providing immigrants with information on Swedish working life, on collective bargaining, labour legislation, and other union-related questions. Basic trade-union courses at workplace level, active recruitment to centrally organised courses, and information in the main immigrant languages were seen as the principal vehicles for activating immigrant membership. The LO's Council for Immigrant Workers had been established in the early 1970s. Starting in 1976, the emphasis was on educating elected and other trade-union officials of the immigrant committees, which started to be set up in local sections and at district level. By 1979, out of a total of 232 LO sections, 110 had their own committees or officials for immigrant questions. Some 600 officials were active in these committees. Migrants made up the majority of committee members, in the proportion of 60 per cent immigrants to 40 per cent Swedes.[60]

The organisation of immigrant-related union issues into separate committees, or as the sole responsibility of specially appointed officials, became over time an issue of concern and critical assessment. This model led to the paradoxical situation that immigrant-related issues were integrated into the trade-union programme, at the same time as being organisationally separated from trade-union concerns at large. Elected representatives at local workplace level or appointed officials in the higher echelons felt they had little support from other union people. They felt overwhelmed by having to take on the entire burden of responsibilities. This often implied dealing as much with problems of a more social character as with strictly work or union-related issues:

> People had the need to talk to someone about their problems. As an elected representative one must have time to listen and it is important to give honest answers. The representatives at the workplaces are over-burdened and often do not find time to listen.[61]

Those working with immigrant issues, often immigrants themselves, were simply too few. At union meetings, immigrant-related questions were given low priority on the agenda, since neither responsibility nor knowledge were distributed among all members of the local union board.[62]

Immigrant women in particular felt at a disadvantage in workplaces where elected representatives were male and Swedish. 'What would a guy like that understand of an immigrant woman's difficulties?', or on a more extreme note: 'What does that male mafia care about us?', were comments made. Shop stewards in female-dominated unions were more sensitive to the special needs of immigrants than those in male-dominated unions. At some workplaces the presence of an 'enthusiast' could make all the difference. In other cases attention would depend on the number of immigrants organised in the particular union and, more specifically, on the kind of support given from the central union level to the local branches.[63]

Immigrants' Trade-Union Activity

Efforts to train and activate the immigrant membership has most commonly been conducted in the form of trade-union study circles. Specially produced study materials such as 'You and your union', began to be offered in Finnish and Serbo-Croat, for example, by the Metal Workers' Union in 1976. Study circles were attended by 7,000 of the approximately 67,000 immigrant members during the first year. No information exists for subsequent years, nor is it known whether the studies were followed by more participation in trade-union activities. Information for immigrants began to be published in the union press both in 'easy Swedish' and in the other most commonly present languages.[64] A quarterly journal, *Trade Union News*, dedicated to the immigrant membership, is still published in several languages by the LO and its affiliated unions. In due course labour law texts, other relevant legislation, and trade-union agreements started to be routinely translated. Unfortunately, though, no systematic evaluations exist of the extent to which the rank and file immigrant members have made use of and actually understood the contents and meaning of the translated materials. As my own investigations show, and as has been confirmed to me by trade-union officials, both the organisational structure and the terminology used in trade unions has remained 'a mystery' for many immigrant members, especially those who have had no prior trade union or political experience in their home countries.

Considering the extensive programmes for information, the number of trade-union courses at different levels, and outreach activities, the question of whether Swedish trade unions have made efforts to include immigrants in their activities has to be answered in the affirmative. The politics of inclusion of Swedish trade unions did not stop at making immigrants join. The unions have never put up any barriers or formal limitations to the eligibility of immigrants, naturalised or foreign citizens, to join local union boards or to take leading positions higher up in the union hierarchy. Apart from basic union courses, courses have been offered at different levels and on different subjects (e.g., trade union structure and organisation, industrial relations, the process of negotiation, health and safety, etc.). Courses have been held in the most commonly present languages, like Finnish and Serbo-Croat, or with the assistance of interpreters, to give immigrants competence for union work. A problem is that no systematic records are kept on either the number or national background of immigrants in elected or leading positions at different hierarchical levels. The general impression, conveyed to me by an LO official (March 1994), is that most nationalities, with the exception of Finns, are still badly under-represented.

There has been little research on the extent to which immigrants participate in union activities. A major survey conducted by LO gives an overall picture,[65] but leaves a number of questions unanswered. What does it mean to be active? How is activity measured or operationalised? The LO report, based on the Standard of Living Studies by Statistics Sweden, presents data on different types of activity. Respondents were simply asked, 'Do you participate actively in the activities of the union?' No definition was given of what was meant by the term 'active'. Answers therefore reflect the respondent's subjective view as to the extent and character of being active.

As an overall result for the entire immigrant group under study, general activity rates were found to be 20–25 per cent lower than for Swedes, a difference that was less than expected.[66] Hypothetically this was attributed to the high presence of Finnish immigrants in the LO's ranks and their supposed familiarity with a similar 'trade union culture'. A more detailed picture of activity, based on individual self-assessment, is presented in Table 8.1.

Throughout, immigrant women report the lowest activity rates. Differences in participation rates at meetings which show higher rates in female-dominated unions compared to the male-dominated ones, which I found in my own study, are not reflected in this table.[67] In the data in Table 8.1, Swedish women and immigrant men have almost identical activity rates. Swedish men show the highest rates in all respects. The most important difference is the proportion of elected representatives, which is around twice as high for Swedish men than for either immigrant men or women. The figure confirms the 'Swedishness' and strong male dominance in influential positions, a fact that has also been confirmed in my own studies.[68]

Apart from the fact that unions are traditionally male strongholds, there is no single-factor explanation for the general under-representation of women immigrants. In my study,[69] language difficulties, not least in trade union terminology, and the burden of the double working day came out as the principal reasons for their lower activity rates.

Table 8.1 *Self-assessment of union activity for immigrant and Swedish women and men (%)*

Type of activities	Immigrant women	Immigrant men	Swedish women	Swedish men
Active	8	18	12	21
Elected rep.	7	9	8	16
Course participant	3	5	6	8
At meeting once p.a.	15	14	15	14
More than once p.a.	17	27	26	34
At meeting in last 12 months	32	42	41	48
Never attended a meeting	57	41	41	32

Source: LO 1981.[67] Non-specified activity rates for second-generation immigrants are 15 per cent, for the naturalised 18 per cent, and for foreign citizens 11 per cent, compared to 16 per cent for indigenous Swedes, both sexes combined (Statistics Sweden 1984).

A general reason with regard to all immigrants, male or female, is that it is onerous first to learn Swedish, and then get familiar with trade union structures and organisation, with the formalised procedures of meetings, with the terminology, and the intricate process of negotiation. One more factor mentioned was that it takes longer for immigrants to make themselves known among fellow workers, and so to get a large enough 'constituency' to become elected.[70] A certain competition from Swedes, though not fierce, seems to occur for the more attractive union posts. Hostility or overt discrimination against immigrants aspiring to a position in the union hierarchy were not reported. The question is whether there are more subtle discriminatory mechanisms at work or whether immigrants themselves are unwilling to take on responsible positions. To explain the under-representation of immigrant workers in the union hierarchy clearly more research is needed.

The LO's Policy Programme in the 1990s

Much has changed since labour immigration began after the war. With the exception of some rapidly jettisoned proposals from the employers during the economic boom at the end of the 1980s, a re-opening of the Swedish border for labour immigration has never been considered. For non-Nordic workers, the LO keeps strictly to the principle of regulated immigration. The 'old' worker immigrants are now well established in society, although many still hold low-skill, low-status jobs. Recent data on long-term illness and early retirement confirm the failure, or unwillingness, of trade unions to help create equal chances and conditions at work for their immigrant members. Great numbers of immigrants, especially among the women, who came as worker immigrants, have become worn out in the monotonous and repetitive jobs they have held.[71] Others are being made redundant in the ongoing structural and technological transformation of the industrial sector, or are hit by unemployment in the present economic recession.

During recent years trade-union concerns have changed in important ways. With the inflow of refugees, now mainly from non-European countries, new priorities have emerged. As mentioned earlier, the immigration of refugees is not supposed to be related to the labour market situation and is therefore not a direct trade-union concern. Yet the LO has an important voice in matters related to refugees, and the following points are laid down in the LO Immigration Policy Programme:[72]

- The position and rights of refugees in the labour market should not differ from those of everyone else,

- Everyone in the Swedish labour market must have the same conditions of employment and be covered by the same labour and social security legislation,
- Every effort must be made to shorten waiting periods for asylum seekers,
- For asylum seekers, special jobs outside the ordinary labour market should be tried out to avoid later problems of adjustment to the labour market,
- Their right to work must be given first priority.

Most of these policy points are very much in line with previous policy and attitudes. The one notable change is the 'special jobs' recommendation for asylum seekers, which in earlier periods was seen as unacceptable from a trade-union point of view. Persons without a residence and work permit were not allowed to hold paid employment or compete for jobs. In this context it is important to point out that Sweden, in contrast with other EU member states, has very few undocumented or so-called illegal immigrants, at least up to now.

As to the women, the first LO Policy Programme of 1979 suggested that their position on the labour market should be strengthened, for example through labour market training. In the second Policy Programme, immigrant women are mentioned twice. First, the programme states that access to language training for immigrant women, who for various periods are engaged in unpaid work at home, should be encouraged through outreach activities and the provision of childcare. Secondly, the programme declares that it may sometimes be justified to offer trade union study circles exclusively for immigrant women. To what extent any of this has happened in practice is not known.[73] The answer from a female LO official, responsible for Equality of Opportunity, on what had been done in the interests of immigrant women, was neither enlightening nor uplifting: 'Well, we have been looking at each other saying that we should do something. But somehow there seems never to have been time.'[74]

Since the early 1980s the main motive for foreigners coming to Sweden, apart from family reunion, has been to seek refuge on political and humanitarian grounds. This has also meant a substantial shift in the countries of origin. As an example, let us look at the composition of refugees who received a residence permit in 1990. Only 12 per cent came from Europe, mainly from the East European countries. The largest share, or 41 per cent, came from Asia, mostly from Iran and Iraq, 24 per cent came from Latin America, and 11 per cent from the African continent. From having been white and European, immigration over the last decade has become non-European, bringing in more dark-skinned people. This reflects in the LO Policy Programme.

Contrary to the period of worker immigration, when racism and xenophobia were little discussed in the union movement, these have now become issues of concern.[75] The LO states in its 1991 Programme the responsibility of the union movement as a creator of public opinion:

> The trade union movement [...] has an important and natural task in opposing and combating all forms of racism, hostility to foreigners and discrimination on ethnic, cultural or religious grounds in working life *as well as in society as a whole.*[76]

A manifestation of the LO's new concerns was, for example, the initiative to launch a highly visible public poster campaign against racism. More importantly, the methods of approaching and seeing to the interests of immigrant members have been reconsidered. The earlier model, with immigrant-related issues being treated in separate committees or as the sole responsibility of a specially appointed representative, became more and more problematic. The 'politics of inclusion' in matters of recruitment did not result in a politics of inclusion of their special problems as part of general union concerns. The policy adopted in the new programme emphasises that immigrant issues must be integrated as a natural part of ordinary trade union activities. *All* elected representatives have now to take on the same degree of responsibility for immigrant members as for indigenous Swedish members.

Information and education on immigrant and refugee-related issues are currently included in all union courses and conferences.[77] The ombudsman argued for increasing the educational level and knowledge about immigrants and refugees, rather than using time and money on occasional campaigns to combat racism and xenophobia. An argument used to convince union members that Sweden can afford more immigrants is that the majority who come are adult and already educated (so Sweden has no reproductive costs), and therefore profitable to the country. 'Fear of the foreign' is seen as the principal root of xenophobia, to be countered by higher levels of knowledge. Racism is still not a term easily used in the internal trade union discourse, or as my informant put it, 'There is little racism in the proper sense in Sweden and there are at maximum 500 active racists in the country.' This, of course, is a matter of definition, going beyond the framework of this chapter.

Conclusions

The Swedish trade-union movement adopted, in contrast with the employers and the government, an initially negative and thereafter restrictive attitude towards postwar non-Nordic immigration of labour, whether it was in the form of bilateral agreements or other forms of recruitment. Instead, like women's organisations, the unions were in favour of mobilising domestic labour reserves, not least married women. No steps, however, were taken by the union movement to stop the immigration of non-Nordic labour. By the mid-1960s, with the spontaneous and uncontrolled inflow of great numbers of workers, mainly from Yugoslavia, Greece and Turkey, the trade union movement requested a regulation of non-Nordic immigration. The regulation came into force in 1967 meaning that a job, a work permit, and housing had to be arranged before entering the country. But it was only in 1972 that a circular letter from the Trade Union Confederation (LO) put a definitive stop to labour immigration from outside the Nordic countries.

During the entire postwar period the trade-union movement had opportunities to exert influence on the immigration of labour. Trade-union local branches could approve or disapprove individual applicants; the union centrals had either consultative status to the labour market authorities or direct representation in decision-making bodies. But it was only with the regulation of 1967 that a consistent immigration policy was adopted by the government. This allowed the union movement to view immigration in terms of the labour market situation instead of taking ad hoc decisions from case to case. With the stop to non-Nordic immigration, union-controlled worker immigration quickly fell to 5 per cent annually. It is currently less than 1 per cent per year of total immigration (156 persons in 1993). According to the 1954 agreement on a common Nordic labour market, only Nordic citizens have the right to free movement for work and settlement.[78]

The trade-union movement insisted from the very beginning on equal wages and employment conditions for foreign workers, principally to avoid wage-pressure. With regard to union membership, an organisation clause was included in the first bilateral agreements with Italy and Hungary (1947), which in 1965 was replaced by an agreement signed by the LO and the SAF making employers responsible for recommending foreign workers to join the union. The organisation of immigrants has not been problematic. It seems to have been taken for granted and sometimes understood as a prerequisite to getting a job. Both female and male immigrants are unionised to the same degree as Swedish workers, with the exception of occupational sectors where union density is generally low, such as hotel and catering, and building maintenance, especially for those in cleaning work.

Information in the union press in different languages, specially designed study circles, and the translation of labour law and industrial relations agreements as well as other relevant texts have all been made available at least since the 1970s. But in the absence of recent studies or evaluations there is little to show the results of the variety of trade-union efforts to activate their immigrant membership. Figures reported by the LO in the early 1980s, and recent information by an LO official, confirm that very few immigrants participate actively in trade-union matters. Attendance at meetings has been generally low, but better in female-dominated than in male-dominated unions. Those data show that the proportion of elected union representatives was low in the early 1980s. At present no information exists on numbers or proportions of elected representatives with an immigrant background.[79]

Towards the end of the 1960s, the LO and especially the Metal Workers' Union started to show concern for the social situation of foreign workers. This resulted in 1970 in the first agreement with the SAF to offer language training, information on Swedish society and introduction at the workplace. The 1973 Act, giving the right to 240 hours of Swedish language training during paid working hours, can be attributed to demands put forward by the Metal Workers' Union.

The LO's first Programme of Action for Migrant Workers was published in 1979, giving attention to the situation of immigrants in society at large, including the right to training in their own language for immigrant children, trade-union information, and education. The second LO Immigration Policy Programme, published in 1991, puts more emphasis on combating xenophobia and racism both at workplace level and in society at large. The shift of emphasis derives from the fact that immigration since the early 1980s has consisted mainly of refugees from countries outside Europe, also implying a changing ethnic composition of people from white and European to black and non-European.

Trade-union policies have reflected an egalitarian and progressive attitude towards the immigrant membership. But what has been done to strengthen the position of immigrants in the union movement and at workplace level, and how much has stayed at the level of declarations? Far too little information exists on immigrants' position in the union movement to give more than a fragmented picture, which, if anything, indicates that immigrants are under-represented in influential positions. As to their situation in working life, the persistent marginalisation of immigrant workers, especially of women, to the least valued tasks in the job hierarchy shows that unions have failed or not exerted enough effort to achieve equality in matters of employment, with the notable exception of wages. As union members, immigrant workers have been paid unionised wages, they have been covered by unemployment benefits, and by insurance against accidents and illness. In the present economic recession, accompanied by cutbacks due to structural and technological change, union membership is no longer a shelter against redundancy, as the rapidly increasing unemployment figures indicate. The Swedish trade-union movement's powerful position in the institutional structure of decision-making during the period of worker immigration, and the politics of including foreign workers as members of the unions has been important in so far as it has protected them from undue exploitation, but it has not helped them to better positions in the hierarchy of working life, or to influential posts in the trade unions.

NOTES

1. Prot. I:24:2, *Parliamentary Discussion on Measures to Transfer Foreign Labour etc.*, 23 March 1947.
2. G. Kyle, *Gästarbeterska i manssamhället*, Stockholm, 1979.
3. G. Ahlberg and I. Svennilson, *Sveriges Arbetskraft och den Industriella utvecklingen*, Stockholm, 1946.
4. Prot. I:24:2, 69; SOU, *Invandrarna och minoriteterna*, Stockholm, 1974, 69.
5. SOU, *Invandrarna och minoriteterna*, 69.
6. J. Nelhans, *Utlänningen på arbetsmarknaden*, Lund, 1973, 139–40.
7. Before 1977, seven years of settlement (five for Nordic citizens) were required before becoming a Swedish citizen. Since then, any person aged eighteen, who has been settled for five years (two for Nordic citizens) and has no serious criminal record, can become a Swedish citizen. In 1992, more than 50 per cent of all immigrants and refugees were naturalised Swedes.
8. SOU, *Invandringen*, 1967, 18.
9. Simultaneously with immigration, Sweden saw a return movement of people back to their home countries. The net surplus of immigrants in the 1950s stayed at 106,000, compared to 134,000 in the 1940s (J. Widgren, *Svensk invandrarpolitik*, Lund, 1980, 13.)
10. The main problem seems to have been friction between Swedish workers and non-unionised foreign workers.
11. Nelhans, *Utlänningen på arbetsmarknaden*, 139–40.
12. Kyle, *Gästarbeterska i manssamhället*, 212.
13. Öberg, oral communication, March 1994.
14. T. Hammar, 'Mellan rasism och reglering: Invandringspolitikens ideologi och historia', *Arbetarhistoria* 12, no. 46 (1988): 11–14.
15. Ahlberg and Svennilson, *Sveriges Arbetskraft och den Industriella utvecklingen.*
16. SOU, *Invandrarna och minoriteterna*, 69.
17. W. Knocke, *Invandrade kvinnor i lönearbete och fack*, Stockholm, 1986.
18. SOU, *Invandrarna och minoriteterna*, 69.
19. Prot. II:37:92, *Parliamentary Discussion on the Immigration of Foreign Labour*, 9 December 1966.
20. SOU, *Kvinnors Arbete: En rapport från Jämställdhetskommittén*, Stockholm, 1979, 89.
21. A. Ålund, 'The Power of Definitions: Immigrant Women and Problem-Centered Ideologies', *Migration*, no. 4 (1989): 37–55.
22. W. Knocke, 'Women Immigrants: What is the "Problem"?', *Economic and Industrial Democracy* 12, no. 4 (1991): 469–86.
23. Nelhans, *Utlänningen på arbetsmarknaden*, 186.

24. G. Ahrne and W. Clement, 'A New Regime?: Class Representation within the Swedish State', in W. Clement and R. Mahon (eds), *Swedish Social Democracy: A Model in Transition*, Toronto, 1994.
25. C. Kellberg and A. Hadjoudes, *Vi sålde våra liv*, Stockholm, 1978, 65.
26. E. Wadensjö, *Immigration och samhällsekonomi*, Lund, 1973.
27. An example is the Metal Workers' Union, which between October 1961 and October 1962 refused 236 applications out of 1,250, due to the low skill-levels of the applicants or the availability of Swedish workers (K. Beckholmen, *Två årtionden 1956–1976*, Stockholm, 1978, 206); Nelhans, *Utlänningen på arbetsmarknaden*, 169–70.
28. SOU, *Invandringen*, 18; Widgren, *Svensk invandrarpolitik*, 14.
29. The agreement with Turkey never meant very much in practice, due to a recession in 1967– 68. The recruitment office established by the Labour Market Board in Turkey was soon redundant, and recruitment through this office only ever amounted to 331 persons (S. Alpay, *Turkar i Stockholm*, Stockholm, 1980, 81, 101).
30. Nelhans, *Utlänningen på arbetsmarknaden*, 140.
31. G. Kyle, *Gästarbeterska i manssamhället*, Stockholm, 1979, 214.
32. Y. Hirdman, *The Swedish Welfare State and the Gender System: A Theoretical and Empirical Sketch*, Uppsala, 1987; R. Mahon, '"Modern Times" Are No Longer Modern': Swedish Unions Confront the Double Shift. Paper presented at the ninth Conference of Europeanists, Chicago, March/April 1994.
33. U. Olsson, 'Planning the Swedish Welfare State', in W. Clement and R. Mahon (eds), *Swedish Social Democracy: A Model in Transition*, Toronto, 1994.
34. T. Hammar, 'Mellan rasism och reglering: Invandringspolitikens ideologi och historia', *Arbetarhistoria* 12, no. 46 (1988): 11–14; translation WK.
35. The war in the former Yugoslavia changed these proportions, in that residence permits for refugees in 1994–95 were more than 60 per cent in the year and around 35 per cent for family reunion.
36. T. Hammar, 'Mellan rasism och reglering: Invandringspolitikens ideologi och historia', 11– 14.
37. Nelhans, *Utlänningen på arbetsmarknaden*, 173; translation WK.
38. Ibid., 143; Prot. I:24:2.
39. Knocke, *Invandrade kvinnor i lönearbete och fack.*
40. Ibid.
41. Ibid.
42. Apart from the LO, Sweden has two other trade union centrals, one for white-collar employees (TCO) and one organising professionals (SACO); W. Clement and R. Mahon, 'Swedish and Canadian Perspectives on the Swedish Model', in W. Clement and R. Mahon (eds), *Swedish Social Democracy: A Model in Transition*, Toronto, 1994.
43. W. Knocke, *Invandrare möter facket*, Stockholm, 1982; Knocke, *Invandrade kvinnor i lönearbete och fack.*
44. LO, *Vem är aktiv i facket?*, Stockholm, 1981.
45. This indicates that immigrants are over-represented in blue-collar jobs, since their share of the total workforce is slightly above 5 per cent for foreign nationals and around 9 per cent for all with an immigrant background.
46. LO, *Migrant Workers and the Trade Union Movement: LO's Programme of Action for Migrant Workers*, Stockholm, 1979, 31; Knocke, *Invandrare möter facket.*
47. S. Alpay, *Turkar i Stockholm.*
48. T.-L. Leiniö, *Städarnas arbetssituation*, Stockholm, 1980.
49. Apart from the Turks, Greek immigrants have also experienced low degrees of union organisation, because almost half of both sexes work in the service sector, principally in cleaning jobs.

50. Immigrants made up 11.3 per cent of all members in 1981 in the Factory Workers' Union, approximately 70 per cent male and 30 per cent female. Of all women in this union, immigrant women made up 15 per cent, which means they were over-represented in this sector compared to immigrant women's share of slightly over 5 per cent of the total labour force (Knocke, *Invandrare kvinnor möter facket: Förstudie och projektplan)*.
51. Beckholmen, *Två årtionden 1956–1976*, Stockholm, 1978, 207.
52. This would hardly be an answer to be expected today, when economic recession and structural change have made unemployment grow to 20.8 per cent among immigrants, as compared to 8.2 per cent for the total workforce (in 1993); Knocke, *Invandrade kvinnor i lönearbete och fack.*
53. B. Schmitter, 'Trade Unions and Immigration Politics in West Germany and Switzerland'. *Politics and Society* 10, no. 3 (1981): 317–34.
54. ILO, *Trade Union Activities of Foreign and Migrant Workers in the Member States of the Council of Europe*, Geneva, 1976.
55. Among the individual unions, the Metal Workers' Union has beyond any doubt been the most influential one.
56. See e.g., Knocke, *Invandrade kvinnor i lönearbete och fack*; C.-U. Schierup and S. Paulson (eds), *Arbetets etniska delning: Studier från en svensk bilfabrik*, Stockholm, 1994.
57. W. Knocke, 'Gender, Ethnicity and Technological Change', *Economic and Industrial Democracy* 15, no. 1 (1994): 11–34; C.-U. Schierup and S. Paulson (eds), *Arbetets etniska delning: Studier från en svensk bilfabrik*, Stockholm, 1994.
58. Nelhans, *Utlänningen på arbetsmarknaden*, 90–91.
59. The legal reform of 1977 entitled children to two hours a week of teaching and tutoring in the language spoken in their home.
60. LO, *Migrant Workers and the Trade Union Movement: LO's Programme of Action for Migrant Workers*, Stockholm, 1979.
61. Local shop steward, in Knocke, *Invandrare möter facket*, 93.
62. Ibid.; Knocke, *Invandrade kvinnor i lönearbete och fack.*
63. Knocke, *Invandrare möter facket*; Knocke, W. *Invandrade kvinnor i lönearbete och fack.*
64. K. Neuhold, *Invandrarna och facket*, Stockholm, 1976.
65. LO, *Vem är aktiv i facket?*
66. Ibid., 33.
67. 80 per cent of the women interviewed in the male-dominated Factory Workers' Union had never attended a union meeting. The corresponding figure for women in the Municipal Workers' Union was 58 per cent (Knocke, *Invandrade kvinnor i lönearbete och fack)*.
68. Knocke, *Invandrare möter facket*; Knocke, W. *Invandrade kvinnor i lönearbete och fack.*
69. Ibid.
70. At one workplace of the Factory Workers' Union, immigrant workers had united to register their discontent with the low priority of their concerns by voting down the chair of the board in the local elections.
71. SIV, *Kvinna och invandrare*, Norrköping, 1992.
72. LO, *The LO Immigration Policy Programme*, Stockholm, 1991.
73. In 1988, on behalf of the Municipal Workers' Union, I produced a study package specially dedicated for courses for women (Knocke, *Våra nya systrar: Invandrade kvinnor i lönearbete och fack)*. Despite many contacts in this union, I never managed to get information on the extent to which study circles had actually taken place.
74. Oral communication, Spring 1994.

75. Racialisation of certain groups, however, is an old phenomenon in popular talk, as shown by the term *blackskull*, which has been used for white persons with dark hair, principally Southern Europeans.
76. Emphasis added; LO, *The LO Immigration Policy Programme*, 17.
77. LO ombudsman; oral communication, March 1994.
78. In 1992 the number of Nordic citizens emigrating from Sweden (8,966) was higher than the number who immigrated (6,403). In 1980 Nordic immigration was 47 per cent of total immigration, but in 1991 only 18 per cent.
79. W. Knocke, *Invandrade kvinnor i lönearbete och fack*, Stockholm, 1986. Oral communication, March 1994.

Chapter 9

Conclusion

Rinus Penninx and Judith Roosblad

In the Introduction (Chapter 1) we specified the questions to be answered, and the steps we would take in order to reach conclusions. As the first of those steps we shall answer the question of how trade unions have faced the three basic dilemmas identified, and what variance of reaction trade unions have shown. In the second section we will turn to the question of how to account for the different attitudes adopted by trade unions in various countries and periods. In doing so we will start from the four sets of potentially relevant factors outlined in the last section of the Introduction. Finally, we shall tentatively try to answer the general question of whether there has been any convergence in the attitudes and actions of trade unions towards immigration, immigrants, and minorities in the period since the Second World War?

It is no accident that we use the word 'tentatively'. The nature of this comparative research is an ex-post comparison and analysis. As was explained in the Introduction, we have developed a common framework before starting, but too rigid an application of the grid derived from that framework would result in the neglect of the special characteristics and contexts in the different countries. The country reports preceding this final chapter are on the one hand rich and inspiring; on the other hand they cannot always cover all the topics in the same detail over a long period in a few pages. That makes comparative analysis more difficult, and a certain degree of interpretation of data is necessary. The consequence is that we are able to formulate relatively clear conclusions in the first descriptive section, but that our conclusions in the second comparative section are more cautious. In many instances they should be read as well-founded hypotheses for further research, rather than as solid conclusions. The same holds for the final conclusions on parallelism and convergence.

Historical Continuity or Discontinuity?

Before describing the variance in the stances adopted by trade unions, it is appropriate to offer a preliminary comment on the question of the historical continuity or discontinuity of immigration in various countries. In some countries the issue of recruiting or admitting labour migrants after the Second World War was experienced as a new phenomenon, while in other countries there had been a long tradition of labour immigration before the war. It transpires from the country accounts that this made for quite variable reactions on the part of trade unions.

Switzerland and France on the one hand are clear cases in which labour immigration after the war was a resumption of an existing prewar phenomenon:[1] 'it seemed almost natural for Switzerland to reinitiate the recruitment of foreign workers', as Schmitter Heisler expresses it in her essay. In general the old existing prewar institutional framework was reinstated. In the case of Switzerland the postwar system seemed to emphasise even more than before the war the ability to control this foreign workforce, having learned the lessons of the Great Depression before the Second World War. Migrants were systematically termed *Fremdarbeiter*, and the system of residence and work permits aimed at keeping them in this special position. In the case of France as well, where immigration had long performed a double function in labour market and demographic terms, postwar immigration was initially resumed on much the same basis as before the war. The newcomers, however, were seen as *immigrés*, and the office that was supposed to regulate these matters went by the name of the National Office of Immigration. These two cases lead to two conclusions: first, in both cases there was no fundamental new dilemma for trade unions, compared to other countries. Secondly, the form the policies took showed great historical continuity within the respective countries, while at the same time the two countries were very different from each other.

In the cases of Austria, the Netherlands and the Federal Republic of Germany, in contrast, the phenomenon of labour immigration was new. Admittedly, all these countries had known significant labour immigration in the past,[2] but such episodes had been followed by too long a period of discontinuity to be relevant to the new situation.[3] In all three cases the institutionalisation of the immigration of labour entailed a much more explicit process of bargaining between the social partners, and of stipulating the aims and means of implementing such policies. The form it took initially was inspired by the Swiss model of temporary employment. The term 'guest workers' was coined in all three countries, expressing the intended temporary nature both of the migrants' stay and of the phenomenon as a whole.

The Swedish case seems to take an intermediate position. On the one hand Sweden was used to participating in a significant exchange of labour between the Nordic countries, with an especially substantial import of Finns into Sweden. This practice of exchange was formalised quite early in the agreement on a common Nordic labour market – a zone of free exchange of labour – in 1954. And in fact Finnish labour immigration turned out to be by far the most important movement throughout the 1960s and early 1970s. Recruitment from outside the Nordic Common Market, however, was perceived as something of a different nature, which required a new stipulation of the rules and a laying down of new procedures, just as in Austria, the Federal Republic of Germany and the Netherlands. In the way this was done, however, it transpires that the experience of the dominant Finnish labour immigration set the rules: a strong accent on equal rights from the beginning, and much less emphasis on the temporary nature. *Invandrare* (immigrants) soon became the dominant term, replacing the initial concept of 'foreign workers'. 'Guest workers' never entered the Swedish terminology.

The case of the United Kingdom is special, in the sense that the immigration dilemma was not formulated as labour immigration in particular. Apart from a short episode immediately after the Second World War (see Wrench's contribution), the issue of immigration as a consequence of decolonisation and the topics of labour shortage and labour immigration have merged in the United Kingdom in such a way that they have been tightly interwoven. The first aspect, of immigration as a consequence of decolonisation, however, has been dominant in the debate on immigration policies: labour market aspects have for the most part remained implicit. Trade unions were not directly involved in decision-making on such policies. There are two major consequences that make the United Kingdom case different from the others. First, the immigrants concerned were United Kingdom citizens, not aliens, and there was no perception of a temporary labour migration system. Instead the dominant political struggle was on how to curb New Commonwealth immigration. Secondly, the ex-colonial origin of most of the immigrants made for another specific United Kingdom feature: the dominant discourse on race and racial relations. It is interesting to note that ex-colonial immigration also took place in France and the Netherlands. In both these cases, however, the discourse on labour immigration was more dominant than the ex-colonial one. In the case of the Netherlands there was considerable immigration from Indonesia (the former Dutch East Indies) between 1945 and 1962, and from Suriname and the Netherlands Antilles between 1970 and 1980. But until the end of the 1970s this was regarded as a category different from 'guest workers' (see Roosblad's contribution, Chapter 5).

What is the significance of these historical differences? Although the dilemmas remain important, it becomes clear that the context in which they were manifested, and thus the involvement of trade unions, was quite different, particularly in relation to the labour immigration dilemma. Where labour migration after the Second World War was in fact an enlargement or continuation of previous labour migrations, the experience of trade unions with these earlier migrations, and the way they defined and perceived it, largely determined the stances they took, with little further discussion. Where immigration was the consequence of ex-colonial and political relations (and not seen as labour migration), the potential involvement of trade unions in decision-making and policies was different, or at least perceived as such. When labour immigration was essentially new, the dilemma manifested itself fully, and an explicit stance was taken.

Answers to the Three Basic Dilemmas of Trade Unions

The core of the descriptive instrument elaborated in the Introduction consists of three basic dilemmas faced by trade unions. The first relates to immigration itself: should trade unions cooperate with employers and the authorities in the employment of foreign workers, or should they resist it? The second dilemma emerges as soon as foreign workers appear: should trade unions include them fully in their ranks, or exclude them as a special category? If trade unions in principle followed a line of inclusion, they were confronted with a third dilemma: should they advocate and implement special measures for the immigrants, or should they insist on the general, equal treatment of all workers? In this section we take the responses of the unions to these dilemmas as a starting point for comparative description. What variance can we identify in the reactions of trade unions in the various countries?

Immigration: Resistance or Cooperation?

A typology of reactions in the early phases of labour migration

On the level of arguments offered by trade unions in different countries there is a considerable degree of consensus: trade unions are worried everywhere about the possible consequences of labour immigration for existing national bargaining and power structures in the socio-economic domain. In that sense it is clear that, although trade unions may commit themselves verbally in varying degrees to the international solidarity of all workers, the dominant frame of reference is that of the nation state and the national arena. We should add that in this period of Cold War, initiatives that tried to organise international solidarity were strongly associated with the Communist movement, and therefore suspect. The reconstruction projects after the Second World War in the various countries reinforced that dominantly national framework, and at the same time excluded Communist trade unions from it. The structures for consensus decision-making in the socio-economic domain which were installed, reinstalled or continued in most of the countries after the war (the Netherlands, Sweden, the Federal Republic of Germany, Austria, the United Kingdom, and in a particular form also in Switzerland) demanded national solidarity of all: workers, employers, the self-employed and the state.

The relative consensus on the level of arguments has nevertheless led to differing outcomes in terms of reactions. We can distinguish a number of different types of reactions on the part of trade unions in relation to the dilemma of whether to cooperate or resist. A first type of reaction we can term cooperation from a position of strength. The initial reaction of unions in Sweden, the Federal Republic of Germany and the Netherlands can be characterised as such. In all three cases unions are substantially involved in socio-economic decision-making and policy formulation. These unions have reformulated their hesitations on the argumentative level: if we cooperate in importing labour, it should be done in such a way that labour relations and bargaining positions will not be jeopardised. Common ways and means to minimise these perceived dangers are as follows:

1. direct control of the recruitment procedure, including a right of veto for trade unions;
2. demands for equal wages and working conditions, and equal industrial rights in general;
3. demands for special provisions (for housing, travel expenses, language courses, etc.) to be provided at the cost of the employer.

In the case of the Federal Republic of Germany and the Netherlands, but less so in Sweden, unions also tried to make provisions to ensure the temporary nature of employment and the possibility of reducing the imported labour force, when appropriate.

Consequently, the reactions of trade unions in these countries to growing 'spontaneous' labour immigration in the 1960s and to the brief economic crisis of 1966–67 were quite uniform: control of inflow and regulation should be guaranteed within a monopoly system, which leaves recruitment open, to be 'agreed upon demand'.[4] Trade unions were part of that system and had a say in the decision-making concerning demand.

A second type of reaction may be called resistance from a position of strength, exemplified by the Austrian case. Throughout the postwar period, Austrian trade unions have practised a policy of what Gächter calls 'protecting indigenous workers from immigrants'. By using their strong position in economic decision-making and their intimate relations with political parties in government, trade unions have opposed any significant inflow by keeping yearly quotas as low as possible, and by defining immigrant labour as a special, temporary category that should not enjoy equal rights in a number of aspects. Although they could not prevent labour immigration completely, this can hardly be called the result of cooperation; unions were simply not able to prevent it completely. But they were able to keep immigration defined as temporary, which compensated for the fact that they could not prevent some arrivals.

The Swiss case, at least in the initial phase, illustrates a third type, that of resistance from a position of weakness. As Schmitter Heisler explains, the structure of Swiss trade unions is fragmented and decentralised. In principle unions are part of a corporatist system of socio-economic decision-making, but in contrast to Austria, their influence is small. They also lack direct lines of influence with political parties in government. Their attitude was one of anti-immigration and restriction.

The situation in France in the immediate postwar period manifests yet another variant, resistance on the part of unions as an opposition movement. As in Switzerland, unions in France were divided, but unlike all other cases mentioned above, French unions were never made part of a system of socio-economic decision-making in any significant way. Politicians and employers in fact practised a rather open policy, by avoiding strict regulation and using lenient regularisation after spontaneous immigration. Not being really involved, unions were free to criticise such policies. The participation of unions on the board of the National Office of Immigration (ONI) seems to have been more of a symbolic engagement: for the trade unions it reflected their intention of creating a planned immigration with guaranteed equal rights, but the ONI soon appeared to be a rather uninfluential body.

The immigration dilemma in the United Kingdom manifested itself in a fundamentally different way from the foregoing cases. Because of the different nature of predominantly colonial and ex-colonial immigration in the United Kingdom, British trade unions had no direct involvement in decision-making relating to immigration policies. But on the level of arguments there was a difference too: trade unions were initially relatively sympathetic to migrants from the ex-colonies, but later, at the end of the 1960s and in the early 1970s, they supported the immigration legislation of both the Conservative and Labour governments which meant that non-white Commonwealth citizens could be kept out, while leaving open the possibility for white colonial citizens to 'return' to Britain. According to Wrench the legitimation of this process was not framed in the classic labour market arguments mentioned above, but predominantly in social terms: 'immigrants failed to integrate properly'.

Later Phases of Labour and Other Immigration: After 1973

Economic circumstances in northwest European countries changed drastically in the early 1970s. National economies had gradually lost their relative autonomy and had become, much more than before, part of worldwide economic processes. Capital and goods could move much more easily than before, as could labour within certain limited areas like the Common Nordic Market and the European Economic Community. A new international division of labour and a restructuring of the economies in the developed countries of Western Europe took shape. Labour-intensive industries were relocated in low-income countries or completely restructured and automated. Capital-intensive, highly productive processes demanded better educated but fewer workers. The first oil crisis of 1973 accelerated these already existing processes and became a turning point. Full employment, an ideal of many governments and trade unions in the 1960s, became an illusion:[5] economic growth, high productivity and profits coexisted from then on with the structural unemployment of part of the working population.

But major changes had also gradually taken place in society at large. The national projects of reconstruction after the war had been so successful that welfare states had developed which implied (among other things) minimum standards for all within the state's territory, rights and facilities for individuals, social security systems procured by the state, and so on. Such developments had particular consequences for the state. On the one hand it was increasingly unable to steer economic developments within the national framework; on the other hand it was dependent on continued economic growth to be able to finance the new facilities of the welfare state. In the changing labour market conditions after 1973, they could try to keep the number of immigrants likely to be dependent on that welfare state as low as possible, which meant restrictive but selective immigration policies.[6]

Viewed in this way, the alliance between governments and trade unions in favour of restrictive immigration policies since the mid-1970s seems to be a natural one. This is particularly true for new labour immigration. As far as we can derive from the preceding chapters, none of the trade unions in the various countries has opposed restrictive policies relating to such new labour migration; many of them have actively endorsed them.

But at the same time this alliance was partial and relative: in those cases where trade unions held the view that legally resident, established immigrants should be incorporated as equals in society,[7] they felt obliged to defend what they saw as their 'acquired rights': protection against deportation in case of unemployment, resistance against involuntary return migration programmes, defence of the right to bring in family and spouse, and equal rights for these new immigrants after arrival, including the right to work. In the Swedish case there is little disagreement between the authorities and the unions in this respect, which is underlined by an absence of stress on the temporary nature of foreigners' labour, and by the early introduction in the 1970s of a general integration policy by the government. In the Netherlands, and more clearly still in the Federal Republic of Germany, however, such topics have often led unions to join other forces in favour of immigrants, in defending such rights or preventing the curtailing of them. Somewhat later, but starting from a rather different position, Swiss trade unions have also endorsed several initiatives to improve the legal position of foreign workers and to facilitate their integration. French trade unions did the same, after it had become clear that most of the immigrants whose stay in France was originally thought to be temporary had actually become established in the country.

In regard to such discussions, the positions adopted by the trade unions in the various countries was largely similar: unlike the direct involvement of many trade unions in recruitment and labour immigration, there was no direct involvement in decision-making on such integration policies. Trade unions have acted in these matters as a partner in or part of a social movement trying to influence the larger political process.

What actually seems to be happening here is that the second dilemma (inclusion versus exclusion) is intervening in the first one. If trade unions ultimately decide to include immigrants in their organisations, they may also feel obliged to defend the immigration rights of their dependents. The exceptional Austrian case makes that clear: the consistent definition of labour immigration as a temporary phenomenon (embodied in the quota system), the fact that migrant workers were always supposed to be sent back 'at the end of their usefulness',[8] and the exclusion of these workers from essential parts of the security system has prevented them from building up any 'acquired rights' which are recognised and endorsed by the unions in that country.

The material on the attitudes of trade unions in relation to refugee and asylum migration is unfortunately partial and uneven. This is probably a direct consequence of the fact that such movements have been unevenly distributed over the countries studied.[9] The political discussion and activity in this regard is related, as a general rule, to the absolute and relative numbers in the country concerned.[10] Again, trade unions often feel obliged to take positions on the subject. To oppose, wholly or partially, categoric restrictive measures, as the Swiss unions did in the case of four referendum initiatives, and some of the German unions did when politicians were changing the German constitutional law in order to make more restrictive policies possible, is one side of union reactions. But it is not the whole story. Ambivalence seems a more common attitude, when it comes to concrete action. More systematic research, however, is needed to support or reject this impression.

The same holds true for the material on attitudes towards 'illegal' or undocumented workers. It transpires that trade unions which have been closely involved in decision-making on labour immigration in an earlier phase regard their endorsement of more comprehensive measures to combat illegal work and residence as a logical consequence. Furthermore, they are institutionally committed. On the other hand, those unions that were not involved, and act in an oppositional role, are much more free to criticise such repressive measures and defend illegal migrants. The French unions are a case in point.[11]

The Inclusion-versus-Exclusion Dilemma

Do trade unions define, in principle, labour migrants as part of the group which they are supposed to represent, and do they in practice welcome and accept these workers as equals? In general, on the formal ideological level, legally resident immigrant workers are regarded as workers who should in principle be included and be organised. Even in the Austrian case, in which labour migrants are kept in special, separate positions, unions are open for the membership of legally resident foreign workers. The ideological base line is thus inclusion, whatever stand was taken regarding the first dilemma.

The evidence in the various chapters, however, suggests that we should make distinctions as to the degree to which inclusionist policies are practised. We shall look at three issues which may shed some light on such differences in practice: membership in general, equality in industrial and social rights, and the behaviour of unions in critical situations such as strikes and other work-related conflicts.

It seems logical that the membership density of migrant workers should be an important indicator of inclusion. The contributions in this collection, however, suggest that such a thesis is misleading.

First, the membership density of West European unions varies immensely from country to country, irrespective of immigrants. Visser and Ebbinghaus give the following membership density for the seven countries studied in 1990:[12] Sweden shows by far the highest score with 82.5 per cent, followed by Austria (46.2), Great Britain (39.1), Germany (32.9), Switzerland (26.7), the Netherlands (25.5), and France (10.8). Trends in the development of membership in the course of time are also different. There has been a clear increase in membership within the Nordic countries, but also in Belgium and Ireland. In all other countries a significant decline in membership has taken place during the last two decades.

In their comparative analysis, Visser and Ebbinghaus try to find an explanation both for the differences themselves, and for the divergent trends in development. Their conclusion is that structural and conjunctural changes in the period since 1975 have significantly limited the opportunities for trade unions to achieve collective results and increase membership. In all countries a less union-friendly climate has grown up, according to these authors. In this climate it is the institutional position of the unions that is decisive for the extent to which they are able to resist the increased pressure.[13] The most important elements of this institutional position, or embeddedness, are, firstly, the presence of unemployment funds directly related to unions; secondly, their regulated access in the workplace; thirdly, the incorporation of unions in structures of socio-economic decision-making; and fourthly, obligatory membership.[14]

This analysis of general differences seems also to fit for the differences in membership levels of immigrants. In the absence of registration and sometimes with an explicit refusal on the part of unions to register separately, the data on membership of immigrants are not always clear. Nevertheless, the general tendency seems to indicate that membership of immigrants does not deviate significantly from the average in the country concerned. As expected, we find high membership in Sweden, but surprisingly in Austria as well, notwithstanding the entirely different attitudes of unions in relation to immigration and immigrants. Membership of immigrants in the Federal Republic of Germany, the Netherlands, and Switzerland has grown in the course of time, but varies considerably between unions. The recent general membership in the Federal Republic of Germany is comparable to indigenous organisation density, while it seems lower in the latter two countries. In the United Kingdom, membership of immigrants is reported to be somewhat higher than average. The French case is not very clear, but here too, membership levels for immigrants do not seem to differ significantly from those of general membership. The degree of organisation of immigrants therefore seems determined much more by structural factors concerning the functioning and embedding of trade unions than by any specific characteristics of the immigrants themselves. The way these structural factors may work is illustrated by Knocke for the Swedish case, where she suggests that the high membership rate in Sweden is due to the fact that unions had included in the recruitment procedure an obligation for employers to ask migrant workers to become members of a union. According to Knocke these migrant workers did so in most cases because they thought that it was the way things had to be done in the new country.

So membership, although indicating the formal openness of unions, cannot necessarily be taken as an indicator of inclusionist policies. There may be first class (indigenous) members and second rank immigrant members. A second indicator, that of equal social and industrial rights, may give us a better idea of inclusion or exclusion.

The extent to which equal industrial and social rights for immigrant workers were guaranteed and defended by unions turns out to be directly related to the logic of how the first dilemma was handled. Austrian trade unions, as explained by Gächter, have manifested their 'resistance from a position of strength' not only in efforts to keep quotas as low as possible, but also in regulations which have put immigrant workers in a weak position when compared to indigenous ones: immigrants could be forced to leave the country once they had difficulties finding employment, immigrants had to be laid off before Austrian workers (in theory), there was unequal access (but equal contributions) to unemployment benefits, no access to works councils, and so on. In the Austrian case the difference between formal and material inclusion becomes clear, particularly when we add the fact that immigrants were excluded from any positions in the unions themselves as long as they were not naturalised Austrian citizens. Although there are signs of gradual change in the Austrian unions' position on these points, the overriding picture is still one of material exclusion.

The position of Swiss trade unions in the early phase of the Swiss *Fremdarbeiterpolitik* very much resembles the Austrian case, with one difference: it was not so much the unions which bargained for such a system, but rather the state that instituted it. Unions were simply required to agree. Being much less involved in that system probably made it easier for at least part of the fragmented union movement in Switzerland to give up their ambivalent and lukewarm position in the 1980s and 1990s, and follow a line of inclusion by campaigning in favour of immigrants and their industrial, social, and residential rights.

This movement of unions away from the original 'guest-worker ideology', with its implicit inequality for migrant workers, took place earlier in the Federal Republic of Germany and the Netherlands. The starting point for those countries was also somewhat different: in their agreements on recruitment, the unions in those countries had in principle already guaranteed equal industrial rights: the ones directly related to the workplace. Inequalities manifested themselves more in social rights, such as access to state-controlled unemployment and social assistance benefits, and the related rights of residence. The more unions became convinced that most of the immigrants would be staying for an extended period or permanently, the more they became aware of these inequalities and took action in favour of immigrants. The coalitions in which they had to campaign for such rights differed: unions in the Federal Republic of Germany had to oppose government policies which insisted on the temporary presence of migrant labour and tried to foster that; Dutch unions, particularly after the launch of the government's policies on minorities in the early 1980s, were obliged to examine their own internal ambivalence on minorities.

The Swedish case seems to have been different from the beginning: the initial idea of the temporary nature of recruited migrant labour was soon replaced by the right to permanent settlement for all migrant workers and their families. The same holds true for the United Kingdom, but for different reasons: the migrants there were citizens with formally equal rights in all spheres from the moment of their arrival. The French case is ambivalent in various respects: policy relating to immigration and the position of immigrants was a matter for government, with insignificant direct involvement on the part of the unions; historically it was an immigration policy, implemented in a decentralised *laissez-faire* manner. This does not mean, however, that equality of rights was the rule, especially for first-generation non-naturalised immigrants, or for those from non-European countries of origin. Although unions have defended equality on an ideological level, they have experienced quite some difficulty in putting it into practice.

A third important indicator of inclusion is to be found in critical situations such as industrial action and strikes. It is in such circumstances that it becomes clear whether unions really regard immigrants as equal members. There are two crucial questions: do unions try to engage immigrants in industrial disputes of a general nature, and mobilise them? And do trade unions back up immigrants in those conflicts which primarily concern the specific problems experienced by immigrants?

As to the first question, the United Kingdom case seems to show a clear participation by black or ethnic minority workers in general labour disputes and conflicts. Wrench attributes this to the fact that most of these workers were already used to organising themselves in the colonies. Unfortunately we have little material on this point from other countries. Only in the Dutch case it is suggested that trade unions, at least until the mid-1970s, tended to forget to inform and organise their immigrant members in general conflicts; this could have been a consequence of the assumption of the temporary position of these workers and the implicit exclusion that followed from that idea.

As to the second question – conflicts concerning the specific problems of immigrants – the material from the United Kingdom and France is rich in this respect. The United Kingdom case suggests that trade unions there moved from an outright racist and exclusionist stand in the early postwar period to a more consistent inclusionist policy from the late 1970s onwards. Virdee points out that particular conflicts in which black workers were involved have served as critical cases which led to changes in the attitudes of unions.[15] Both Wrench in this volume and Virdee make it clear that 'black self-organisation' has played a significant role in bringing about these changes.[16] It also becomes evident from both studies that racism and racial relations are the keywords of the dominant discourse in the United Kingdom, rather than the status of alien or temporary workers.

The French case suggests a similar evolution towards more inclusionist policies from the mid-1970s onwards, although the starting point, the public discourse, and the strength of immigrant organisations are quite different. In the French case too, a number of notorious labour conflicts, in which immigrants were closely involved, have triggered off discussions within unions and sometimes led to new policies of inclusion.

The picture in other countries is less clear. On the basis of the reports included here one might assume that such specific conflicts have been smaller in number or even absent in other countries. But if that were so, how can we explain this absence? One could argue that the existence of specific immigrant conflicts is the result of an earlier neglect by trade unions in failing to prevent unequal treatment or an unequal position for immigrants. The argument is plausible, particularly in cases where industrial conflicts are based on complaints that refer to basic inequality, such as unequal wages for the same work, unequal access to specific jobs, and the like. According to this interpretation, the extent and frequency of such specific conflicts are themselves indications of non-inclusion. Following this line of argument, the absence of specific conflicts in countries like Sweden, the Federal Republic of Germany, and the Netherlands could be explained by the fact that equal treatment was insisted upon from the beginning, and to a great extent materialised through the influence of the unions on the way immigrant labour was organised. But it makes little sense in the Austrian and the Swiss cases, where unequal rights and treatment were part of the system. In the latter cases the almost total absence of significant forms of organisation among the immigrants themselves, combined with (and as a consequence of) their alien and temporary status, seems to be a plausible additional argument.[17]

Up to now we have treated the inclusion-exclusion issue in the strict sense, directly pertaining to social and industrial relations. In a broader definition of the issue we now include the question of whether immigrant workers are or should be regarded as full citizens (inhabitants) of the new society as a whole, having the same rights as nationals. The question is then what attitudes trade unions adopt on general policies relating to immigrants in society. We have already touched on this to a certain extent under the first dilemma, in so far as such attitudes had consequences for the admission of new immigrants. Here we are concerned with such things as resistance to laws which curtail the rights of immigrants, anti-racist policies, stands against extreme-right and anti-immigrant mobilisation, and so on. But it also relates to active policies of endorsing integration programmes, affirmative action programmes for immigrants, and the like.

On the basis of the admittedly uneven material collected here, we can make three observations which could lead towards more detailed research and comparison. The first is that trade unions which are not strongly committed to central socio-economic decision-making tend to participate more strongly as partners in social movements in favour of immigrants, and in anti-racist policies. They take on the role more of an opposition movement against the state's and the employers' policies, and against general tendencies in society. This has been the case for the French trade unions over the whole period, but also seems more and more the case in the Federal Republic of Germany and the United Kingdom, where trade unions have lost power in central decision-making and where former coalitions between the state authorities (and dominant political parties) and the unions have weakened or vanished. But it also works the other way around: those unions which are strongly committed to common socio-economic decision-making have tied their hands much more, and tend to stick more closely to the core activities of trade unions. One of the areas in which this comes clearly to the fore is the question of illegal or undocumented immigrants, particularly when it comes to surveying and policing of immigrants, and concrete measures to exclude illegals from all the provisions of the welfare state.

A second observation is that the issues and topics on which trade unions may be mobilised as part of a social movement differ considerably. These issues are generated in particular national contexts, and are formulated in specific, national discourses. In the United Kingdom, one of the most dominant discourses over the whole period has been that of racial relations and anti-racism. In France too, that has become a major issue. Discussions in Sweden and the Netherlands since the mid-1970s and early 1980s have been framed in terms of multiculturalism and minorities policies (of which combating racism and discrimination is an element). In the Swiss case, *Überfremdung* is a keyword for mobilisation and counter-mobilisation.

The last example brings us to a third observation: the agenda of trade unions, whether voluntary or imposed, is often set by other actors in the national context and by structural factors in that context. An extreme example is the Swiss case where, through the legal provision of referendum initiatives, unions have several times been obliged to take positions against anti-immigration and anti-immigrant referenda. An example of a different nature is the Dutch case: Dutch unions have, particularly since the beginning of the 1980s, taken firm stands on the rights of legally resident immigrants and on integration policies. But stating this is only half the truth: the other side of the coin is that it was precisely the introduction of a general minorities policy in the Netherlands in the 1980s (which was not a result of trade-union efforts) that forced the trade unions hesitantly to formulate internal inclusion policies. The fact that at the present time such policies have only been introduced in a very piecemeal fashion within the unions, and the number of immigrants in organisational positions is very low, reminds us again that we need to draw a distinction between statements and actual behaviour. In the Dutch case, then, the general context obliges trade unions to formulate explicitly anti-racist and inclusionist policies, rather than the other way around.

The case of the Federal Republic of Germany seems to have shown exactly the opposite since the mid-1970s: there trade unions have actually been the major institutional force for integration, in the absence of adequate government policies in this field. In the 1980s and 1990s the German Trade Union Federation (DGB) has resisted, wherever possible, any measures that it regarded as counter-productive to integration, but they have not been able to force the national government to change its policies.

Equal versus Special Treatment

As was explained in the Introduction and illustrated in the previous section, inclusion may mean several things. Moreover, inclusion may be attained by different strategies. At this point we formulated the third dilemma faced by trade unions:[18] should they concentrate exclusively on the common interests of indigenous and migrant workers and follow general policies for all workers, or should they also stand up for the specific interests and needs of their migrant members, and devise specific policies in order to attain material equality? These special policies may be of various kinds. In the workplace, they can entail practical measures to do with communication, and special policies that take the position of the migrant into account, but which also help to create cultural or religious facilities for migrant and minority workers. In the area of integrating immigrant and minority workers into the organisational structure of the unions, measures can cover a range of activities, from facilities encouraging immigrant workers to organise themselves as special groups within the union at one end of the spectrum, to active anti-discrimination policies within the unions at the other, possibly combined with affirmative or positive action in the training and employment of immigrants or members of minorities, and actually changing trade union structures to accommodate them.

Some of the trade unions that were actively involved in recruiting systems have introduced special arrangements for recruited workers as migrants from the beginning, for example by making the employer responsible for housing the newcomers, or by including travel expenses for an annual vacation in the country of origin in the employers' costs package. However, the test of whether such provisions were intended primarily to increase the costs of recruiting for employers, or as genuine protection of fellow workers, came soon after they had arrived, and particularly later on, when it became clear that many of them were not temporary visitors after all.

Looking at all the chapters, the general historical evolution seems clear: in the course of time, but at different points in time, most of the national trade-union organisations had to admit that the specific situation and characteristics of migrant workers required special attention and policies. On the practical level this led to special basic measures concerning communication and organisational facilities such as special immigrant commissions or secretariats, in most cases at some time in the 1970s. Once again Austria formed the exception, and Switzerland followed the trend rather late.

Where trade unions actually take up the special interests of immigrants or minorities in collective bargaining and in crisis situations, it turns out to be a highly sensitive issue. If such special interests are directly related to work and work conditions, it appears that certain unions, in the course of time, after long hesitation and sometimes strong pressure from outside, may change their position. Some of the more recent industrial disputes in the United Kingdom and France, as described by Wrench and Lloyd, bear witness to such changes. When the specific measures concern the cultural characteristics of immigrant workers, such as claims for the opportunity to pray during working hours, the question is more sensitive and difficult to handle for the unions. The French case described by Lloyd illustrates that point clearly: unions had to reformulate such cultural and religious claims in more neutral and apparently work-related terms of 'hygiene', before being able to back them up.

In the Netherlands there has been some pressure on trade unions to incorporate certain cultural or religious rights in collective agreements, such as the right of workers to take leave on non-Christian religious holidays. Although such phrases were incorporated in a limited number of agreements, it has transpired that it was easier in the Dutch context to have such rights recognised for Muslim and Hindu workers in the courts.[19]

In quite another way, Dutch minorities policies have confronted trade unions with a particular form of the general-versus-special-treatment dilemma that has not occurred anywhere else: the Employment Equity Act (WBEAA) was introduced in the context of minorities policies in order to reduce the relatively high unemployment in a number of immigrant groups. Unions were asked to endorse a weak form of affirmative action for immigrants; their reaction was ambivalent and evasive: by making a voluntary agreement between employers and unions to employ more immigrants, they were able to avoid the introduction of the law for a number of years. When it became clear that the voluntary agreement was not yielding results, and the law was introduced, they reacted by renewing a new common 'commitment' on the part of employers and unions in 1996, and negotiated what amounted to a revision of the law.

The general-versus-special-treatment dilemma manifests itself most clearly when it comes to the internal organisation of trade unions. The awareness that migrant workers ought to be equally represented within trade union organisations, and that the existing organisational structure hinders migrants and minority members from reaching positions of power and therefore requires special measures, seems to have evolved quite differently in the various national contexts. Special organisational forms within the unions, such as committees for migrant workers or separate secretariats, formed the first response, starting in the early 1970s in a number of countries: France, the United Kingdom, Sweden, the Federal Republic of Germany, and the Netherlands. The experience with these organisational forms often proved unsatisfactory in the long run: they tended to be located on the periphery of the organisation, devoid of access to the centres of decision-making and power, and came to perform only a token function in the eyes of many participants.

A more fundamental approach added to or following these early experiences was to establish special training or affirmative action programmes which aimed at a larger or even equal representation of immigrants within the organisation and power structure of trade unions. Swedish unions, again, seem to have taken the lead in this regard, starting their action programme as early as the 1970s. The German unions have also invested seriously in this course of action. Other countries have been much slower and more ambivalent; the Dutch and British cases in particular highlight the ambivalent nature of these endeavours. In the United Kingdom such policies, in so far as they exist, seem to result from a serious campaign by immigrants both within and outside the unions; immigrant organisations outside traditional unions play a significant role as pressure groups, which is a unique feature of the British case.

Explaining Differences

In explaining differences in attitudes and actions between trade unions we have assumed that the following set of factors could be of importance (see the Introduction):

- the position of trade unions in the power structure of society;
- economic and labour market conditions;
- factors connected with society as a whole; and
- factors connected with the characteristics of the immigrants.

We will look at each of these elements briefly, and estimate the extent to which they may help to explain the differences. We will treat them, however, in a different order.

Characteristics of the Immigrants

We concluded in a previous section that differences between countries in the membership density of immigrants cannot be explained by the special characteristics of the immigrants or by their special experiences or behaviour; it is primarily the institutional embeddedness of unions in the national context that explains differences in general membership, and also that of immigrants to a large extent. Immigrants with the same Turkish background are highly organised in Sweden and Belgium, but have a relatively low membership density in France, Switzerland and the Netherlands. Within this main conclusion there are, of course, variations due to special efforts of certain unions or to specific circumstances in certain sectors.[20] But once again these differences tend to confirm the thesis that it is not the specific features of immigrants that are decisive, but rather the variables in the receiving society or the unions concerned. We found no support for the commonly expressed hypothesis that immigrants' lack of experience with unions and industrial working conditions is an important explanatory factor.

As far as the characteristics of immigrants are concerned, factors like a special historical background appear to be more important. In the British case, for example, the first dilemma never played a major role because Commonwealth immigrants were usually United Kingdom citizens. Another example is the different approach taken by Dutch trade unions towards colonial immigrants and 'guest workers'. The important variables seem to be the characteristics which have been allocated to immigrants by the receiving society: their legal status, their being regarded as temporary workers, their confinement to insecure or part-time sectors especially where women are concerned, and the like. Their legal and residential status as temporary aliens may have a particularly strong effect, in a direct sense because unions do not regard these workers as proper members, and indirectly, because low status makes it more difficult to form the strong organisations which oblige unions to take them seriously later on. The British case underlines the point: it is unique in the sense that organisations representing minorities, who were United Kingdom citizens, fulfilled a function in forcing unions to change their position.

There is, however, more to the matter than simply the membership density among immigrants. Equal or even higher membership density of immigrants compared to indigenous workers does not automatically predict the influence of immigrants and minorities on the policies and behaviour of trade unions. We have seen that only gradually, and by no means everywhere, has the awareness grown that there are structural factors which prevent these groups from participating in trade union structures, and that active policies are needed to remove those barriers. We have to conclude that only in exceptional cases and under very special circumstances could the degree of organisation of immigrants and minorities possibly be a direct explanatory factor for the attitudes and behaviour of trade unions, and thus for the differences between the various countries.

Economic and Labour Market Factors

Economic and labour market conditions were quite different in the seven countries immediately after the Second World War. Some of them had to build up an entirely new economy on the ruins left by the war. Those not involved in the war, or whose industrial potential had not been destroyed, were able to get a flying start. These circumstances have made for differences of timing between countries, particularly up to the beginning of the 1960s. Since then, however, economic and labour market developments have increasingly run in parallel. Processes of financial and economic internationalisation have rendered national economies more and more interwoven and interdependent.

Clearly, a great economic shift took place in the early and middle years of the 1970s, partly triggered off by the first oil crisis, but building on processes which had started long before. The years 1974–75 thus form a watershed between two distinct phases: it marked the end of large-scale, labour-intensive production along 'Fordist' lines, and the advent of a new profile of Western European economies, in which capital-intensive production and high-quality international services became dominant. That kind of economy requires highly skilled workers, but fewer of them. The direct relationship between economic growth and a growing demand for labour, which had been the rule before, was broken. The need for labour immigration, particularly of the low skilled variety, was over.

We have argued that this development led to new alliances between states and trade unions on restrictive policies relating to *new* labour immigration. At the same time, the issue of the right of legally resident immigrants to bring in dependants and marriage partners became a new point of dispute between those same partners in many countries.

It is clear that these economic and labour market developments have also had consequences for the attitudes of unions to immigration in general. The ambiguous attitudes of unions on the issue of asylum seekers and undocumented immigrants illustrate that point.

However, apart from generating a general agreement to restrict new labour immigration, the parallel development in economic and labour market developments cannot explain the significant differences in attitudes to the immigration of the dependants and partners of legally resident immigrants, to asylum seekers, or to undocumented migrants.

The Position of Trade Unions in Socio-economic Decision-making

The positions of trade unions differ markedly in this respect: in Austria, in Sweden, and to a lesser degree in the Netherlands, unions have had a continuous involvement in socio-economic decision-making over the whole period. In the United Kingdom and the Federal Republic of Germany, a significant change has taken place over time in the degree of involvement. In France, trade unions have never have been a significant partner in national socio-economic decision-making. Swiss unions are involved in central policy-making, but their influence is weak. A point directly related to the influence of unions in consensus decision-making is the structure of unions and of union federations: a strongly centralised and unified union structure is clearly more influential than fragmented union movements.

A consequence of a close involvement and co-responsibility on the part of trade unions is that they are obliged to adopt attitudes on all kinds of issues. They are often forced to take positions even on questions on which their rank and file is divided. This may lead to ambivalent situations in which formal positions adopted at the central level may differ significantly from practice and behaviour down in the organisations. In the Netherlands, such discrepancies have recently surfaced once more in relation to affirmative action policies in favour of minorities. At the other end of the scale, trade unions not involved in national consensus decision-making are more free to choose the matters about which they wish to express their opinions, and whether to join social movements. In such circumstances, decisions are also easier to make for individual unions in a fragmented union movement.

A particular factor relating to the influence of unions is their relationship with political parties in government. It is no accident that in the cases of Austria and Sweden, where close relations have existed between unions and the Social Democrat parties in power throughout most of the postwar period, the influence of unions has been considerable. And by the same token, changing coalitions of parties in government have led to significant increases and decreases in union influence. The coming to power of the Conservatives in the United Kingdom, and of the coalitions of Christian Democrats and Liberals in the Federal Republic of Germany, for example, have caused the unions to lose considerable influence. The arrival of a Social Democrat as President of France in the late 1970s, on the other hand, led to a short period of cooperation and some influence for the unions there.

Such observations over the whole period tend towards the obvious and self-evident. An important additional question is whether relations between trade unions and 'parented' parties in general did not change in the course of the period concerned. From the material presented here, that appears to be the case. The political scene has changed, between the period after the war in which national consensus projects of 'reconstruction' were dominant, and the more recent period of welfare states. Leftist parties and policies have often shifted to the centre. Trade unions have had to adapt to that new situation: their position in welfare states is often less evident and clear-cut than it used to be, and their relations with parties have often had to be revised. In general the ground of common interest between parties of the left and trade unions has become narrower and less distinct than it was before. Having linked or 'parent' political parties in power seems to have lost at least part of its importance in the course of time.

Although the degree of involvement of trade unions in consensus decision-making is probably a good indicator of their effectiveness in influencing socio-economic policies, it does not, however, predict the content or direction of decisions relating to immigrants. Two comparisons make this clear. The first concerns the Swedish and Austrian trade unions: in both cases, unions had a strong influence on socio-economic decision-making, strong centralised union structures, and a direct axis with the Social Democrats in power; the way they handled the three dilemmas of immigration and immigrants, however, could not have been more divergent.

One could argue that the differences in approach between the Swedish and the Austrian trade unions – which both have strong influence in socio-economic decision-making – are caused by contextual and historical factors such as political continuity or discontinuity. Sweden has not been involved in a war for the last two centuries. In much earlier periods, craftsmen were brought into the country and the German Hansa had an important place in Sweden, but since then it has been an ethnically homogeneous country. This may have led to a more self-confident Swedish identity, and more openness towards the 'other'. Swedish attitudes towards foreigners were decidedly anti-semitic in the first half of the twentieth century (the 'J stamp' in passports was supported by Sweden) and racist, but not nationalistic. Since the 1954 Aliens Act, which stipulated that there should be a free exchange of workers and of those persecuted on grounds of race or creed, Swedish immigration has been dictated by economic needs. Perceived socio-cultural threats to Swedish national identity from immigrant populations are formulated largely at the popular and not at the political level.

Austria, on the other hand, is characterised by historical and political discontinuity. After its re-establishment and independence in 1918, at the end of the Habsburg era, it had to defend its existence and overcome the severance from its great imperial past. This may well have led to a strong nationalistic Austrian identity, which could have had an effect on the way immigrants were perceived.[21]

This explanation, however, is rather speculative and ad hoc.[22] It is also possible to adhere more closely to the contributions in this volume and to the assumptions we have formulated, in accounting for the differences, and argue that looking at the explanatory factors separately as monocausal explanations does not bring us very far, but that looking at the interaction between these factors might shed some light on differences as yet unaccounted for. Then it becomes clear that what at first glance looks like a strange difference between two countries with the same strong influences in socio-economic decision-making is illuminated by the dominant type of immigration in the countries (or how the dominant type of immigration is perceived). In the Swedish case, immigration was predominantly from partners within the Common Nordic Market. It was within the agreements of this free exchange of workers within the Common

Nordic Market that the rights and integration of these immigrants were regulated and guaranteed. This has led to the inclusion of the Nordic immigrants both in Swedish society and in Swedish trade unions.[23] In this respect Sweden resembles the United Kingdom case. This dominant framework has largely functioned as a frame of reference for later immigration from non-Nordic countries.

This strongly differs from the Austrian case, where there was another type of immigration, namely the immigration of predominantly 'guest workers'. In the Austrian case, immigrants were perceived as aliens not belonging to Austrian society, and with whom Austria had no special ties as in the Swedish or British cases. So unlike the Swedish trade unions, which had cooperated in the establishment of a free Common Nordic Market – and as a consequence did not look upon these immigrants as temporary and tried to integrate them in Swedish trade unions – the Austrian trade unions used that same strong position in the socio-economic decision-making structure to make sure that labour immigration remained a temporary 'guest worker' immigration.[24]

But if this explanation is a plausible one, how can the differences in a second comparison, between Austria and the Federal Republic of Germany, be explained? Both the German and Austrian trade unions had considerable direct influence in their countries in the 1950s and 1960s, they were structurally involved in decision-making, and they both had a 'guest worker system'. The Austrian trade unions used their influence to protect the interests of indigenous workers exclusively, and succeeded. The German trade unions have developed over time towards a position in which they now represent the major force for the integration of those same immigrants, both within their own ranks and within society at large. They are relatively successful, it would seem, with the integration into their own organisations, but not with integration into German society at large. It seems plausible that in the German case the massive immigration of Italians in the first phases of 'guest-worker' immigration set a tradition of cooperation with Italian trade unions, and of inclusionist policies on the part of German unions.

Contextual Factors

Thus in retrospect we have to admit that the assumptions which we formulated to account for differences in behaviour and legitimating arguments in different countries, when taken separately, turn out to have a limited explanatory power. They account to a certain extent for parallel developments that have taken place in the different countries, and thus for the similarity of the kind of dilemmas with which unions have been confronted; this is particularly the case for economic and labour market factors. They may also account for the extent to which unions have been able to influence developments; here the position of unions in socio-economic decision-making and the internal structure of unions are important. But they do not convincingly account for the variance in attitudes and legitimations that unions have adopted. While the factors that we have treated so far are not located in their national and historical contexts we see them as quasi-monocausal explanations. That brings us to the most important explanatory factor: national contextual and historical factors.

We have argued earlier that although trade unions may ideologically have an internationalist orientation, their actual effectiveness has to be struggled for within national contexts. The way dilemmas present themselves, or are represented by other actors and resolved, cannot be understood without knowledge of these national contexts. Trade unions are an inextricable part of that context, much more than they might themselves realise.

In the course of our analysis we have referred several times to such historical and contextual factors. At the very start we stressed the factor of the continuity or innovation of labour immigration after the Second World War. Such immigration was perceived quite differently in the light of differing historical experience, was regulated by different instruments and to a varying degree, and the 'regimes' for immigration and the position of immigrants differed accordingly. Dominant discourses, terminology and issues varied considerably, reflecting the perceptions and problem definitions of society at large. The policies and structures of state and society embody these different perceptions. To put it plainly, in view of the many aspects of structure and position of unions which resemble each other, an explanation for the contrasting attitudes of Swedish and Austrian unions in relation to the three dilemmas can only be given in terms of the logic of the specific nationally bound traditions and experiences of unions and society at large in relation to immigration and immigrants or foreigners.

By emphasising these contextual and historical factors we do not mean to say that unions are no more than chameleons. They may and do try to influence and change that context, but at the same time they are also strongly influenced by it. The extent of their influence will depend on their position in the decision-making structure of the national framework.

Parallelism and Convergence?

The foregoing analysis has shown that there have been strong parallel developments in the various countries. External factors in particular, like the growing internationalisation of economic processes, have confronted unions in different countries with the same kind of dilemmas and situations. In recent decades such developments have also tended to be more synchronised than in earlier periods. The fact that all migration systems, however temporary they may have been when they started, have ended up with significant immigrant populations staying for a long period, and thus in democratic welfare states with substantial rights for those immigrants, forms another parallel development. Growing migration pressure in the form of asylum seekers and undocumented immigrants is again a parallel development. Such parallel developments, however, do not necessarily lead to convergence, or in this particular case to the convergence of the attitudes of trade unions in different countries. To claim convergence we need to be able to demonstrate that differences in the stances adopted by trade unions are diminishing or have diminished in the course of time.

Looking back at the variance in attitudes to the three dilemmas, the extent of convergence seems to vary considerably. As to immigration, particularly new waves of labour migration, the convergence is great: restrictive policy has been a strong common denominator since the mid-1970s.[25] Such convergence, however, is much less strong when it concerns the immigration of the dependants and marriage partners of legally resident immigrants, asylum seekers, and undocumented immigrants.

As for the inclusion-exclusion dilemma, there has been consensus from the beginning that formal exclusion was not in conformity with union ideology, nor in union interests. That is, on the whole, hardly surprising. On looking more closely at indicators for material inclusion or exclusion, the picture becomes more complex. In the course of time unions in most countries have developed more inclusionist attitudes and policies, particularly for long-stay immigrants, but this is not always the case. Furthermore, both the degree to which this happens and the commitment of unions to more inclusionist policies vary.

The thesis of convergence seems most problematic in relation to the third dilemma. If we look at indicators for the recognition by unions of the special needs of immigrants and minority workers, we may assume a tendency towards more sensitivity and acceptance, sometimes enforced by immigrant organisations or by other factors such as state policies of multiculturalism; but such a tendency is by no means general or uniform. Measured in terms of efforts to include immigrants in union organisation, the picture is still more diversified. Trade union confederations in some countries have seriously committed themselves to affirmative action programmes in order to achieve at least a reasonable representation of immigrant or minority workers in the union organisation, but many stick to a 'colour-blind' approach. In some cases, like the Austrian unions, no serious effort is made to remove fundamental hindrances preventing immigrants from taking up positions in the union movement.

In conclusion, one can certainly see convergence over time on certain points, but in general convergence is much less than the strong parallel developments might suggest. Here again we have to recognise that unions act and react within their specific national contexts, conditions and traditions.

Postscript: Prospects for a European Trade Union Movement

In his analysis of the position of European trade unions at the end of the twentieth century, Visser paints a gloomy picture of the future of these unions against a background of growing European integration and of the internationalisation of economic processes and industrial relations in general.[26] Transnational collective action and transnational organisation of labour appear to be extremely difficult. The European Trade Union Confederation, established as early as 1973, is potentially a powerful organisation, representing 30 per cent of all workers in twenty-two European countries. But in fact this potential has not materialised, according to Visser, for two internal and two external reasons.

The external obstacles are first the organisation of the European Union: this union is in a number of aspects ‘a market without a state’. Where historically trade unions have gained their position nationally within the tripartite structure of employers, organised workers and state, with the latter playing an influential role in forcing or persuading the other partners to avoid conflict and find compromises, at the European level that powerful partner is largely absent, as are the mechanisms that partner might apply. And secondly, the employers – in the absence of clear international rules and mechanisms and of a powerful international labour movement – are playing the game more sharply.

The internal obstacles are embodied in the specific history of national unions and the resulting organisation. Trade unions have developed in national contexts, and it is there that they are (or were) able to exert their power. And these national contexts have differed significantly, which expresses itself in social, political, cultural and organisational diversity. Our analysis of trade unions in relation to one specific issue – that of immigration and immigrants – has confirmed that thesis.

How to establish unity from such diversity? How to overcome real or perceived divergent interests, in view of inequalities of membership density and of the ensuing power relations? Searching for a possible answer, Visser looks at two historically analogous situations. The first is the transition of unions from local to central negotiations and the organisation of unions within national histories: in the present European situation, however, the third party in the triangle, a strong state, is sorely missed. The second is the analogy of the growth of central negotiation and unions within the United States of America: here he concludes that the main conditions which have led to centralisation in the case of the USA are not yet powerful enough to force unions to cooperate across borders in the present European situation.

We have no fundamental arguments in objection to Visser's analysis. On the basis of the material presented in this volume, however, we can suggest that it would be worthwhile for trade unions to have a closer look at whether they are able to overcome diversity issues as a consequence of immigration in their national context. If that answer is positive, then that experience should also be relevant for this larger European integration project. And those who have had a major share in realising real unity in a fragmented trade union should be the ones with the relevant experience and skills to work on the European issue.

NOTES

1. The same holds true for Belgium, which resumed recruitment of Italians immediately after the Second World War (see A. Martens, 'Belgium'. Paper at the International Seminar, 'Cultural Diversity in Trade Unions: A Challenge to the Class Identity', Hoger Instituut voor de Arbeid, Katholieke Universiteit Leuven, Leuven 6–7 February, 1977).
2. In the Netherlands labour immigration had been very strong in the period 1580–1780, had then declined until 1880, and was – apart from the employment of foreign miners and domestic servants in the Interbellum – virtually absent in the period 1880–1955 (J. Lucassen and R. Penninx, *Nieuwkomers, nakomelingen, Nederlanders: Immigranten in Nederland 1550– 1993*, Amsterdam, 1994). The German Reich (1871–1914) employed 1.2 million workers from Poland and the Austro-Hungarian Empire: see Kühne's chapter. It also used the forced employment of foreigners on a massive scale in the period, 1935–45.
3. The huge forced labour of foreigners in Germany during the Second World War can clearly not be regarded as a relevant experience for continuity.
4. As explained by Knocke in her chapter, the new instruments for control had already been developed in Sweden prior to 1966–67. But it was only in 1967 that the regulation of non-Nordic labour immigration came into effect.
5. Except where all-embracing welfare state policies, including the creation of a strong service-based sector, are implemented, as in Sweden, at least until recently (see G. Esping-Andersen, *Three Worlds of Welfare Capitalism*, Cambridge, 1991).
6. The restrictions were not categoric ones: those migrants whose presence was perceived as functional and fitting the economic interests of the country were welcomed: these tended to be highly skilled workers, company-linked migrants, and the like.
7. N.B. 'incorporation in society at large', and not 'incorporation in labour organisations': we will show later that trade unions may well plead for equal positions to

be brought about by government policy, while at the same time being very hesitant in implementing such policy within their own organisations.

8. Foreign workers were forced to leave the country once they experienced difficulty finding employment. The explanations accompanying the Austrian Foreigners Employment Law in 1975, drafted in collaboration with the trade unions, spoke of 'the end of their usefulness' as the point at which they might be repatriated, according to the law.
9. R. van der Erf, *Asylum Seekers and Refugees: A Statistical Report*, Luxembourg, 1994.
10. Koopmans (see R. Koopmans, 'Explaining the Rise of Racist and Extreme Right Violence in Western Europe: Grievances and Opportunities?', *European Journal of Political Research*, no. 30 (1996): 198 calculated the number of asylum seekers per million inhabitants for the period 1988–93. Sweden (26,500), Switzerland (23,800) and the Federal Republic of Germany (19,200) showed the highest records. The Netherlands took a position in the middle (7,800). France (4,300) and the United Kingdom (2,400) had relatively small inflows. Koopmans argues that numbers do seem to matter, but their significance is mediated strongly by the way in which policies and debates on these issues are framed politically.
11. Wrench forthcoming, 'Trade Unions, Migrants and Ethnic Minorities in the European Union: National differences and common dilemmas', in J. Gundara and S. Jacobs (eds), *Intercultural Europe: Cultural Diversity and Social Policy in the European Union*) suggests a North-South divide within Europe on this subject: countries like Spain and Italy do not have a tradition of immigration, nor an institutional framework to regulate it. Further, they have recently experienced a specific type of unregulated immigration. Trade unions in these countries tend to be more willing to respond in favour of undocumented migrants.
12. J. Visser and B. Ebbinghaus, 'Een halve eeuw verandering: Verklaringen voor convergentie en diversiteit van werknemersorganisatie in West-Europa', in Jelle Visser (ed.), *De vakbeweging op de eeuwgrens: Vijf sociologische studies over de vakbeweging*, Amsterdam, 1996, 24.
13. Ibid., 45.
14. In their study Visser and Ebbinghaus test six possible explanations for changes in the period 1975–1990: (a) changes in the economic environment, (b) changes in the political environment, (c) changes in the social structure, such as the decline of industry, the disappearance of traditional artisans, a higher participation of women and the increase of small-scale entrepreneurs, (d) cultural changes (e.g., individualisation, postmaterialism), (e) the replacement of trade unions by other interest groups, and (f) the increased opposition of employers through international competition. These structural and conjunctural variables, however, do not yield significant correlations. Next they look at four indicators of the institutional embeddedness and the structure of unions: (a) the presence of 'voluntary' unemployment funds directly related to unions (for example in Sweden and Belgium), (b) regulated access of unions in the workplace (strong in Sweden, Austria, the United Kingdom, and to a lesser degree in the Federal Republic of Germany), (c) the corporatist embeddedness of unions, which is strong in Sweden, Austria, the Federal Republic of Germany, the Netherlands, and Switzerland, and more or less absent in France and the United Kingdom (in recent periods), and (d) the presence of obligatory membership, especially closed-shop systems.
15. S. Virdee, *Racism and Resistance in the British Trade Union Movement: A Critical Analysis of Historical and Contemporary Developments.* Paper at the International Seminar, 'Cultural Diversity in Trade Unions: A Challenge to the Class Identity', Hoger Instituut voor de Arbeid, Katholieke Universiteit Leuven, Leuven, 6–7 February, 1997.

16. Ibid.
17. One might also consider the organisation of industrial relations in general in different countries as an explanatory factor. Industrial relations in France and the United Kingdom are organised less along principles of common socio-economic decision-making, and are more confrontational, which expresses itself in more labour conflicts and strikes. Employers and unions which normally operate within a common decision-making system (as in the Netherlands or Austria) will be more inclined to apply agreed rules, and will therefore less easily engage in industrial action.
18. The Austrian case is not taken into account in this section; as we have seen, union policies there have not pursued any significant form of inclusion except the acceptance of passive membership. As Gächter points out in his chapter, official positions within the unions are often restricted to members of works councils. However, to become a member of a works council, Austrian citizenship is required. In none of the other countries do unions have such requirements.
19. See J.R. Rath, R. Penninx, K. Groenendijk and A. Meyer, *Nederland en zijn islam: Een ontzuilende samenleving reageert op het ontstaan van een geloofsgemeenschap*, Amsterdam, 1996.
20. In the Dutch case there is the exceptional example of very early active recruitment of Turkish employees of the National Railway Company by the Christian Transport Union, achieving a membership density of more than 75 per cent among Turkish workers.
21. See M. John, *Historical Mass-migration in Habsburg Austria 1848 to 1914: Multicultural Options vs. National Hegemony*. Paper presented at the international conference 'Mass-migration in Europe, Implications in East and West', Vienna, 5–7 March 1992.
22. The argument could be reversed: a stable and homogeneous society like Sweden would supposedly have more problems in accepting newcomers than a mixed society like Austria.
23. Being strongly incorporated in the socio-economic decision-making structure, trade unions had also agreed upon the establishment of a free Nordic market, so they were committed to the agreements.
24. An additional argument could be the differences in the social systems of the two countries. Sweden developed a much more elaborated system of social security with strong involvement from the unions. That makes the position of unions less dependent on development of the labour market on the one hand, but also makes it more urgent to have immigrants included in that system.
25. One may wonder what will happen in the near future if for demographic reasons a number of countries have to resort once more to immigration; the age structure of the economically active population in a number of countries is already at a point which gives cause for concern among politicians and policy-makers. Since fertility rates are low, difficult to influence and have only long-term effects, selective immigration is being proposed by some of those politicians as a remedy. Such developments could unmask the present convergence among unions as being somewhat conditional.
26. J. Visser, 'Tussen nationale ontwikkeling en Europese uitdaging', in J. Visser (ed.), *De vakbeweging op de eeuwgrens: Vijf sociologische studies over de vakbeweging*, Amsterdam, 1996, 13–6.

APPENDICES

1. Trade Unions in Austria[1]

August Gächter

After the Second World War all efforts of the unions were focused on national rehabilitation and economic reconstruction. After 1945 Socialist unionists began to set up an organisation covering all political groups, and they were joined by both Communist and Christian unionists. An inter-party agreement led to the establishment of the Austrian Federation of Trade Unions (Österreichischer Gewerkschaftsbund-ÖGB) in 1945.

Although the ÖGB was founded as a suprapartisan organisation, there were close informal links between political subgroups and political parties from the very beginning. These connections were formally centralised in the early 1950s, although the ÖGB's articles of association have never been adapted to reflect this fact. In the late 1940s, the Socialists and the Christians, who preferred an unequivocally moderate policy towards employers, increasingly resented Communist interference.[2]

It was the declared goal of all political actors to achieve economic recovery. The ÖGB in particular played a leading role in attempts to guide trade unions in a corporatist direction, and experiments followed one another. In 1946, a Central Wages Commission was established, to be replaced in 1947 by the Economic Commission. Between 1947 and 1951, annual agreements were arrived at to restrain the wage-price spiral, and in 1957 the Joint Commission on

Wages and Prices was established. This was complemented by a Council of Economic and Social Advisers. Henceforth, the Joint Commission stood at the heart of a specifically Austrian kind of corporatist social partnership.

With respect to the structure of the social partnership, it is necessary to distinguish between two dimensions: one autonomous and one not. The non-autonomous social partnership covers the statutory corporations with compulsory membership, such as the Chamber of Labour and the Chamber of Commerce. Both have certain legal rights, including extensive co-determination in questions of social security, employment, agrarian policy, money and credit policy, and labour jurisdiction.

Autonomous social partnership refers to the voluntary cooperation between employers' federations and trade-union organisations. The secret of Austria's corporatist success lies in the fact that both types of social partnership combine to constitute an effective power in industrial relations and in the political arena. Regardless of whether or not they are entitled to by law, the trade-union associations have a decisive say on all government bills before they are put to the vote in parliament. One of the most important examples is the Works Industrial Relation Scheme, part of the new Employment Constitution Law (*Arbeitsverfassungsgesetz*) of 1974, which was approved by the 'social partners' before it was passed by parliament.

Scholars agree that the stability of the Austrian social partnership stands or falls with the strength of the ÖGB. For this reason, it is necessary briefly to deal with the specific conditions of union power. To an important extent this rests on the Chamber of Labour, which relieves the unions of various tasks. In addition, the works councils (*Betriebsräte*) hold a key position for union power. Incorporated in the Works Industrial Relation Scheme, their members are elected by all the employees of a plant, not only by union members. They are protected by law and carry on the day-to-day work of the unions. The relationship between works councils and unions is one of interdependence. The enterprise is the domain of the works council, whereas the union is dominant at the supraplant level. The works council relies upon information, legal advice, and various support services provided by the union. The union depends on the activities of the works council which undertakes the recruitment of and service to members. What at first sight seems to be a dual system of representation in fact reveals itself to be a peculiar kind of monism.

All things considered, Austrian trade unions are highly immune to the imponderable challenges of everyday life. The ÖGB, which includes about 60 percent of Austrian wage and salary earners, holds a monopoly in representing the interests of all workers. This makes it the strongest union federation among developed capitalist countries with the possible exception of Israel. But the picture of total harmony must be qualified: The ÖGB's powerful position may not suffice to protect it in the face of recent world-wide changes in industrial relations. For one thing, the official number of members is greatly exaggerated since the statistics include retired members, credited as active employees. The real degree of organisation of the employed workforce barely exceeds 50 percent. Also, in Austria as elsewhere, there has been a continuous growth of white-collar workers in the labour force. Although it has become the strongest group within the ÖGB, the Union of White-Collar Workers is the worst organised affiliate, with a rate of organisation under 30 percent.

Throughout its history, the ÖGB has been dominated by the Socialist sub-group, which in 1989 had a majority in thirteen of the fifteen affiliated unions. Far behind it ranks the group of Christian unionists, with a majority in only one affiliate, the Union of Public Servants (Gewerkschaft Öffentlicher Dienst). The fifteenth affiliate, a small union covering the arts and media, has a non-party chairperson. In recent years however, the Christian subgroup has grown and has claimed increased representation in the leading organs of the ÖGB. While Socialist hegemony remains secure, competition has therefore increased, with each side keeping a sharp eye on the activities of the adversary. Meanwhile, both the Socialists and the Christians have prepared separate articles of association, in case the federation should split up. This might be no more than sabre rattling, but, in any event, it represents something new in Austrian postwar unionism.

NOTES

1. Principal source: Ferdinand Karlhoffer and Anton Pelinka, 'Austria', in Joan Campbell (ed.), *European Labour Unions*, Westport/London, 1992, 13ff..
2. Ibid., 17.

2: Trade Unions in the United Kingdom[1]

John Wrench

Although British trade unions do have a much longer history, according to Phillips the foundations for the present trade-union structure in the UK were laid in the period between 1900 and 1920.[2] It was particularly in that period that, on the one hand, unionism was more and more accepted politically – partly through an alliance of unions and socialist bodies – and wage-bargaining became a regular practice. On the other hand, unions gained ground: whereas before unionisation had been mainly a matter of non-manual male workers, now also many manual workers and women joined unions. Total union membership rose to 8.3 million by 1920.

The Trades Union Congress, established officially as early as 1868, brought most of the old and new powerful unions together, though some of the clerical and professional unions did not participate in this 'national forum of manual unionists'.[3]

Although the depression of the 1920s put the new system under pressure – industrial disputes intensified and the unions suffered defeats – the main elements of the structure survived. Collective bargaining seemed an established and familiar part of the industrial scene.

> Even during the Great Depression of 1929–1933, although unemployment rose substantially, neither the economy nor the social order suffered the catastrophic dislocation experienced in other industrial nations.[4]

According to Phillips trade unions in Britain had advocated a collectivist ideology, but had not been able to realise such demands in the

1920s and 1930s. When in 1945 the Labour government came to power, this

> carried the union hopes of a collectivised economy, a welfare state, and improved conditions of life for the mass of working people. In many ways, the aspirations (…) were in fact fulfilled. The nationalizaton of the mines and the railways, as well as statutory reform of casual employment in the docks.[5]

The influence of unions was also substantial because postwar governments were inclined to involve the union leadership in the discussion of state policy through informal and formal mechanisms of consultation.

> This kind of 'negotiated corporatism' meant that labor representatives were treated as the confidants of ministers and were given a political status to which they had aspired since the late 1920s. The most visible mark of their elevation was the establishment in 1960 of a permanent National Economic Development Council, in which TUC representatives joined with those of the employers and with government to discuss current economic issues and problems.[6]

In the mid-1970s, according to Phillips, the union movement achieved unsurpassed heights of membership and political influence. Its leaders were successful in obtaining new legislation that enhanced their bargaining strength, enabling them to enforce recognition from employers, to command access to confidential company information, and to extend negotiated agreements to non-signatories. In return, they conceded a form of voluntary incomes policy that the TUC General Council itself devised.

The late 1970s brought an abrupt end to this period of union power. The return of a Conservative government could be seen as a turning point in British labour history. But at the same time it has to be recognised that the movement had itself laid the foundations of these changes. A first element had been the ambivalent strategy of the unions by using its influence to promote collectivist policies of government and partipating in 'negotiated corporatism', and at the same time not committing itself to that corporatism by maintaining its counterveiling power and independence. This aroused suspicion among the partners involved – politicians and employers. Secondly, the union movement had not come to grips with two important shifts in the postwar period: the first were changes in the economic structure and consequently the occupational structure of the work force. The second pertained to a shift in political thinking away from interventionist governmental policies towards internationally determined market economies. The strong position of unions – in a period of practically full employment – led to the negation of these phenomena, although several earlier conflicts had signalled these trends. Furthermore, the union movement had alienated itself to a great extent from public sympathy by using its strong position and an ambivalent strategy. Frequent industrial strikes – whether they could be justified or not – and the mass picketing – and physical violence that accompanied it – caused an adverse reaction. On top of that it coincided with a high rate of price inflation: a vicious spiral of costs and prices for which trade unions seemed an important responsible actor.[7]

Throughout the 1980s the trade unions have been in retreat. The traditionally high union membership declined markedly in both the private and public sectors. The proportion of employees in union membership – union density – fell from 58 percent in 1984 to 48 percent in 1990. In 1984 union membership stood at 10.8 million. By 1994 this was down to 7.09 million, a figure which represents about one third of employees in Great Britain.[8] The TUC still organises virtually all the trade unions in Britain, and is the only federation of its kind, but its political influence has declined drastically. Its traditionally strong links with the Labour Party, which were influential when Labour governments were in power, particularly during the 1970s, have come increasingly under pressure. And more importantly, as far as they still function, they have had no direct political relevance since Conservative governments took over power in 1979.

The Conservative government's long-term policy to undermine trade-union structures and activities in Britain has been of particular importance in diminishing the influence of trade unionism. Between 1979 and the end of 1993 nine pieces of legislation, including five Employment Acts, eroded trade-union rights and functions, in particular the right to strike. These measures circumscribed the right to strike by giving the legal industrial dispute a narrow definition and rendering the unions liable to prosecution for actions outside these limits. For example, secondary action in support of other workers has been outlawed, picketing severely restricted and unions are made liable for the unofficial actions of members. Enforcement of the closed shop was likewise subjected to restrictions and safeguards. The Conservatives withdrew Labour government legislation that had allowed unions to compel recognition from employers and that had extended the coverage of voluntary trade agreements. Furthermore, ballots must be held for all industrial action, and employers are entitled to know the identity of all workers who are being balloted. There is no right to strike enshrined in UK law.

The significance of Conservative employment legislation has been twofold. On the one hand they have been effective in stimulating the desertion of members who had the feeling that the unions could do little to protect their jobs: they could now abandon unions with comparative impunity. On the other hand the principal significance of these measures has been to deny workers access to resources of collective power.[9] This has had a particularly significant influence on union attempts to recruit new groups of ethnic minority and migrant workers. This political onslaught, in conjunction with the economic changes over the last fifteen years, has caused a crisis for the British trade-union movement. As sectors which have traditionally provided the mainstay of trade-union membership have declined, this has increased the proportional significance of sectors that are difficult to unionise. There is an expanding cohort of workers in part-time work, contract work, low-paid sweatshops and service sector work, illegal and unregulated work, and home-work. Unions feel they need to target such new groups of workers for replacement membership at a time when government policies have made recruitment more difficult. Within this picture, ethnic minority, migrant and refugee workers form an extra dimension. They are disproportionately concentrated in these 'poor work' sectors. Therefore, the issue of union policies in relation to ethnic minority workers has an added significance in Britain in the 1990s.

NOTES

1. Principal sources: Gordon Phillips, 'The United Kingdom', in Joan Campbell (ed.), *European Labor Unions*, Westport/London, 1992, 481–514; P. Smith and G. Morton, 'Union Exclusion and the Decollectivisation of Industrial Relations in Contemporary Britain', *British Journal of Industrial Relations* 31, no. 3 (1993).
2. Ibid., 481–514.
3. Ibid., 494.
4. Ibid., 497.
5. Ibid., 498.
6. Ibid., 501–2.
7. Ibid., 498–503.
8. Labour Research, May 1994.
9. Smith and Morton, 'Union Exclusion and the Decollectivisation of Industrial Relations in Contemporary Britain', 99.

3: Trade Unions in Sweden[1]

Wuokko Knocke

The Swedish Trade Union Confederation (Landsorganisationen i Sverige – LO) was founded in 1898. The Swedish trade-union movement has been highly centralised since about 1910; only a few unions remained outside the LO. These were mainly the unions for state employees, which only decided to join the LO in the 1920s and 1930s. Left-wing opposition has never been powerful in Sweden. Always dominated by reformist Social Democrats, the LO has cooperated closely with the Social Democratic Party and the government. In 1910, after the General Strike, the syndicalists left the LO to found the Swedish Workers' Central Organisation (Sveriges Arbetas Centralorganisation – SAC), which for a time played a role in the stone-cutting, mining, construction, and forestry industries. Since the 1930s, however, the SAC has become a marginal phenomenon. The Swedish Communist Party (Sveriges Kommunistiska Parti, SKP, 1921–67; since 1990 Vänsterpartiet or Left Party) had a certain influence on some trade unions during the 1920s, but lost much of its power after a split in 1929. The Communists have been strongest in the engineering, construction, mining, and pulp industries. Various other left-wing groups have operated on the local level since the late 1960s, but trade union and LO congresses have usually been dominated by the Social Democrats since the 1950s. This means that the Swedish trade-union movement is extraordinarily homogeneous, with no important divisions along religious, ethnic or political lines.[2]

White-collar workers in Sweden have chosen to organise themselves outside the LO. The two major white-collar trade-union confederations are the Swedish Confederation of Professional Employees

(Tjänstemännens Centralorganisation-TCO) and the Swedish Confederation of Professional Associations (Sveriges Akademikers Centralorganisation-SACO). There is some cooperation among the three main organisations: the TCO cooperates principally with the LO and to a certain extent with the SACO, which is conceived as a competing organisation by the TCO. The LO and the SACO rarely cooperate with each other. The LO has much closer contacts with the Social Democratic Party than do the white-collar confederations.

Trade-union membership in Sweden is entirely voluntary, and closed shops do not exist. About 90 percent of blue-collar and 80 percent of white-collar workers belong to trade unions – an exceptional degree of organisation, especially for white-collar workers. At the end of 1991, the LO unions had a membership of 2.2 million; 1.3 million belonged to unions affiliated with the TCO, and 343,000 belonged to SACO unions.

From the end of the nineteenth century until the mid-1930s, Sweden was a conflict-ridden country with frequent strikes of long duration. This situation led to demands for the promotion of labour peace through legislation. Several such attempts were made by Conservative governments after 1900, but they were stopped by the LO and the Social Democrats. The labour movement itself was divided on the issue: whereas some union leaders favoured legislation in principle, others, backed by wide support from the rank and file, strongly opposed state intervention. In 1928 parliament passed the Collective Agreement Act and established a Labour Court to interpret the collective agreements.[3]

Victory in the parliamentary election of 1932 enabled the Social Democrats to form a government. This was the beginning of a period of Social Democratic rule that lasted without interruption until 1976. With the Social Democrats in power, the LO undertook to revise its general policy of opposition. Representatives of the export industries within the LO were particularly eager to put an end to the long and costly trade-union conflicts. Seeking cooperation with the employers, they strove for peace on the labour market. By promoting industrial rationalisation and economic growth they hoped to ease the struggle over the distribution of profits.[4]

An important symbol of the new spirit was the Saltsjöbaden Agreement or Main Agreement between the LO and the SAF (Swedish Employers Association), which was concluded in 1938. This agreement set out the procedures for handling disputes and for the interpretation of collective agreements, and instituted safeguards against unfair dismissal. The Saltsjöbaden Agreement laid the basis of the 'Swedish model' of industrial relations: negotiations between the employers and unions and the absence of state intervention or a state incomes policy.[5]

A wages policy based on solidarity began to be discussed at the time of the Saltsjöbaden Agreement, and was formally adopted by the LO in 1951. The solidarity wage policy called for the reduction of wage differentials and promoted equal pay for equal work, independent of the company or branch of industry in which the worker was employed. The LO tried to enforce the solidarity wage policy in the central negotiations with the SAF.[6]

Towards the end of 1960s there were increasing conflicts between workers and employers, and within the trade-union movement. One of the reasons was discontent with the results produced by the peaceful negotiations conducted in accordance with the Swedish model. Many workers opposed the policy of wage restraint that the LO leadership had accepted out of a sense of responsibility to the Social Democratic government. Rank and file disaffection expressed itself in a number of wildcat strikes. These strikes usually also served as protests against the official policy of the LO.[7]

One major issue confronting the Swedish trade unions as they entered the 1990s was that of wage policy. High inflation meant that high nominal wage increases no longer translated into rising real wages. This created difficulties for both the trade unions and the Social Democratic government.[8] Although the Social Democratic government's numerous attempts after 1982 to keep wages down ended in failure, these efforts created serious tensions between the SAP and the LO. In 1990 the government suggested a freeze on wages and prices, combined with a two-year strike ban. Surprisingly enough, this scheme was supported by the LO chairperson and most chairs of the affiliated unions. Vigorous protests from the LO rank and file against both the SAP and the LO leadership led the SAP to emphasise the need to make compromises in parliament, even against the wishes of the LO. The response of the LO was to withdraw to a degree from general politics and to concentrate instead on its task as a trade-union organisation.

The continuous public controversies between the LO and the SAP contributed to the defeat of the SAP in the general election of 1991. For the first time since 1930, Sweden had a Conservative as prime minister. Inspired by the United Kingdom and its former Prime Minister Margaret Thatcher, the new coalition government tried to carry through a major 'shift of system', including privatisation of public services and of state-owned companies. At the same time, employers in the SAF decentralised the collective agreement system to the company level, in spite of protests from the trade-union movement. Many of these changes were part of the process of securing Sweden's membership of the European Community.

Table A3.1 *Immigration and emigration 1967–79 (foreign citizens only)*

Year	Immigration			Emigration			Immigration Surplus		
	Nordic	Non-Nordic[1]	All	Nordic	Non-Nordic	All	Nordic	Non-Nordic	All
1967	14,100	13,000	27,100	9,500	5,100	14,500	4,600	7,900	12,500
1968	21,800	11,000	32,900	10,200	7,000	17,200	11,600	4,000	15,600
1969	44,300	16,500	60,800	9,300	5,100	14,400	35,000	11,300	46,300
1970	48,000	25,600	73,500	15,600	5,700	21,300	32,300	19,900	52,300
1971	20,700	18,000	38,700	23,800	7,600	31,400	–3,000	10,400	7,400
1972	13,600	12,000	25,600	22,200	10,100	32,300	–8,600	1,900	–6,700
1973	12,700	12,200	24,900	20,000	10,200	30,200	–7,300	2,000	–5,300
1974	18,000	13,900	31,900	13,900	6,300	20,100	4,200	7,600	11,800
1975	25,400	12,600	38,000	13,300	7,100	20,400	12,100	5,500	17,600
1976	22,200	17,600	39,800	12,200	6,500	18,700	10,000	11,100	21,100
1977	19,600	19,100	38,700	10,600	4,300	14,900	9,000	14,800	23,800
1978	15,300	16,400	31,700	10,100	5,500	15,600	5,300	10,800	16,100
1979	16,400	16,000	32,400	10,700	5,600	16,300	5,700	10,400	16,100

Source: Widgren 1980.

1. Non-Nordic immigration after 1972 consists of family reunion and refugees.

NOTES

1. Principal source: Klas Åmark, 'Sweden', in Joan Campbell (ed.), *European Labour Unions*, Westport/London, 1992, 429ff..
2. Ibid., 435.
3. Ibid., 431.
4. Ibid., 432.
5. Ibid.
6. Ibid., 432–3.
7. Ibid., 433.
8. Ibid., 436.

Bibliography

Ackermann, E., 'Editorial', *Gewerkschaftliche Rundschau* 86, no. 2 (1994): 3.

Ahlberg, G. and I. Svennilson, *Sveriges Arbetskraft och den Industriella utvecklingen*. Stockholm: Industriens Utvecklingsinstitut, 1946.

Ahrne, G. and W. Clement, 'A New Regime?: Class Representation within the Swedish State', in W. Clement and R. Mahon (eds), *Swedish Social Democracy: A Model in Transition*. Toronto: Canadian Scholars' Press Inc., 1994.

AK (Chamber of Labour), *Jahrbuch 1962*. Vienna: Arbeiterkammer, 1963 and consecutive years.

———, *Fremdenrechtsänderungsgesetz*. Unpublished manuscript, 3 June 1996.

Albert, Michel, *Kapitalismus contra Kapitalismus*. Frankfurt am M./New York: Campus Verlag, 1992.

Alpay, S., *Turkar i Stockholm*. Stockholm: LiberFörlag, 1980.

Ålund, A., 'The Power of Definitions: Immigrant Women and Problem-Centered Ideologies', *Migration*, no. 4, 1989, 37–55.

Åmark, Klas, 'Sweden', in Joan Campbell (ed.), *European Labour Unions*. Westport/London: Greenwood Press, 1992, 429ff.

Amersfoort, H. van, *Immigration and the Formation of Minority Groups: The Dutch Experience 1945–1975*. Cambridge: Cambridge University Press, 1982.

——— and R. Penninx, 'Regulating Migration in Europe: The Dutch Experience, 1960–92', in M.J. Miller, *Strategies for Immigration Control: An International Comparison*, Annals AAPPS, no. 534, July 1994: 133–46.

Amnesty International, *France: Shootings, Killings and Alleged Ill-treatment by Law Enforcement Officers*, AI Index Eur. 21/02/94. London: Amnesty International, 1994.

Anderegg, H., 'Stellenabbau wirkt sich auf Mitgliederzahl aus', *Dokumentation no. 12*. Bern: Schweizerischer Gewerkschaftsbund, 1994.

Armingeon, Klaus, *Die Entwicklung der westdeutschen Gewerkschaften 1950–1985.* Frankfurt am M./New York: Campus Verlag, 1986.

Bade, Klaus-J. et al. (eds), *Deutsche im Ausland, Fremde in Deutschland: Migration in Geschichte und Gegenwart.* München: C.H. Beck, 1992.

Bauböck, Rainer, 'Demographische und soziale Struktur der jugoslawischen und türkischen Wohnbevölkerung in Österreich', in Hannes Wimmer (ed.), *Ausländische Arbeitskräfte in Österreich.* Frankfurt: Campus, 1986, 181–239.

———, 'Kein Kurswechsel des ÖGB in der Ausländerpolitik', *Kurswechsel* 90, no. 1, 1990, 48–56.

———, *Immigration Control in Austria.* Second draft. Unpublished manuscript, 1996.

——— and H. Wimmer, 'Social Partnership and 'Foreigners Policy': On Special Features of Austria's Guest-Worker Sstem', *European Journal of Political Research* 16, no. 6, 1988, 659–81.

Beckholmen, K., *Två årtionden 1956–1976.* Stockholm: Svenska Metallindustriarbetareförbundet, 1978.

Beirat für Wirtschafts- und Sozialfragen, *Möglichkeiten und Grenzen des Einsatzes ausländischer Arbeitskraft.* Vienna: Überreuter, 1976.

Bentley, S., 'Industrial Conflict, Strikes and Black Workers: Problems of Research Methodology', *New Community*, no. 1–2, Summer, 1976.

Biffl, Gudrun, 'Auswirkungen des Ausländerzustroms auf den Arbeitsmarkt', *WIFO Monatsberichte*, 65, no. 10, 1992, 526–35.

———, *SOPEMI-Report on Labour Migration 1995–96.* Vienna: WIFO, 1996.

Blanchet, Didier and Olivier Marchand, 'Au-delà de l'an 2000, s'adapter à une pénurie de main-d'oeuvre, *Economique et Statistique*, no. 243, 1991.

BMAS (Ministry of Labour and Welfare), *Bericht über die soziale Lage 1990.* Vienna: BMAS, 1991.

———, *Arbeitsmarktvorschau 1992.* Vienna: BMAS, 1992.

Bonnechère, M., 'La condition juridique des travailleurs immigrés et la crise en France', *Questions de l'Immigration et Syndicalisme, Etudes et documents économiques*, February (CGT). Paris, 1981.

Bouamama, Said et al., *La Citoyenneté dans tous ses etats: De l'immigration à la nouvelle citoyenneté.* Paris: L'Harmattan, 1992.

Bovenkerk, F., *Een eerlijke kans: Over de toepasbaarheid van buitenlandse ervaringen met positieve actie voor etnische minderheden op de arbeidsmarkt in Nederland.* The Hague: Ministerie van Binnenlandse Zaken, 1986.

Brass, Tom and Marcel van der Linden (eds), *Free and Unfree Labour.* International and Comparative Social History Issued by the International Institute of Social History Amsterdam 5. Bern etc: Peter Lang, 1997.

Brassé, P. and W. van Schelven, *Assimilatie van vooroorlogse migranten: Drie generaties Polen, Slovenen en Italianen in Heerlen.* The Hague: Staatsuitgeverij, 1980.

Bridgeford, Jeff and Peter Morris, 'Labour Confederations and Socialist Governments in France 1981–86' in W. Brierly (ed.), *Trade Unions and the Economic Crisis of the 1980s.* Aldershot: Gower, 1987.

Briefs, Götz, *Zwischen Kapitalismus und Sozialismus.* Bern: Franke, 1952.

Brown, C., *Black and White Britain: The Third PSI Survey.* London: Heinemann, 1984.

———, '"Same difference": The Persistence of Racial Disadvantage in the British Employment Market', in P. Braham, A. Rattansi and R. Skellington (eds), *Racism and Antiracism: Inequalities, Opportunities and Policies.* London: Sage, 1992.

Bundesamt für Ausländerfragen, *Die Ausländer in der Schweiz: Bestandergebnisse Ende Dezember 1993.* Bern, 1993.

Bundesamt für Industrie, Gewerbe und Arbeit and Bundesamt für Ausländerfragen (BIGA), *Bericht über Konzeption und Prioritäten der Schweizerischen Ausländerpolitik der Neunziger Jahre.* Bern: Eidgenössische Drucksachen- und Materialzentrale, 1991.

Butschek, Felix and Norbert Geldner, *Kurzfristige Arbeitsmarktvorschau 1992.* Revidierte Fassung. Vienna: WIFO, 1991.

——— and Norbert Geldner, 'Aspekte der Ausländerbeschäftigung', *WIFO Monatsberichte* 47, no. 4, 1974, 214–24.

Büyüm, M., *The Burnsall Strike: Account of a Struggle.* MA dissertation, Department of Sociology, University of Warwick, 1993.

BWK (Chamber of Employers), *Jahrbuch der österreichischen Wirtschaft 1962.* Vienna: BWK, 1963 and consecutive years.

Capdeville, Jacques and René Mouriaux, 'Conflit Social et Immigration: Le cas de la Cellophane', *Projet*, 22 February, 170–8. Paris, 1968.

Carassus, Emilien, *Les grèves imaginaires.* Paris: Eds CNRS, 1982.

CARF 'From Red Scar Mill to Burnsalls: Black Workers Today', *Journal of the Campaign against Racism and Fascism*, March/April 1994.

Castles, S. and G. Kosack, *Immigrant Workers and Class Structure in Western Europe.* London: Oxford University Press, 1973.

——— and G. Kosack, 'How the Trade Unions Try to Control and Integrate Immigrant Workers in the German Federal Republic', *Race* 15, no. 4, 1974, 497–514.

——— and M.J. Miller, *The Age of Migration: International Population Movements in the Modern World.* Basingstoke/London: MacMillan, 1993.

Clement, W. and R. Mahon, 'Swedish and Canadian Perspectives on the Swedish Model', in W. Clement and R. Mahon (eds), *Swedish Social Democracy: A Model in Transition.* Toronto: Canadian Scholars' Press Inc., 1994.

CNV, *De vreemdeling binnen de poort.* Utrecht: CNV, 1980.

Commissie Verwey-Jonker, *Ambonezen in Nederland: Rapport van het Ministerie van Maatschappelijk Werk uitgebracht door de daartoe ingestelde commissie onder voorzitterschap van Mevr. Dr. H. Verwey-Jonker.* The Hague: Staatsuitgeverij, 1959.

Compston, H., 'Union Participation in Economic Policy-Making in Austria, Switzerland, the Netherlands, Belgium and Ireland, 1970–1992'. *West European Politics* 17, no. 1, 1994, 123–45.

Confédération Française Démocratique du Travail, *Textes de base.* Paris: CFDT, 1974.

Confédération Générale du Travail, *La CGT et le mouvement syndicale.* Paris: CGT, 1925.

———, *Pour une politique de l'immigration conforme aux intérets des travailleurs français et immigrés mémoire remis au Premier Ministre le 21 Mai 1970.* Paris, 1971.

———, *La CGT.* Paris: CGT, 1989.

———, 'Mesures sur l'immigration et la lutte contre le racisme: Rapport au Premier Ministre', 21 March 1990. Paris, 1990.

Courtois, Stéphane and Gilles Kepel, 'Musulmanes et Prolétaires', *Revue Française de Science Politique* 37, no. 6, 1987.

CRE, *Part of the Union?: Trade Union Participation by Ethnic Minority Workers.* London: Commission for Racial Equality, 1992.

Cross, M., J. Wrench and S. Barnett, *Ethnic Minorities and the Careers Service: An Investigation into Processes of Assessment and Placement.* Department of Employment Research Paper no. 73. London, 1990.

Danimann, Franz, 'Das neue Ausländerbeschäftigungsgesetz', *Arbeit & Wirtschaft* 30, no. 2, 1976, 16–19.

Davy, Ulrike, 'Stimmungsmache zuerst: Jörg Haiders Forderungskatalog ist juristisch obsolet – Was begehrt er wirklich?', *Der Standard,* 2 November 1992.

——— and August Gächter, 'Zuwanderungsrecht und Zuwanderungspolitik in Österreich', *Journal für Rechtspolitik* 1, no. 3, 1993, 155–74; 1, no. 4, 1993, 257–81.

DGB-Bundesvorstand, *'Es ist Zeit zu widerstehen...': Beispiele gewerkschaftlicher Aktivitäten gegen Fremdenfeindlichkeit und Rassismus.* Düsseldorf, 1993.

DGB-Bundesvorstand and Pro Asyl, *'Flüchtlinge schützen!: Nein zum Bonner Asylkompromiß'.* Düsseldorf, 1993.

Edye, D., *Immigrant Labour and Government Policy.* Hants: Gower 1987.

Eidgenössische Konsultativkommission für das Ausländerproblem (EKA), 'Menschliche und Soziale Probleme der Ausländischen Saisonniers', *Information Nr. 17.* Bern: EKA, 1988.

Engelbrektsson, U-B., *The Force of Tradition: Turkish Migrants at Home and Abroad.* Gothenburg, 1978.

Entzinger, H., 'The Netherlands', in T. Hammar (ed.), *European Immigration Policy: A Comparative Study.* Cambridge: Cambridge University Press, 1985, 50–88.

Erf, van der R, *Asylum Seekers and Refugees; A Statistical Report.* Eurostat, Luxembourg 1994.

Esping-Andersen, G., *Three Worlds of Welfare Capitalism.* Cambridge: Polity Press, 1991.

Europäisches Gewerkschaftsinstitut, *Gewerkschaften: Mitglieder in Europa.* Brussels, 1993.

EUROSTAT, *Demandeurs d'asile et réfugiées: Rapport statistique.* Vol. 1, 3D. Rapporteur R. van der Erf. Bruxelles/Luxembourg, 1994.

Fluder, R., *Stability Under Pluralist Conditions: Trade Unions and Collective Bargaining in Switzerland.* Paper presented at the 12th World Congress of Sociology, Madrid, Spain, 1990.

———, H. Ruf, W. Schöni and M. Wicki, *Gewerkschaften und Angestelltenverbände in der schweizerischen Privatwirtschaft.* Zürich: Seismo Verlag, 1991a.

———, H. Ruf, H. Schöni and M. Wicki, *Schweizerische Arbeitnehmer-organisationen im Vergleich: Binnenstruktur und Verbandspolitik.* Schlussbericht zum Forschungsprojekt Nr. 12– 26587.89. Zürich: Soziologisches Institut der Universität Zürich, 1991b.

FNV, *Samen, beter dan apart: De FNV en de buitenlandse werknemers.* Amsterdam: FNV, 1982.

———, *'Onder ons gezegd, maar niet meer gezwegen': Naar een implementatie van anti-discriminatiebeleid bij FNV en bonden.* Amsterdam: FNV, 1992.

———, *Non-discriminatie code voor FNV en bonden: Richtlijnen voor de vereniging en werkorganisatie.* Amsterdam: FNV, 1993.

Fonds d'Action Sociale, *Circulaire d'information sur la procédure de dépot des dossiers.* Campagne 1995 Juillet. Paris: FAS, 1994.

Freeman, G.P. *Immigrant Labor and Racial Conflict in Industrial Societies: The French and British Experience 1945–1975.* New Jersey: Princeton University Press, 1979.

———, 'The Consequences of Immigration Policies for Immigrant Status: A British and French Comparison', in A.M. Messina et al. (eds), *Ethnic and Racial Minorities in Advanced Industrial Democracies.* New York: Greenwood Press, 1992, 17–32.

Frick, A., 'AusländerInnen sind nicht mehr Konjunkturpuffer', *Gewerkschaftliche Rundschau* 86, no. 2, 1994, 4–6.

Fryer, P., *Staying Power: The History of Black People in Britain.* London: Pluto Press, 1984.

Gächter, August, 'Forced Complementarity: The Attempt to Protect Native Austrian Workers from Immigrants', *New Community* 21, no. 3, 1995a, 379–98.

———, *Preventing Racism at the Workplace in Austria: Report to the European Foundation for the Improvement of Living and Working Conditions.* Vienna: IHS, 1995b.

———, *Ein Arbeitsmarkt unter Druck: Über die Wirkung von Zugangsbeschränkungen zum Arbeitsmarkt.* Unpublished manuscript, 1996a.

———, *Gleicher Zugang zur Notstandshilfe: Eine Folgenabschätzung.* Unpublished manuscript, 1996b.

Gani, Léon, *L'attitude des syndicats ouvriers à l'egard de l'immigration en France 1945–1968.* Thèse de Doctorat. Paris, 1969.

———, *Syndicats et travailleurs immigrés.* Paris: Editions sociales, 1972.

Geiger, Theodor, *Die Klassengesellschaft im Schmelztiegel.* Köln/Hagen: Kieleuer, 1949.

Gewerkschaft Bau und Holz, *Saisonnierstatut im Wandel.* Schriftenreihe der Gewerkschaft Bau und Holz, no. 5.1., 1992.

Gitmez, A. and C. Wilpert, 'A Micro-Society or an Ethnic Community?: Social Organisation and Ethnicity amongst Turkish Migrants in Berlin', in J. Rex, D. Joly and C. Wilpert (eds), *Immigrant Associations in Europe.* Aldershot: Gower Publishing, 1987.

Gorz, André and P. Gavi, 'La Bataille d'Ivry', *Les Temps Modernes*, March. Paris, 1970.

Grillo, Ralph, *Ideologies and Institutions in Modern France.* Cambridge: Cambridge University Press, 1985.

Guidice Fausto, *Arabacides: Une chronique française 1970–1991*. Paris: La Decouverte, 1992.

Hagmann, H.-M., *Les travailleurs étrangers: Chance et tourment de la Suisse*. Lausanne: Payot, 1966.

Hammar, T. (ed.), *European Immigration Policy: A Comparative Study*. Cambridge: Cambridge University Press, 1985.

———, 'Mellan rasism och reglering: Invandringspolitikens ideologi och historia', *Arbetarhistoria* 12, no. 46, 1988, 11–14.

Handboek, *Handboek Buitenlandse Werknemers*. Alphen aan den Rijn: Samsom Uitgeverij, 1973.

Harman, C., *Gramsci versus Reformism*. Bookmarks, 1983.

Haut Conseil à l'Intégration, *La Connaissance de l'Immigration et de l'Integration*. Paris: HCI, 1991.

Heijke, J.A.M., *Sociaal-economische aspecten van gastarbeid*. Rotterdam: Het Nederlands Economisch Instituut, 1979.

Heintz, P. and H.J. Hoffmann-Nowotny, *Bericht über eine Survey Analyse des Fremdarbeiterproblems*. Part I: 1–120. Zürich: Soziologisches Institut, 1990.

Heisler, B.S., 'From Conflict to Accommodation: The "Foreigners Question" in Switzerland', *European Journal of Political Research*, no. 16, 1988, 683–700.

Hetfleisch, Gerhard, 'Rotation statt Integration?: AusländerInnengesetze in Österreich und AusländerInnenbeschäftigungspolitik am Beispiele Tirols', in Gesellschaft für politische Aufklärung and Verein zur Betreuung und Beratung von AusländerInnen in Tirol (eds), *AusländerInnen: Integration oder Assimilierung?* Innsbruck: Österreichischer Studien Verlag, 1991, 30–88.

Hirdman, Y., *The Swedish Welfare State and the Gender System: A Theoretical and Empirical Sketch*. Uppsala: Maktutrednigen, 1987.

Hollifield, James F., 'l'Etat Français et l'Immigration', *Revue Française de Science Politique*, no. 1, 1993, 943–63.

——— and George Ross, *Searching for the New France*. London: Routledge, 1991.

Holthoon, Frits van and Marcel van der Linden (eds), *Internationalism in the Labour Movement 1830–1940*. Contributions to the History of Labour and Society Issued by the International Institute of Social History Amsterdam 1, 2 vols. Leiden, 1988.

Höpflinger, F., *Industriegewerkschaften in der Schweiz*. Zürich: Limmat Verlag, 1976.

Horak, Kurt, 'Ausländer raus oder rein?', *Arbeit & Wirtschaft* 44, no. 3, 1990a, 2.

———, 'Ausländerbeschäftigung: Was wir wollen', *Arbeit & Wirtschaft* 44, no. 5, 1990b, 2.

Hotz-Hart, B., 'Switzerland: Still as Smooth as Clockwork?', in A. Ferner and R. Hyman (eds), *Industrial Relations in the New Europe*. Oxford: Blackwell, 1992.

Hug, K., 'Ausländerpolitik – eine mittel – und längerfristige Betrachtung', *Die Volkswirtschaft*, no. 5, 1989, 8–29.

Hyman, R., *Marxism and the Sociology of Trade Unions.* London: Pluto Press, 1971.

ILO, *Trade Union Activities of Foreign and Migrant Workers in the Member States of the Council of Europe.* Geneva: ILO, 1976.

INSEE, *Les Étrangers en France.* Collection Contours et Caractères, 1994.

Jaarverslag van de Personeelsraad, 1951.

Janssen, J.W., 'Opvattingen en beleid van de werkgevers- en werknemers-organisaties', in R. Wentholt et al., *Buitenlandse arbeiders in Nederland.* Leiden: Spruyt, Van Mantgem and De Does NV, 1967, 33–56.

John, M., *Historical Mass-migration in Habsburg Austria 1848 to 1914: Multi-cultural Options vs. National Hegemony.* Paper presented at the international conference 'Mass-migration in Europe, Implications in East and West', Vienna, 5–7 March 1992.

Jones, Peter, 'Race, Discourse and Power in Institutional Housing: The Case of Immigrant Workers Hostels in Lyons', in M. Silverman (ed.), *Race, Discourse and Power in France.* Aldershot: Avebury, 1991.

Jones, T., *Britain's Ethnic Minorities.* London: Policy Studies Institute, 1993.

Jongh, R. de, M van der Laan and J. Rath, *FNV'ers aan het woord over buitenlandse werknemers.* Uitgave 16. Leiden: Rijksuniversiteit te Leiden, Centrum voor Onderzoek van Maatschappelijke Tegenstellingen, 1984.

Josephides, S., 'Principles, Strategies and Anti-racist Campaigns: The Case of the Indian Workers' Association', in H. Goulbourne (ed.), *Black Politics in Britain.* Aldershot: Avebury, 1990.

Joshi, S. and B. Carter, 'The Role of Labour in the Creation of a Racist Britain', *Race and Class* XXV, no. 3, 1984.

Karlhoffer, Ferdinand and Anton Pelinka, 'Austria', in Joan Campbell (ed.), *European Labour Unions.* Westport/London: Greenwood Press, 1992, 13ff.

Kaske, Rudolf ,'Einleitungsstatement', in Plattform gegen Fremdenhaß (ed.), *Gegen Rassismus und Ausländerfeindlichkeit.* Vienna, 1992, 1ff.

———, 'Keine Apartheid in den Betrieben!', in Österreichische Hochschülerschaft (ed.), *Zwischen Mit- und Selbstbestimmung.* Vienna: ÖH, 1993, 48–50.

Katzenstein, P., 'Capitalism in One Country?: Switzerland in the International Economy', *International Organization*, no. 34, 1980, 507–40.

———, *Corporatism and Change: Austria, Switzerland and the Politics of Industry.* Ithaca, N.Y.: Cornell University Press, 1984.

———, 'Small Nations in an Open International Economy: The Converging Balance of State and Society in Switzerland and Austria', in P. Evans, D. Rueschemeyer and T. Skocpol (eds), *Bringing the State Back In.* Cambridge: Cambridge University Press, 1985.

Kay, D. and R. Miles, 'Migration, Racism and the Labour Market in Britain 1946–1951', in M. van der Linden and J. Lucassen (eds), *Racism and the Labour Market: Historical Studies.* Bern: Peter Lang, 1995.

Kayser, B., *Cyclically Determined Homewards Flows of Migrant Workers.* Paris: OECD, 1972.

Kellberg, C. and A. Hadjoudes, *Vi sålde våra liv.* Stockholm: Askild and Kärnekull, 1978.

Kelly, J., *Trade Unions and Socialist Politics.* London: Verso, 1988.

Kittner, Michael (ed.), *Gewerkschafter heute: Jahrbuch für Arbeitnehmerfragen.* Köln: Bund Verlag, 1995.

Klandermans, B. and J. Visser, *De vakbeweging na de welvaartstaat.* Assen: Van Gorcum, 1995.

Klose, Jürgen, '"*Die Zigeuner kommen!*": Aufnahme von Roma-Familien durch den DGB-Landesbezirk Baden-Württemberg', in Peter Kühne et al., *Gewerkschaften und Einwanderung.* Köln: Bund Verlag, 1994, 62ff.

Knocke, W., *Invandrare möter facket.* Stockholm: Arbetslivscentrum, 1982.

———, *Invandrare kvinnor möter facket: Förstudie och projektplan.* Unpublished mimeograph. Stockholm: Arbetslivscentrum, 1983.

———, *Invandrade kvinnor i lönearbete och fack.* Stockholm: Arbetslivscentrum, 1986.

———, *Våra nya systrar: Invandrade kvinnor i lönearbete och fack.* Stockholm: Svenska kommunalarbetare-förbundet och Brevskolan, 1988.

———, 'Women Immigrants: What is the "Problem?"', *Economic and Industrial Democracy* 12, no. 4, 1991, 469–86.

———, 'Gender, Ethnicity and Technological Change', *Economic and Industrial Democracy* 15, no. 1, 1994, 11–34.

Köbben, A.J.F., *De zaakwaarnemer: Inaugurele Rede Erasmus Universiteit Rotterdam.* Deventer: Van Loghum Slaterus, 1983.

Kok, H., 'Beleid belicht', *Tijdschrift voor maatschappij-vraagstukken en welzijnswerk* 32, no. 6, 1978, 178–83.

Koopmans, R., 'Explaining the Rise of Racist and Extreme Right Violence in Western Europe: Grievances and Opportunities?', *European Journal of Political Research,* no. 30, 1996, 185–216.

Kraak, J.H., P. Ploeger and F.O.J. Kho, *De repatriëring uit Indonesië: Een onderzoek naar de integratie van de gerepatriëerden in de Nederlandse samenleving.* The Hague: Staatsuitgeverij, 1957.

Kriesi, H., *Entscheidungsstrukturen und Entscheidungsprozesse in der Schweizer Politik.* Frankfurt a.M./New York: Campus, 1980.

Kriesi, H., 'The Structure of the Swiss Political System', in G. Lehmbruch and P. Schmitter (eds), *Patterns of Corporatist Policy Making.* Beverly Hills: Sage, 1982.

———, *Political Mobilization and Social Change: The Dutch Case in Comparative Perspective.* Aldershot: Avebury, 1993.

Kyle, G., *Gästarbeterska i manssamhället.* Stockholm: LiberFörlag, 1979.

Labbe, Dominique, 'Trade Unionsm in France Since the Second World War', *West-European Politics* 17, no. 1, 1994, 146–68.

Labour Research 1988, 1989, 1994

Layard, Richard, Olivier Blanchard, Rudiger Dornbusch and Paul Krugman, *East-West Migration: The Alternatives.* Cambridge/MA: MIT Press, 1992.

Lechner, Mario, 'ImmigrantInnen im Betriebsrat? Firma Head: Nein Danke!', *Die Alternative* no. 9, 1995, 16.

Lee, G., *Trade Unionism and Race: A Report to the West Midlands Regional Council of the Trades Union Congress*. Birmingham, 1984.

———, 'Black Members and their Unions', in G. Lee and R. Loveridge (eds), *The Manufacture of Disadvantage*. Milton Keynes: Open University Press, 1987.

——— and J. Wrench, *Skill Seekers: Black Youth, Apprenticeships and Disadvantage*. Leicester: National Youth Bureau, 1983.

Leiniö, T.-L., *Städarnas arbetssituation*. Stockholm: Arbetslivscentrum, 1980.

Leutner, Richard, 'Sozialpartnerschaft und Ausländerbeschäftigung', *Kurswechsel*, no. 1, 1990, 42–8.

Leveau, René, Cathérine Wihtol de Wenden and Gilles Kepel, 'Syndicalisme Française et Islam', *Revue Française de Science Politique* 37, December. Paris, 1987.

Lijphart, A., *The Politics of Accomodation: Pluralism and Democracy in the Netherlands*. Second revised edition. Berkeley, California: University of California Press, 1975.

Linden, Marcel van der (ed.), *Social Security Mutualism: The Comparative History of Mutual Benefit Societies*. International and Comparative Social History Issued by the International Institute of Social History Amsterdam 2. Bern etc.: Peter Lang, 1996.

——— and Jan Lucassen (eds), *Racism and the Labour Market: Historical Studies*. International and Comparative Social History Issued by the International Institute of Social History Amsterdam 1. Bern etc.: Peter Lang, 1995.

——— and Jürgen Rojahn (eds), *The Formation of Labour Movements: A Comparative Approach*. Contributions to the History of Labour and Society Issued by the International Institute of Social History Amsterdam 2, 2 vols. Leiden, 1990.

Linder, W., *Swiss Democracy: Possible Solutions to Conflict in Multicultural Societies*. New York: St. Martin's Press, 1994.

Lis, C., J. Lucassen and H. Soly, 'Introduction', in C. Lis, J. Lucassen and H. Soly, *Before the Unions: Wage Earners and Collective Action in Europe, 1300–1850*. Supplement 2 of the *International Review of Social History*, 1994, 1–11.

Lloyd, Cathie, 'Racist Violence and Anti-racist reactions: A view of France', in R. Witte and T. Bjørgo (eds), *Racist Violence in Europe*. New York: St. Martin's Press, 1993, 207–220.

———, 'Universalism and Difference: The Crisis of Anti-racism in Britain and France', in A. Rattansi and S. Westwood (eds), *On the Western Front: Studies in Racism, Modernity and Identity*. Cambridge: Polity, 1994.

LO, *Migrant Workers and the Trade Union Movement: LO's Programme of Action for Migrant Workers*. Stockholm: LO, 1979.

———, *Vem är aktiv i facket?* Stockholm: Landsorganisationen i Sverige, 1981.

———, *The LO Immigration Policy Programme*. Stockholm: The Swedish Trade Union Confederation, 1991.

Lucassen, Jan and Leo Lucassen (eds), *Migration, Migration History, History: Old Paradigms and New Perspectives*. International and Comparative Social History Issued by the International Institute of Social History Amsterdam 4. Bern etc.: Peter Lang, 1997.

——— and R. Penninx, *Nieuwkomers, nakomelingen, Nederlanders: Immigranten in Nederland 1550–1993*. Amsterdam: Het Spinhuis, 1994.

Mahon, R., *'Yesterday's "Modern Times" Are No Longer Modern': Swedish Unions Confront the Double Shift*. Paper presented at the ninth Conference of Europeanists, Chicago, March/April, 1994.

Marshall-Goldschwartz, A.J., *The Import of Labour: The Case of the Netherlands*. Rotterdam: Rotterdam University Press, 1973.

Marquis, J.-F. and G. Grossi, *Einwanderer-Minderheit ohne politische Rechte*. Bern: Schweizerischer Gewerkschaftsbund, 1990.

Martens, A., *Belgium*. Paper at the International Seminar, 'Cultural Diversity in Trade Unions: A Challenge to the Class Identity', Hoger Instituut voor de Arbeid, Katholieke Universiteit Leuven, Leuven 6–7 February 1997.

Matuschek, Helga, 'Ausländerpolitik in Österreich 1962–1985: Der Kampf um und gegen die Arbeitskraft', *Journal für Sozialforschung* 25, no. 2, 1985, 185–98.

Maucorps, F., A. Memmi and H.-F. Held, *Les Français et le racisme*. Paris: MRAP/Payot, 1965.

Mayer, K., 'Migration, Cultural Tensions and Foreign Relations: Switserland', *The Journal of Conflict Resolution*, no. 11, 1967, 139–52.

Miles, R. and A. Phizacklea, *The TUC, Black Workers and Immigration 1954–1973*. Working Papers on Ethnic Relations no. 6. Birmingham: University of Aston, 1977.

——— and V. Satzewitch, 'Migration, Racism and "Postmodern Capitalism"', *Economy and Society* 19, no. 3, 1990, 334–58.

Miller, M., *The Problem of Foreign Worker Participation and Representation in France, Switzerland and the Federal Republic of Germany*. PhD thesis, University of Wisconsin USA, 1978.

Miller, M.J., *Foreign Workers in Western-Europe: An Emerging Political Force*. New York: Praeger Publishers, 1981.

Ministerie van Binnenlandse Zaken, *Minderhedennota*. The Hague: Staatsuitgeverij, 1983.

Morris, L., 'Women's Poor Work', in P. Brown and R. Scase (eds), *Poor Work: Disadvantage and the Division of Labour*. Milton Keynes: Open University Press, 1991.

Mouriaux, René and Francoise Subileau, *Approche quantitative du syndicalisme francais 1945– 1986*. Paris: CEVIPOF, 1987.

——— and Cathérine Wihtol de Wenden, 'Syndicalisme Française et Islam', *Revue Française de Science Politique* 37, December. Paris, 1987.

Mouvement Contre le Racisme et Pour l'Amitié Entre les Peuples (MRAP), *Chronique du flagrant racisme*. Paris: La Découverte, 1984.

Müller-Jentsch, Walther, *Soziologie der industriellen Beziehungen*. Frankfurt am M./New York: Campus Verlag, 1986.

Nelhans, J., *Utlänningen på arbetsmarknaden*. Lund: Studentlitteratur, 1973.

Neuhold, K., *Invandrarna och facket*. Stockholm: Svenska Fabriksarbetareförbundet, 1976.

Neurath, Erich and Günther Steinbach, *Ausländerbeschäftigungsgesetz*. Vienna: Verlag des ÖGB, 1976.

Nicolet, Claude, *L'idée républicaine en France: Essai d'histoire critique*. Paris: Gallimard, 1982.

Niederberger, J., 'Die politisch-administrative Regelung von Einwanderung und Aufenthalt von Ausländern in der Schweiz: Strukturen, Prozesse, Wirkungen', in H.-J. Hoffmann-Nowotny and K.-O. Hondrich (eds), *Ausländer in der Bundesrepublik Deutschland und der Schweiz*. Frankfurt a.M.: Campus, 1982.

NN, '"Tun was WIR wollen!": Verein Wiener Jugenzentren wählte türkischen Kollegen in den Betriebsrat', *Die Alternative*, no. 2, 1992, 22–23.

Noiriel, Gerard, *Vivre et Lutter à Longwy*. Paris: Maspero, 1986.

———, *Le Creuset Française*. Paris: Seuil, 1988.

Notitie Vreemdelingenbeleid, 1979.

Nowotny, Ingrid, 'Ausländerbeschäftigung in Österreich: Die Gesamtproblematik und aktuelle Situation', *WISO* 14, no. 1, 1991, 37–64.

OECD/SOPEMI, *Trends in International Migration: Annual Report 1993*. Paris: OECD, 1994.

ÖGB (Austrian Trade Union Federation), *Tätigkeitsbericht 1961*. Vienna: ÖGB, 1962 and consecutive years.

———, *Entwurf eines Bundesgesetzes, mit dem das Fremdengesetz, das Asylgesetz und das Bundesbetreuungsgesetz geändert werden sowie das Aufenthaltsgesetz 1996 erlassen wird* (Fremdenrechtsänderungsgesetz/FRÄG). Unpublished manuscript, 4 June 1996.

——— Landesexekutive Vorarlberg/Tirol/Salzburg, *Leitlinien gewerkschaftlicher Ausländerpolitik*. Vorgelegt bei der ARGE-Alp Sitzung am 15–16 Oktober in Mailand. Salzburg: ÖGB, 1992.

Öllinger, Karl, 'Der ÖGB und "seine" AusländerInnen', *Die Alternative*, no. 4, 1994, 9–16.

Olsson, U., 'Planning the Swedish Welfare State', in W. Clement and R. Mahon (eds), *Swedish Social Democracy: A Model in Transition*. Toronto: Canadian Scholars' Press Inc., 1994.

Overlegorgaan NVV-NKV-CNV, *Aktieprogramma 1971–1975*, n.d.

Owen, D., *The Location of Ethnic Minorities in Great Britain*. National Ethnic Minority Data Archive, 1991 Census Factsheet no. 1. Warwick: Centre for Research in Ethnic Relations, University of Warwick, 1992.

Parri, L., 'Staat und Gewerkschaften in der Schweiz (1873–1981)', *Politische Vierteljahresschrift*, no. 28, 1987, 35–58.

Pelz, Sylvia, *Ausländerbeschränkungen Österreichs in der Zwischenkriegszeit*. Diplomarbeit Universität Salzburg, 1994.

Penninx, R., *Towards an Overall Ethnic Minorities Policy: Preliminary Study of the WRR Report 'Ethnic Minorities'*. The Hague: Staatsuitgeverij, 1979.

———, *Immigrant Populations and Demographic Development in the Member States of the Council of Europe*. Part I (Analysis of General Trends and Possible Future Developments), Part II (Country reports), Part III (Statistical Annexes, Population Studies Series nos 12 and 13). Strasbourg: Council of Europe, 1984.

———, 'International Migration in Western Europe since 1973: Developments, Mechanisms and Controls', *International Migration Review* 20, no. 76, 1986, 951–72.

———, 'Immigrants and Organised Labour in the Netherlands as a Field of Research in Social History', *Dutch Crossing, a Journal of Low Countries Studies*, no. 37, 1989, 120–30.

———, 'Immigration, Minorities Policy and Multiculturalism in Dutch Society since 1960', in R. Bauböck, A. Heller and A.R. Zolberg (eds), *The Challenge of Diversity: Integration and Pluralism in Societies of Immigration*. Vienna/Aldershot: European Centre Vienna/Avebury, 1996, 187–206.

——— and H. van Renselaar, *A Fortune in Small Change: A Study of Migrant Workers' Attempts to Invest Savings Productively through Joint Stock Corporations and Village Development Co-operatives in Turkey*. The Hague: REMPLOD/NUFFIC, 1978.

———, J. Schoorl and C. van Praag, *The Impact of International Migration: The Case of the Netherlands*. Netherlands Interdisciplinary Demographic Institute (NIDI) Report 37. The Hague: NIDI, 1994.

——— and L. van Velzen, *Internationale arbeidsmigratie: Uitstoting uit 'thuislanden' en maatschappelijke integratie in 'gastlanden' van buitenlandse arbeiders*. Nijmegen: SUN, 1977.

Phillips, Gordon, 'The United Kingdom', in Joan Campbell (ed.), *European Labor Unions*. Westport/London: Greenwood Press, 1992, 481–514.

Phizacklea, A. and R. Miles, *Labour and Racism*. London: Routledge and Kegan Paul, 1980.

Pichelmann, Karl and Ewald Walterskirchen, *East/West Integration and its Impact on Workers: The Austrian Example*. Paper presented at the OECD conference on 'Regional Integration and Globalization: Implications for Human Resources', Vienna, January 1994.

Prot. I:24:2, *Parliamentary Discussion on Measures to Transfer Foreign Labour etc.*, 23 March 1947.

Prot. II:37:92, *Parliamentary Discussion on the Immigration of Foreign Labour*, 9 December 1966.

Quataert, Donald and Erik Jan Zürcher (eds), *Workers and the Working Class in the Ottoman Empire and the Turkish Republic 1839–1950*. Library of Modern Middle East Studies 3. London and New York: Tauris Academic Studies, I.B. Tauris Publishers, in association with the International Institute of Social History Amsterdam, 1995.

Radin, B., 'Coloured Workers and British Trade Unions', *Race* VIII, no. 2, 1966.

Ramdin, R., *The Making of the Black Working Class in Britain*. Aldershot: Gower, 1987.

Rand-Smith, W., 'Towards Autogestion in Socialist France', *West European Politics* 10, no. 1, 1987.
Rath, J., R. Penninx, K. Groenendijk and A. Meyer, *Nederland en zijn islam: Een ontzuilende samenleving reageert op het ontstaan van een geloofsgemeenschap.* Amsterdam: Het Spinhuis, 1996.
Redaktion, 'Angebotsschock am Arbeitsmarkt', *Wirtschaft und Gesellschaft* 17, no. 2, 1991, 131–39.
Reubsaet, T.J.M., J.A. Kropman and L.M. van Mulier, *Surinaamse migranten in Nederland, deel 2: De positie van Surinamers in de Nederlandse samenleving.* Nijmegen: ITS, 1982.
Riedo, R., *Das Problem der ausländischen Arbeitskräfte in der schweizerischen Gewerkschaftspolitik von 1945–1970.* Bern: Lang, 1976.
Ritsema, G., *De participatie van Turkse werknemers in de FNV.* Amsterdam: Wetenschapswinkel Universiteit van Amsterdam, 1993.
Rojahn, Jürgen (ed.), *The Communist International and its National Sections, 1919–1943* (forthcoming).
Runnymede Trust, 'Trade Unions and Immigrant Workers', *New Community* 4, no. 1, 1974.
Schierup, C.-U. and S. Paulson (eds), *Arbetets etniska delning: Studier från en svensk bilfabrik.* Stockholm: Carlssons, 1994.
Schmidt, M., *Der Schweizerische Weg zur Vollbeschäftigung.* Frankfurt: Campus, 1985.
Schmitter, B., *Immigration and Citizenship in West Germany and Switzerland.* Unpublished Dissertation, University of Chicago, 1979.
Schmitter, B.E., Trade Unions and Immigration Politics in West Germany and Switzerland'. *Politics and Society* 10, no. 3, 1988, 317–34.
Schumacher, P., *De minderheden: 700.000 migranten minder gelijk.* Amsterdam: Van Gennep, 1987.
Schweizerischer Gewerkschaftsbund, 'Das Dokument: Die SGB Vorschläge', *Gewerkschaftliche Rundschau* 86, no. 2, 1994, 12–13.
Schweizer Metall- und Uhrenarbeiterverband (SMUV), *Geschaftsbericht SMUV.* Bern: SMUV, 1955.
———, *Unsere Zukunft hat Geschichte: Eine Festschrift zum hundertjährigen Bestehen des Schweizerischen Metall- und Uhrenarbeiter-verbandes.* Bern: SMUV, 1988.
Schwidder, Emile (ed.), *Guide to the Asia Collections at the International Institute of Social History.* Amsterdam: Stichting beheer IISG, 1996.
Sensenig, Eugene, 'Interkulturelle Mitbestimmung vor Ort', *Die Alternative*, no. 9, 1994, 6–7.
Siegenthaler, J. *Die Politik der Gewerkschaften.* Bern: Francke Verlag, 1968.
Silverman, Max, *Deconstructing the Nation: Immigration, Racism and Citizenship in Modern France.* London: Routledge, 1992.
SIV, *Kvinna och invandrare.* Norrköping: Statens invandrarverk, 1992.
Sivanandan, A., 'Editorial', *Race Today*, August 1973.
———, *A Different Hunger: Writings on Black Resistance.* London: Pluto Press, 1982.
———, 'Racism 1992', *Race and Class*, January-March 1989.

Slob, A., *De buitenlandse werknemers en de Nederlandse vakbeweging*. Unpublished manuscript, Vakgroep Sociologie, Faculteit der Economische Wetenschappen, Erasmus Universiteit Rotterdam, 1982.

Smeets, H. and J. Veenman, 'Steeds meer "thuis" in Nederland: Tien jaar ontwikkelingen in de Molukse bevolkingsgroep', in: H. Vermeulen and R. Penninx (eds), *Het democratisch ongeduld: De emancipatie en integratie van zes doelgroepen van het minderhedenbeleid*. Amsterdam: Het Spinhuis, 1994, 15–43.

Smith, P. and G. Morton, 'Union Exclusion and the Decollectivization of Industrial Relations in Contemporary Britain', *British Journal of Industrial Relations* 31, no. 1, 1993.

SOU, *Invandringen*. Stockholm: Arbetsmarknadsdepartementet, 1967, 18.

———, *Invandrarna och minoriteterna*. Stockholm: Arbetsmarknadsdepartementet, 1974, 69.

———, *Kvinnors Arbete: En rapport från Jämställdhetskommittén*. Stockholm: Arbetsmarknadsdepartem entet, 1979, 89.

Statistics Netherlands, *Monthly Bulletin of Population Statistics* 43, no. 7, 1995, 11.

Statistics Sweden, *Theme Immigrants*. Stockholm/Örebro, 1984.

Steijlen, F., *RMS: van ideaal tot symbool: Moluks nationalisme in Nederland 1951–1994*. Amsterdam: Het Spinhuis, 1996.

Stevens, Anne, *The Government and Politics of France*. London: Macmillan, 1996.

Stichting van de Arbeid, *Méér werk voor minderheden*. Publication no. 6/90. The Hague: Stichting van de Arbeid, 1996.

Stokman, H., *De toegankelijkheid van de FNV voor allochtonen*. Amsterdam: Wetenschapswinkel Universiteit van Amsterdam, 1995.

Streeck, W., *Gewerkschaftliche Organisationsprobleme in der sozialstaatlichen Demokratie*. Königstein/Ts.: Athenäum, 1981.

Stuurman, S., *Het ontstaan van de verzuiling in Nederland*. Amsterdam: Universiteit van Amsterdam, 1981.

Tournier, Maurice, 'Les Jaunes: Un mot-fantasme à la fin du 19e siècle', *Mots*, no. 8, 1984, 125– 46.

Tripier, Maryse, 'Concurrence et différence: Les problèmes posés au syndicalisme ouvrier par les travailleurs immigrés', *Sociologie de Travail*, July 1972.

———, 'Syndicats, Ouvriers Français, Immigration et Crises', *Pluriel*, no. 21, 1980.

———, 'Français et Immigrés', *Questions de l'Immigration et Syndicalisme, Etudes et documents économiques*, February (CGT). Paris, 1981.

TUC, 1981.

TUC, *Involvement of Black Workers in Trade Unions*. London: Ruskin College/Northern College, Trades Union Congress, 1991.

Tunçay, Mete and Erik J. Zürcher (eds), *Socialism and Nationalism in the Ottoman Empire 1876– 1923*. London and New York: British Academic Press/Imprint of I.B Tauris Publishers, in association with the International Institute of Social History Amsterdam, 1994.

Twist, K. van, *Gastarbeid ongewenst: De gevestigde organisaties en buitenlandse arbeiders in Nederland.* Baarn: In den Toren, 1977.

Velde, B. van de and J. van Velzen, 'De Nederlandse vakbonden, internationale solidariteit en buitenlandse werknemers: Ideologie en werkgelegenheid', in F. Bovenkerk (ed.), *Omdat zij anders zijn: Patronen van rasdiscriminatie in Nederland.* Amsterdam/Meppel: Boom, 1978, 166–88.

Vermeulen, H. (ed.), *Immigrant Policy for a Multicultural Society: A Comparative Study of Integration, Language and Religion in Five Western European Countries.* Brussels/Amsterdam: Migration Policy Group/IMES, 1997.

Vervoersbond CNV, *Leven en werken in Nederland: Een sociologisch onderzoek onder Turkse werknemers in dienst van de N.S.* Utrecht: Vervoersbond CNV, 1976.

Virdee, S., *Racism and Resistance in the British Trade Union Movement: A Critical Analysis of Historical and Contemporary Developments.* Paper at the International Seminar, 'Cultural Diversity in Trade Unions: A Challenge to the Class Identity', Hoger Instituut voor de Arbeid, Katholieke Universiteit Leuven, Leuven 6–7 February 1997.

———, *Organised Labour and the Racialised Worker in England: Racism, 'Racial' Formation and Working Class Militancy.* Ph.D. thesis (forthcoming).

——— and K. Grint, 'Black Self Organization in Trade Unions', *Sociological Review* 42, no. 2, 1994.

Visser, J., 'Tussen nationale ontwikkeling en Europese uitdaging', in Jelle Visser (ed.), *De vakbeweging op de eeuwgrens: Vijf sociologische studies over de vakbeweging.* Amsterdam: Amsterdam University Press, 1996, 7–19.

——— and B. Ebbinghaus, 'Een halve eeuw verandering: Verklaringen voor convergentie en diversiteit van werknemersorganisatie in West-Europa', in Jelle Visser (ed.), *De vakbeweging op de eeuwgrens: Vijf sociologische studies over de vakbeweging.* Amsterdam: Amsterdam University Press, 1996, 20–53.

Voorden, W. van, 'The Netherlands' in Joan Campbell (ed.), *European Labor Unions.* Westport/London: Greenwood Press, 1992.

Vranken, J. 'Industrial rights', in Zig Layton-Henry (ed.), *The Political Rights of Migrant Workers in Western Europe.* Sage Modern Politics Series 25. London: Sage, 1990, 47–73.

Wadensjö, E., *Immigration och samhällsekonomi.* Lund: Studentlitteratur, 1973.

Wallner, Josef and Georg Ziniel, 'Ausländerpolitik in Österreich', *Arbeit und Wirtschaft* 44, no. 6, 1990, 32–36; 44, no. 7–8, 1990, 24–28; 44, no. 10, 1990, 3.

Wandaller, Peter, *Daten und Fakten: Ausländer in Salzburg: Finanzielle Beiträge der Ausländer zum österreichischen Sozialstaat.* Unpublished manuscript, Salzburg: AK-WiPol, 1993.

Wayland, Sarah, 'Mobilizing to Defend Nationality Law in France', *New Community* 20, no. 1, 1993.

Webster, Paul, *Petain's Crime*. London: Macmillan, 1990.

Widgren, J., *Svensk invandrarpolitik*. Lund: Liber Läromedel, 1980.

Wihtol de Wenden, Cathérine, *Les Immigrés et la politique*. Paris: Presses de la Fondation Nationale des Sciences Politiques, 1988.

Willi, V., *Überfremdung: Schlagwort oder bittere Wahrheit*. Bern: Lang, 1970.

Wimmer, Hannes, 'Die Arbeitswelt der ausländischen Arbeitnehmer', in Hannes Wimmer (ed.), *Ausländische Arbeitskräfte in Österreich*. Frankfurt: Campus, 1986, 241–80.

Windmuller, J.P., C. de Galan and A.F. van Zweden, *Arbeidsverhoudingen in Nederland*. Derde herziene druk. Utrecht: Het Spectrum, 1979.

Wolff, R. and R. Penninx, 'Donkere wolken boven de arbeidsmarkt', *Migrantenstudies* 10, no. 1, 1994, 1–18.

Wrench, J., 'Unequal Comrades: Trade Unions, Equal Opportunity and Racism', in R. Jenkins and J. Solomos (eds), *Racism and Equal Opportunity Policies in the 1980's*. Cambridge: Cambridge University Press, 1987, 160–86.

———, *Ethnic Minorities and Workplace Organisation in Britain: Trade Unions, Participation and Racism*. Paper at the conference, 'Ethnic Minorities and Their Chances of Participation: A Comparison between France, Great Britain, the Netherlands and the Federal Republic of Germany', Bonn, December 1992.

———, 'Trade Unions, Migrants and Ethnic Minorities in the European Union: National Differences and Common Dilemmas', in J. Gundara and S. Jacobs (eds), *Intercultural Europe: Diversity and Social Policy*, Aldershot: Ashgate/Arena, 2000.

——— and S. Virdee, 'Organizing the Unorganized: "Race", Poor Work and Trade Unions', in P. Ackers, C. Smith and P. Smith (eds), *The New Workplace and Trade Unionism*. London: Routledge, 1996.

Wetenschappelijke Raad voor het Regeringsbeleid (WRR), *Ethnic Minorities*. The Hague: Staatsuitgeverij, 1979.

Wubben, H.J.J. *Chineezen en ander Aziatisch ongedierte: Lotgevallen van Chinese immigranten in Nederland, 1911–1940*. Zutphen: De Walburg Pers, 1986.

Yuval-Davis, M., 'Women, Ethnicity and Empowerment', in K.-K. Bhavanani, and A. Phoenix (eds), *Shifting Identities, Shifting Racisms*. London: Sage, 1994.

Zolberg, A.R., A. Suhrke and S. Agayo, *Escape from Violence: Conflict and the Refugee Crisis in the Developing World*. New York/Oxford: Oxford University Press, 1989.

Zwinkels, A., 'Buitenlandse arbeiders en vakbonden', *Informatiebulletin werkgroepen buitenlandse arbeiders*, no. 3, 1972, 71–9.

Notes on Contributors

August Gächter is a research fellow at the Institute for Advanced Studies, Vienna. His work focuses on the economic and social absorption of immigrants, on migration processes, and on industrial relations. His publications in English include a piece on 'forced complementarity' in *New Community* (1995), and a research report on *Migration Potential and World Economic Development.*

Wuokko Knocke, who is a sociologist, has been working since 1979 as a senior researcher at the National Institute for Working Life. Her research has focused on the working life and labour market situation of immigrants, with an emphasis on issues related to gender, class and ethnicity. Apart from empirical working life studies, she has worked on the theoretical understanding of the processes and mechanisms which lead to the marginalisation of female and male immigrants in the world of work. In 1994 and 1995 she acted as an expert member of the *Joint Specialist Group on Migration, Cultural Diversity and the Equality between Women and Men* of the Council of Europe, Strasbourg. Her publications in English include 'How to Be a Woman, A Worker, and an Immigrant', *International Studies of Management and Organization* (1990); 'Women Immigrants – What is the "Problem"?', *Economic and Industrial Democracy* (1991); 'Gender, Ethnicity and Technological Change', *Economic and Industrial Democracy* (1994).

Peter Kühne is Professor of Sociology at the Sozialakademie Dortmund. His main fields of research are the sociology of literature; sociology of the trade unions, and comparison of German and French trade unions, and the sociology of migration. Major publications: *Arbeiterklasse und Literatur*, Frankfurt/Main, 1972; *Gewerkschaftliche Betriebspolitik in Westeuropa*, Berlin, 1981; *Verlust der politischen Utopie in Europa?*, Berlin, 1991 (with Klaus W. West); *Gewerkschaften und Einwanderung*, Cologne, 1994 (with Nihat Öztürk and Klaus W. West).

Cathie Lloyd is Director of the Centre for Cross Cultural Research on Women, Queen Elizabeth House, University of Oxford, United Kingdom, and a member of the National Council of the Mouvement Contre le Racisme et Pour l'Amitié entre les Peuples (MRAP) in France. She has published widely on antiracism, notably *Discourses of Racism in France*, Ashgate, 1998.

Rinus Penninx is academic Director of the interdisciplinary research Institute for Migration and Ethnic Studies (IMES) at the Universiteit van Amsterdam. He recently published on minority formation in the Netherlands, on the institutionalisation of Islam and on multiculturalism. His publications in English include 'Immigration, Minorities Policy and Multiculturalism in Dutch Society since 1960', in R. Bauböck et al. (eds), *The Challenge of Diversity: Integration and Pluralism in Societies of Immigration*, Aldershot, 1996; *Newcomers: Immigrants and Their Descendants in the Netherlands 1550–1995*, Amsterdam, 1997 (with J. Lucassen). A book on the institutionalisation of Islam (with J. Rath, K. Groenendijk and A. Meyer) appeared in 1996.

Judith Roosblad is a researcher at the Institute for Migration and Ethnic Studies, Universiteit van Amsterdam. Her research focuses on the responses of trade unions to immigrants and (labour) migration since the 1960s. Currently she is working on a Ph.D. thesis on 'Trade Unions, Immigration and Immigrants in the Netherlands 1960–1997'. Publications include *Nederland en de islam*, Nijmegen, 1992 (with R. Hampsink).

Barbara Schmitter Heisler is Professor of Sociology at Gettysburg College, USA. Her research interests centre on the processes of social inclusion and exclusion in advanced industrial societies. She has published numerous articles in the areas of immigration and poverty. She is co-editor (with M.O. Heisler) of *From Foreign Workers to Settlers? Transnational Migration and the Emergence of New Minorities*, The Annals of the American Academy of Political and Social Science. Vol. 485 (1986). Recent articles include 'A Comparative Perspective on the Underclass: Questions of Urban Poverty, Race and Citizenship', *Theory and Society* (1991); 'The Future of Immigrant Incorporation: Which Models? Which Concepts?', *International Migration Review* (1992); and 'Housing Policy and the Underclass', *Journal of Urban Affairs* (1994).

John Wrench is a senior researcher at the Danish Centre for Migration and Ethnic Studies, South Jutland University centre, and an associate fellow of the Centre for Research in Ethnic Relations, University of Warwick. He has researched and published on issues of racism and discrimination in the labour market in the United Kingdom and in a broader European context. Publications include *Racism and Migration in Western Europe*, Oxford 1993 (co-edited with John Solomos) and *Preventing Racism at the Workplace: A Report on 16 European Countries*, Luxembourg 1996.

Index